Major · mrs. Somervell

With appreciation
The Salvation Army
Lt Colonel and Mrs Wm J. McHarg

Christmas 1561

THE HALLELUJAH ARMY

THE
HALLELUJAH
ARMY

Harry Edward Neal

CHILTON COMPANY · BOOK DIVISION · *Publishers*

PHILADELPHIA AND NEW YORK

Foreword

Throughout the world today there are countless friends of The Salvation Army who take for granted the need for and effectiveness of its work because they have confidence in its basic spiritual motives. Nowhere is this more true than in America. Our generous friends frequently approve and applaud our methods and activities without actually knowing much about them.

We prefer, however, that loyalty to and support of The Salvation Army be predicated on full knowledge of what it is and what its purposes are, and on some familiarity with the wide range of its religious and humanitarian services.

Thus, when Mr. Harry Edward Neal expressed to us his interest in telling the story of The Salvation Army through the stories of the men and women who wear the familiar caps and bonnets, and the stories of human beings helped by this Army, we quickly agreed that this might be a very effective way to give our friends a clear, sharp, three-dimensional picture of the structure and program of our organization.

Mr. Neal confined his close-range observation and personal interview research to our New York City operations, but the pattern of service traced out in the following pages is repeated, in part or *in toto*, in nearly every community across our country in which The Salvation Army is established.

Ironically enough, in this era of "images," we are not so much concerned with the public "image" of The Salvation Army which, happily, seems quite satisfactory, but we are deeply concerned with clarifying the solid, practical, down-to-earth reality behind that image. This, we believe, is the substance of Mr. Neal's work.

We are grateful for his distillation of the human factors of our day-by-day program and his appreciation of the religious convictions and objectives which motivate our service. We sincerely hope that, through these pages, many readers will enjoy the process of "getting to know us."

COMMISSIONER NORMAN S. MARSHALL
National Commander
The Salvation Army

Preface

If you should ask an officer of The Salvation Army how he or she happened to join the organization, there is a good chance the answer would be, "I felt that I was called by God. This is what He wanted me to do."

To many people this would seem a good reason, but to some others it may sound corny. There are those who squirm, or smile, raise a skeptical eyebrow or cock a quizzical eye whenever God comes into their conversation with others. In the Bible we read how Moses and the prophets heard God's voice and even spoke with Him—but in this enlightened age of the atom, the satellite, the ballistic missile and other instruments of destruction, how many of us have ever heard of God making a personal visit?

After weeks of talking with officers of The Salvation Army and seeing them in action, I am satisfied that when one says, "God called me," he means it. Not only did he answer the call, but also he (or she) tries his utmost to live and act as God would have all of us live and act—in peace and with love for our fellow man.

This is not to say that every Salvation Army officer is a model of perfection. They are as human as the rest of us. A few "backslide" and resign. Some have personal or family problems which make normal living difficult. For these and other reasons some relinquish the uniform and return to civilian life. Most, however, follow the "Blood and Fire" banner until they retire or die.

Seeing the derelicts, the bums, the prostitutes, the drunks, the thieves, and so many other human beings The Salvation Army tries to save and serve, I was convinced that the only people who could face up to the filth, the despair, the trials and tragedies of forgotten men and homeless and hungry individuals, must be truly dedicated Christians, else they could never do what they do.

I am sure there are many other people so dedicated in homes, in churches, and in various welfare organizations, but I have come face to face with those in The Salvation Army and it is their story and thus the story of the Army itself that I have sought to tell.

The Salvation Army works in many countries of the world, and in several parts of this book I have tried to show what it does in some of these places. However, it was neither possible nor practicable for me to make personal visits to these other lands, and in order to get a really close look at the operations of this unique organization I went to its national headquarters for the United States in New York City. There I associated with its people and visited numerous installations where I saw them at work. I know now that its activity in and around New York reflects the kind of help it gives to troubled souls everywhere.

The World War I doughnut and The Salvation Army military canteen combine with the bass drum, the tambourine, the Christmas kettle, the street-corner worship service and the red Salvation Army salvage trucks to create the image of The Salvation Army that flits through the mind of the average man, if indeed he thinks about it at all. It is a false image because it portrays only an infinitesimal part of the dramatic and fascinating humanitarian tasks performed day and night by thousands of dedicated people around the world.

For example, how many people are aware that the infamous

French penal colony called Devil's Island was abolished as the result of a 25-year battle by a French Salvation Army officer?

Or that some 27,000 Salvation Army officers and cadets (not counting many thousands of "soldier" Salvationists) serve humanity in 86 countries of the globe, preaching in 136 different languages?

Or that these officers are *not* people who have been saved from a life in the gutter, but are well-educated, specially trained, legally ordained ministers of the Gospel?

Or that The Salvation Army has a navy?

Or that the Army, throughout the world, operates 367 hostels for homeless men and women, 66 employment bureaus, 39 general hospitals, 37 maternity hospitals and 61 dispensaries and clinics, 8 leprosaria, 90 maternity homes for unwed mothers, 141 children's homes, 30 boarding schools, and 27 hotels; publishes 137 periodicals in 38 languages and dialects; and serves more than 20 million meals a year to people who might otherwise go hungry?

Or that there are several Salvation Army colleges, called Schools for Officers' Training, where dedicated young men and women study to become Salvation Army officers and ordained ministers, guided by the Army's doctrines?

What are these doctrines? Eleven in number, they carry a quiet power of their own, in striking contrast to a tense world of cold wars, hydrogen bombs, intercontinental ballistic missiles and a nation-by-nation race for military supremacy. Of all the armies in our turbulent world, only The Salvation Army has no guns, no bayonets, no bombs, choosing to fight "with hand to man and heart to God."

The Salvation Army believes:

1. That the Scriptures of the Old and New Testaments were given by inspiration of God and that they only constitute the divine rule of Christian faith and practice.

2. That there is only one God, who is infinitely perfect, the Creator, Preserver and Governor of all things, and who is the only proper object of religious worship.

3. That there are three persons in the Godhead: the Father, the Son, and the Holy Ghost, undivided in essence and co-equal in power and glory.

4. That in the person of Jesus Christ the divine and human natures are united so that He is truly and properly God, and truly and properly man.

5. That our first parents were created in a state of innocency but by their disobedience they lost their purity and happiness, and that in consequence of their fall, all men have become sinners, totally depraved, and as such are justly exposed to the wrath of God.

6. That the Lord Jesus Christ has, by His suffering and death, made an atonement for the whole world, so that whosoever will may be saved.

7. That repentance toward God, faith in our Lord Jesus Christ, and regeneration by the Holy Spirit are necessary to salvation.

8. That we are justified by grace through faith in our Lord Jesus Christ, and that he that believeth hath the witness in himself.

9. That continuance in a state of salvation depends upon continued obedient faith in Christ.

10. That it is the privilege of all believers to be "wholly sanctified" and that "their whole spirit and soul and body" may "be preserved blameless unto the coming of our Lord Jesus Christ."

11. In the immortality of the soul, in the resurrection of the body, in the general judgment at the end of the world, in the eternal happiness of the righteous, and in the endless punishment of the wicked.

Symbolic of the Army and its doctrines are the soup kettle and the bass drum, which came into use for good reasons. One night before Christmas in 1894 a terrific gale screamed out of the Pacific near San Francisco, hurling schooners off course, ripping sails of ships at sea, tearing cargo loose in the holds, and swamping decks and seamen. One ship, its rudder damaged, plunged helplessly shoreward and slammed into the rocks with a sickening, splintering groan.

Spectators ashore included Salvation Army people, who helped to bring the crew and passengers to safety. Once on land, the survivors were taken to the Salvation Army building nearby, where they were warmed while hot soup was prepared. Other seamen and longshoremen, wet, cold and tired, had come to the shelter during the day to eat and rest as they had done many times before, and the soup ingredients were almost gone. The Army would have to buy more, but its own funds were extremely low and had to be conserved, if possible, for its winter work.

An inspired Salvation Army lassie, whose name has been lost to posterity, grabbed a huge black soup kettle and a piece of cardboard. On the cardboard she printed, in large pencilled letters, the words: "KEEP THIS KETTLE BOILING!" She took the kettle, the sign, and a bell into the cold night and stood with them on a street corner. People were attracted by the clanging bell, and within a short time passers-by had thrown enough coins into the kettle to buy plenty of food for the victims of the shipwreck and others who came to The Salvation Army asking to be fed.

By the next Christmas (1895), word of this unique appeal had spread and the soup kettle was used in the 30 Salvation Army Corps along the West Coast. In 1897 the idea moved Eastward and was used in Boston, where the Army's kettles provided Christmas dinners that year for 150,000 needy men, women and children. It has been said that the "S" on the Salvation Army uniform stands for "Soup, Soap and Salvation." The Army people will tell you that it means "Save" and "Serve."

Today the soup kettles are bright red, still in use, and as symbolic of Christmas as holly or mistletoe. A brief episode in New York City in 1959 shows that the spirit of Christmas —and giving—is not active only in December. A Spring snowstorm whitened the city's streets—a very belated "white Christmas." One Salvation Army girl suggested that the red

Christmas kettle be put on the sidewalk in front of Macy's department store. The kettle was set up, a Salvation Army lassie clanged the bell, and whenever a pedestrian dropped a coin in the pot the lassie called, "Thank you! Merry Christmas!" Oddly enough, no one seemed surprised at the greeting, and when the snowstorm stopped about an hour later, the kettle was taken away. It contained several dollars in dimes, nickels and pennies.

I am deeply appreciative of the willing assistance and excellent suggestions given to me by Miss Marian F. Tuthill, then Assistant Director of the National Information Service, and by members of her staff—especially Sophia Perry, Evelyn Hart, and Catherine M. Podolin, who were my "girl guides" in Army establishments in and around the New York metropolitan area. Without the help of these four girls, without the kindness of Lieutenant Commissioner Llewellyn W. Cowan, and except for the hearty cooperation extended to me by a great many officers, including those named in the book, I could not have told this story.

I think that it is an exciting and inspiring story, and I pray that my telling of it has been adequate, clear, and straightforward.

HARRY EDWARD NEAL

Contents

Chapter 1

IN DARKEST ENGLAND

A thirteen-year-old boy who prepared for his future by being apprenticed to a pawnbroker in a pinched community sees little but the sordid side of life. William Booth, born April 10, 1829, in Nottingham, England, was such a boy.

For five years young Booth watched, listened to, and waited upon destitute men and women who came to the Nottingham pawnshop to borrow money for food, rent, or other necessities. A chimney-sweep pawned a suit given to him by an old lady. A carpenter pawned his saws and hammer between hard-to-get jobs and redeemed them by pawning clothes and furniture so that he could work at his trade when the opportunity offered; and after he was paid his meager wage he would redeem what he could until his funds were again exhausted.

Pale, scrawny housewives borrowed a few shillings against wedding rings taken from rough, vein-ridged hands. Some were weekly customers who redeemed the rings every Saturday when their husbands received their pay. Others never came back.

William Booth, who knew poverty with his own parents, understood these needy souls and tried, in a shy, youthful way, to comfort and encourage them, unknowingly preparing himself even then for a partnership with God in a company that would flourish the world over.

Booth was baptized in the Church of England, but to him the Church seemed to center more upon ritual than upon practical Christian activity. Almost a hundred years before Booth was born, an English cleric named John Wesley had founded the Methodist Church, traveling tirelessly from village to town on horseback, preaching to greater and greater crowds, pleading with his listeners to seek the personal salvation of their souls. As a result, thousands of people separated from the Church of England to become Methodists.

Perhaps curiosity led young William Booth to a meeting of a Methodist Bible Class in the Broad Street Wesleyan Chapel, where members declaimed Bible quotations and uttered prayers that were spontaneous and earnest, not given by rote and not devoid of deep feeling. As each spoke, joyous cries of "Hallelujah!" and "Amen!" punctuated their sentences, and at intervals the members would sing hymns so enthusiastically that the windows rattled.

When finally the congregation was invited to come forward and repent of their sins, accepting Christ as their personal Savior, Booth was among those who responded. With others he knelt at a small wooden table where he was aware of a new and strange sensation—a feeling of extraordinary peace and cleanliness surging through his thin body. On that historic night William Booth became a real, honest-to-God Christian, vowing to separate himself from the world of the godless. He was fifteen years old.

Sometime within the next two years Booth was indelibly impressed by the zeal and fire of an itinerant American preacher, the Reverend James Caughey, who drew great crowds in many churches and who often held services in an open field, a sidewalk, or a vacant lot. Caughey's straightforward speech and manner influenced Booth in the years ahead and some of Caughey's remarks might even have subconsciously inspired the formation of the amazing Army that Booth was ordained to assemble.

"The sword that gives the soldier victory on the field is accounted trusty and true," Preacher Caughey once declared, "but the Gospel is a sword as well as a sceptre of mercy. St. Paul says it is quick and powerful and sharper than any two-edged sword, dividing asunder the joints and the marrow, and is a discerner or lays open the very thoughts of the heart as the knife of the surgeon lays open the seat of the disease or the cause of death. The Gospel is a science of war against the world, the flesh and the devil. In the hand of a Christ-sent preacher the Gospel is a sword as well as a sceptre, but of what use is a sword, however much adorned, if not wielded energetically and if it fail in execution? A sword that hath an hilt of gold, set with diamonds, is no good sword, says an old divine, if it have no edge to cut or wants a good back to follow home the stroke."

Fired by Caughey's eloquence and by his own fervor, Booth at seventeen cast aside his youthful shyness to deliver his first sermon as a lay preacher at a "cottage meeting" in Nottingham —a meeting held in the home of a Methodist family, attended by other Methodist families. His earnest manner and simple delivery resulted in invitations to speak at other meetings, and before long Booth was the leader of a group of young men in Wesleyan Chapel.

The young men, however, were steady churchgoers, and Booth's aim was to bring salvation to those outside the church, the outcasts whose only altar was a bar in a local "pub," whose only sermons came from a jovial barkeep and were peppered with profanity. Following Caughey's pattern of evangelism, Booth invaded the world of beer and skittles and gradually persuaded several boozers and bums to attend Sunday services with him at the Wesleyan Chapel.

On Sunday morning, when Booth marched into the church leading his shabby, almost ragged, penitents, the "good" folk of Nottingham, dressed in their Sunday best, squirmed in their pews; and when Booth failed to herd his flock into special seats reserved for the poor, the congregation stared, glared, whispered and snorted. A few changed seats to avoid any danger of contact with the riff-raff.

3

When the last echo of the benediction had faded, a committee of the respectable brethren approached Booth.

"Now, lad," they said, "it's a fine thing you are doing to help these poor souls, but you should have sat them in the reserved section."

"I don't see why," Booth said. "They came for the same reason you and I did—to worship God. Are they to be set apart for that?"

"No, no, lad, of course not. But—well, they may be crawling with lice and vermin, and they make our good women uneasy."

"They cleaned themselves as best they could for this occasion," Booth answered. "Their clothes may be threadbare, but I'm not interested in their clothes. I'm interested in their souls."

"That's another thing," one churchman put in. "Walking in the front door of the church wearing those rags and patches, they give decent people the wrong impression about our congregation." He glanced around at his supporters. "We must insist that if you bring this rabble here again, you bring them in through the back door and seat them in the poor section."

"They're not rabble," Booth said. "They're men seeking salvation—and it seems to me that in the House of God they should be free to sit where they please. Good day, gentlemen." He walked away, externally unruffled but inwardly disturbed by this first clash with church society.

In 1849 Booth ended his apprenticeship in the pawnshop, and being unable to find other work in Nottingham he went to London, but the only job he could get there was in a Walworth pawnshop. In his spare time he continued his preaching, and at one revival session on April 10, 1852, he had a fateful meeting with a British bootmaker named Edward H. Rabbits, who was so favorably impressed by Booth's earnestness that he urged the youth to give up his job and devote his full time to evangelism.

"Even a preacher must eat to live," Booth told him. "I need my job."

"I'll get you started," Rabbits said. "I'll guarantee you one pound a week for three months."

On this basis Booth quit his job and took to full-time preaching. Rabbits introduced Booth to his middle-class friends in their comfortable homes and made him welcome in the Rabbits household. At the end of the three months, when no further support came from Rabbits, Booth sold his furniture and some personal belongings, the money from which enabled him to live until the following November. Walking through the Walworth slums with his last sixpence in his pocket, Booth came upon an old woman searching a pile of refuse for food. He gave her the sixpence and a prayer for her welfare.

A few days later Booth was invited to take charge of a Methodist Reform Movement in Spalding, Lincolnshire, where he labored for some eighteen months. As a lay preacher, Booth was often confronted with people in his congregations whose education was far superior to his own, and he had an intense desire not only to broaden his knowledge, but also to become an ordained minister of the church. With this aim he left the Reformers and joined the Methodist New Connection as a theological student in London.

In the London home of his friend Rabbits, Booth met a pretty girl named Catherine Mumford who, with her parents, was associated with the Society of Friends, the Quakers. They were married on June 16, 1855.

After serving four years as a probationary assistant pastor, Booth was ordained a Methodist minister in Hull, England, in May, 1858, and assigned to a circuit at Gateshead. When he arrived at the Bethesda Chapel there he learned that an average of 120 people attended the Sunday night services. Within a few weeks Booth's preaching drew crowds of 2000, including so many converts that the chapel became known as "the conversion shop."

For three years Catherine and William Booth ministered to the people of Gateshead and the surrounding area. In May, 1861, at a Methodist Conference in Liverpool, debate centered on the feeling that Booth's drawing power was depleting the congregations of less-spirited ministers. The Reverend William Cooke proposed that Booth concentrate on his own church,

5

minimize his evangelism, and refrain from holding any revival meetings in other districts without the consent of the ministers in those districts.

Booth, seated among the conferees, glanced at his wife standing in the gallery. Catherine shook her head proudly. "No, never!" she cried.

Calmly, Booth picked up his hat, walked up the aisle to meet Catherine at the front of the building and they strolled out arm in arm. At home, Booth wrote a letter of resignation in which he said, "Knowing that the future will most convincingly either vindicate or condemn my present action, I am content to await its verdict."

The Booths went from town to town holding revival meetings which attracted thousands of people, many of whom were merely curious and many already churchgoers. Some of the meetings were held in churches or on church property, but gradually denominational officialdom increased its opposition to Booth's methods until church doors were closed in his face and he was compelled to find dance halls, theaters, vacant stores, or other secular locations for his meetings. Some of his most successful revivals were held in a circus tent at Cardiff, where Booth noticed that several derelicts and prostitutes came to hear him speak. These were the people he wanted most to reach, and it was here that he conceived the idea of reaching them through converts of their own levels.

When some of the downtrodden came forward to repent, Booth proposed sending them to the churches, but he soon discovered that this was a mistake. First, many would not go where they were sent. Second, those who did go found that they were not welcome. Third, Booth decided he wanted them himself to help him save others of their class.

Why, he asked himself, did these people, who would not go to a church, come to a circus tent to hear an evangelist? The answer was plain. They lived in a world of saloons and honky-tonks, and the open flap of a tent was much more inviting and less formidable than the oaken door of a church.

Even in the tent, however, a "churchly" air was created by

the music of the small organ which was used for hymn accompaniments, and Booth was aware that his wayward newcomers did not appreciate organ music and in fact were repelled rather than attracted by it. The music they enjoyed and understood came from the twanging banjo, the mellow guitar, the blaring trumpet and the boom-boom-boom of the big bass drum. This, then, was the kind of music he would give them.

The Booths decided to concentrate their activity in London, where they organized an agency called The East London Christian Revival Society, later known as The East London Christian Mission, and subsequently as The Christian Mission. In the London slums the road became rough. With a few musicians and loyal followers, Booth would march to open-air meetings or to revivals in a tent he pitched on a Quaker burial ground. Along the way he and his people were bombarded with stones, tomatoes, eggs, or other missiles by drunkards and blasphemers, yet in the midst of the barrages and the mockery William Booth would hold high his Bible and proclaim the gospel of love to those who were most antagonistic.

One day when a heavy windstorm (and some enemy sabotage) destroyed Booth's tent, he hired a saloon and dance hall for his Sunday services. He preached in butcher shops, carpenter shops, an old wool-shed, in stables—anywhere he could find space. In 1867 he rented the Effingham Theatre, one of the lowest resorts then in London, and packed it to the rafters. Later he took over a dingy, disreputable saloon, "The Eastern Star," cleaned it up and used it as an administrative headquarters for his movement.

As Booth's converts increased, so did the antagonism of the "pub" owners, who were losing some of their best bar customers. "That old fool wants to take away the only pleasure you 'ave," the saloon-keepers warned. "You can't be like them rich toffs wot spends their money for the ballet and flipperies and such. We're poor people, we are, and we've got to stick together like poor people should."

It was a forceful argument because the pubs were truly the social recreation centers for the low-paid working class. There

7

were no movies, no other forms of entertainment as inexpensive or so satisfying as a flagon of ale or a few gulps of whiskey. The fact that hard-earned money was often used to quench a thirst rather than to feed and clothe a family was promptly buried, ostrich-like, in the far recesses of the mind, and it was William Booth's chosen mission to divert the flow of shillings from the bulging pockets of the liquor barons to cleaner, better living for the families in need.

Booth's converts, men and women alike, were former drunks, thieves, prostitutes and other notorious characters who used their new-found moral strength to stand on the streets and testify openly and proudly that they had found a wonderful way of life through Jesus Christ.

One night three men and a woman, standing outside a saloon and shouting the glories of the Lord, were suddenly rushed by men carrying boxes of garbage which they dumped over the heads of the four penitents.

"Father, forgive them," one man said.

"God bless you and make you see the light," the woman told the attackers.

"Hallelujah!" another man shouted.

The garbage heavers laughed and yelled, and the quartette then began to sing a hymn. The attackers closed in, shoving the four down the street as they continued to sing.

This was a typical episode among Booth's followers, except that some encounters were more violent. Many of their street services were broken up by hired goons who beat the converts, both men and women, into masses of bruises. Parading Salvationists were frequently stoned and trampled, even smeared with whitewash, only to continue marching to their meeting halls and hold services with bloody faces.

Women who had accepted the Lord invaded saloons to seek new converts, defying jeers, insults, and orders to get out. After a brief testimony a girl would kneel on the sawdust-covered floor and pray aloud, even though she might not be heard above the din of laughter and derision. Frequently the bartender or barmaid would draw free ale and beer for men

8

who delighted in pouring it over the head of the kneeling woman, yet she knelt calmly until her prayer was finished, and before leaving she would smile at her tormentors and say, "God bless you all. Hallelujah!"

In 1882 William Booth took a bold step in his fight against the liquor interests. He bought an unexpired lease on a saloon called the Eagle Tavern and promptly closed the place. The barflies and steady customers, fired up by other saloon-keepers who were secretly frightened by Booth's victory, armed themselves with stones, sticks and empty bottles (courtesy of the pub owners) and stormed the Eagle Tavern, where Booth was holding worship services.

Amid a chorus of catcalls, curses and murderous threats, the mob hurled its missiles through all of the tavern's windows. Inside, Booth called his flock to kneel in prayer (they called it "knee drill"), and in the crash and jangle of breaking glass his supplication, loud and clear, was punctuated by the voices of his men and women shouting, "Hallelujah!" and "Bless the Lord!" and "Amen!"

Some of the converts were struck by stones or jagged fragments of glass, and others ministered to them even as they sang their hymns. The mob finally dispersed, the siege was broken, and the defenders set about cleaning up the debris.

On another occasion Booth's daughter, Evangeline, was stoned and fell to the street, blood flowing from her forehead. She was seized by a British constable who forcibly dragged her to the police station to charge her with disorderly conduct. His superior officer refused to support the charge and Evangeline was released.

After more experiences with the violence of unsympathetic crowds Evangeline developed a technique that proved highly effective. If a knot of people interfered with her marching, Evangeline tried to identify the ringleader and would then approach him with a wide-eyed appeal for his help and protection.

"You seem a kind man," she would say. "We need protection from this crowd. Won't you help me, please?"

Nine times out of ten the man would respond to her plea and escort her and her company to their destination.

A time came when William Booth was under a new kind of attack. His antagonist was the law itself. The lease on the Eagle Tavern was accompanied by a license to sell liquor. The license was renewable each year, and if he continued to hold the saloon he was compelled to meet the demands of the license and to sell liquor. He could, of course, give up his lease and license, but they had been purchased with the contributions of his followers and Booth decided it would be unfair to them to give up what they had paid for. Reluctantly he took the only alternative—he designated one small room in the building as a saloon and, as compelled by the law, marked its door with his name and a declaration that he was licensed to sell alcoholic beverages. He had comparatively few customers, because in his eyes they were all potential converts and he did his best to win them over, even as they guzzled their drinks.

The constant pleading by the converted thieves and prostitutes, and the testimony offered by them and by drunks-turned-sober gradually made an impression upon other wayward souls who, one by one, left the jeering opponents to join the ranks of the penitents and the Reverend William Booth.

At the same time, Booth was also winning the sympathy and support of higher-income groups in England, and his appeals for money to help the downtrodden drew satisfying results.

Throughout all this activity Catherine Booth conducted revival services of her own, not only to rehabilitate fallen women, but also to gain support for her activity from the educated classes. Her work was interrupted at intervals for twelve years, during which time she bore eight children. While all of these were to become active in Booth's movement, three in particular —William Bramwell Booth, Ballington Booth, and Eva (Evangeline) Booth—were destined to play noteworthy roles in the story of The Salvation Army.

William Bramwell Booth became the second General of the Army when his father died (1912).

Ballington Booth, who commanded the Army in the United

States, had a disagreement which resulted in his separation from the Army and the formation, by him and his wife, of a similar organization, The Volunteers of America.

The first news of this separation was a story in *The War Cry* on February 29, 1896, a curt announcement that the Ballington Booths had resigned from The Salvation Army. The beginning of the break occurred the previous January, when Bramwell ordered his brother Ballington to leave the United States for reassignment. Ballington protested that relations between Britain and America were strained because the United States was backing Venezuela in a border dispute between that country and England, and that a new Salvation Army commander coming to the United States from England might dim the favorable light in which Americans held The Salvation Army.

In addition, the Ballington Booths had not enjoyed a close relationship with General Booth for some time, and the General had not even communicated with them for six months or more. Over Ballington's objections, the old man had already placed certain parts of the Army's organization in the United States under the jurisdiction of Salvation Army headquarters in Toronto, Canada.

These were the principal reasons why Ballington and his wife chose to leave the Army. Some people, not knowing the whole story, declared that Ballington was insane. Others tried character assassination, calling him an ingrate and names even worse.

To clarify his position and perhaps (according to some) aiming to promote the separation of the entire Army in America from the international organization, Ballington held a mass meeting in the Army's New York headquarters. When the hall was filled with Salvation Army personnel, the doors were locked to outsiders.

Ballington's sister, Evangeline, who had tried in vain to change his mind about the resignation, was forbidden to attend the meeting. Characteristically, she went to the back of the building, climbed a fire escape and opened a window near the auditorium. Making her way backstage, Evangeline swept out

11

to the platform and cried out that she was entitled to speak her piece.

A great actress as well as a dedicated humanitarian, Evangeline held the crowd spellbound with her eloquence, her sincerity and her forceful arguments in favor of her beloved father. When she finished, her arms held outward in a symbolic plea, there were a few cries of "Hallelujah!" and "God bless General Booth!" The cries were echoed through the hall and soon the whole gathering pledged its allegiance to the General. Ballington strode out of the hall, never again to return to the Army's national headquarters.

On March 9, 1896, Mr. and Mrs. Ballington Booth established the philanthropic organization known as The Volunteers of America. Ballington became its first General, and although The Volunteers of America was a "democratic American organization" whose commanders were to be elected for five-year terms, Ballington held the top post for more than 30 years. He built well, however, for the organization grew steadily and is today active throughout the United States.

Eventually Evangeline Booth became General of The Salvation Army and carried its standard and message to throngs of people throughout the world. She was probably the most famous of all the Army leaders and had a sense of showmanship that was a tremendous asset to her and her entire organization.

Incidentally, Evangeline Booth's mother, after reading *Uncle Tom's Cabin*, had wanted her daughter called "Eva," but William Booth recorded his daughter's given name as "Evelyne," and she was called "Eva" at home but was addressed as "Dear Evelyne" in letters from her father. When she came to the United States as a grown woman she took the name "Evangeline" at the suggestion of Frances Willard, founder of the Women's Christian Temperance Union, who evidently felt that the name was more euphonious and more suited to a public figure. Evangeline herself often signed correspondence with her middle name, Cory, which was bestowed in appreciation of considerable financial support which William Booth received from two close friends, John and Richard Cory, well-known Welsh coal merchants.

As the work of The Christian Mission broadened, William Booth hired a young Scot, George Railton, to handle administrative details. In 1878, when Railton was preparing an annual report of the group's accomplishments, he proposed saying that "The Christian Mission has organized a volunteer army to carry the Blood of Christ and the Fire of the Holy Ghost to every corner of the world."

William Booth, reading the draft, shook his head. "Not 'volunteer army,'" he said. "The members of our Mission are 'regulars'."

With a pencil he crossed out the word *volunteer* and wrote in the word *salvation*. Thus was The Salvation Army christened. Later he drew up "Orders and Regulations" which were modeled upon the military orders of the regular British Army. His posts were designated as "Corps," military ranks were established, and the first flag was designed by Catherine Booth.

The flag today has a dark blue border around a red rectangle in the center of which is a yellow star inscribed with the words, "Blood and Fire." The blue symbolizes the purity of God; the crimson center the atoning Savior; and the yellow star the Fire of the Holy Spirit.

"Blood and Fire," the Army's motto, was taken from the Bible: "And I will shew wonders in the heavens and in the earth, blood, and fire, and pillars of smoke" (Joel 2:30). To the people of the Army it means "the Blood of Jesus Christ and the Fire of the Holy Spirit."

Booth began publication of a magazine, *The War Cry,* to keep his "soldiers" abreast of each other's work, and to be sold to the public to promote conversions and to raise operating funds. Sample items from the edition of September 13, 1883: "Teems (Gateshead on Tyne) has captured a man who lives in a room over the hall and who used to disturb the meeting by rolling potatoes and turnips on the floor. He rolls the chariot along now."

"WANTED: Within the next six months, 300 men, 200

13

women, who are willing to forsake their friends, who are willing to leave their homes and suffer persecution, who are willing to work for nothing but food and clothing, in fact to give themselves up to God and The Salvation Army for the salvation of the people."

When William Booth was asked, "Why a weekly *War Cry?*" he answered, "Because our Army means more war! Because millions cry to our inmost souls to arise and fight more furiously than ever for the salvation of our fellows. We shall conquer! To that end, let *The War Cry* go everywhere. Quick!"

The War Cry was then, as it still is, an effective fund-raising device which also spread the Gospel among its readers and kept the Salvationists informed of the Army's accomplishments. Evangeline Booth, at 17, was one of the most successful *War Cry* salesgirls. As each issue came off the press she would memorize the names of various cities, towns or countries mentioned in some of the columns, and like a hawking newsboy she would follow a prospective buyer down the street, calling out the list of places in the hope that one or more would be of special interest to the customer. Perhaps this technique was responsible for her sales record, or maybe her hard-sell persistence motivated prospects to buy the paper to get rid of Evangeline.

Many supporters who could not afford to give money to the Salvationists responded to appeals for worn furniture, castoff clothing or other unwanted possessions which the Army might then renovate and use or sell.

This salvage of merchandise was both secondary and essential to the spreading salvage of sinners. The penitents who had been outcasts of "respectable" society, the great unwashed, the undernourished, many living in squalor, began the uphill climb to clean and decent living, deriving material help from William Booth and spiritual strength from their growing faith in God.

Not all were in earnest, any more than are all those who today profess to be "saved." Some acted a part in order to get food, lodging, or other benefits, secretly (and erroneously) believing that Booth and his assistants were genuinely fooled. To some the desire to be cleansed was subordinate to a more powerful feeling, a longing of the weak to be looked after and cared for as a child seeks the comfort of its parents. Others who entered into pacts with God and William Booth often found temptation stronger than redemption and became "backsliders" who reverted to the old life and old ways. A growing number, however, clung to hope and repentance, and the force that began as a kind of worshipful rabble was slowly becoming an organized regiment of dedicated volunteers.

Clothing this volunteer Army became a problem. Catherine Booth felt that some officers dressed in too worldly a fashion and that others, going to the opposite extreme, wore costumes that were unsuitable if not downright ridiculous. She suggested that uniforms be worn, and the members agreed. However, no attempt was made immediately to design a distinctive uniform, and the officers improvised as best they could, often wearing clothing contributed by supporters. Some wore second-hand British Army uniforms of varying styles and periods. Some wore postmen's caps with red ribbons, or firemen's blue jackets with do-it-yourself brass "S"'s on the lapels. In 1880 George Railton punched the words "Salvation Army" in a piece of tin which he tied across the front of the derby worn by an officer named Henry Howard. Some "soldiers" tore the printed title, *The War Cry*, from the top of the Army's publication and fastened it around their caps or hats.

Catherine Booth finally designed standard uniforms of red and blue—the colors of the Army. Since headgear was important for the women, Catherine and her daughter Emma collected an assortment of straw bonnets, closeted themselves in a room, and tried on all the hats to find one that would be suitable for both mother and daughter. None actually satisfied them so Catherine chose the one she considered most suitable and made certain modifications in the design. She summoned a young cadet who was a milliner by trade and had him produce a sample bonnet to her specifications. After she approved the model, the cadet produced twenty-five of the new hats

15

which were first worn by twenty-five women officers marching from Hackney to Whitechapel on June 16, 1880, for the silver wedding anniversary celebration of William and Catherine Booth.

The bonnet was called "the Hallelujah Bonnet," just as the Army was often called "The Hallelujah Army," mostly because its members in their enthusiasm were given to frequent shouts of "Hallelujah!" during services or even in discussions with potential converts. The brim of the original bonnet was considerably wider than it is today, and the wide brim was especially effective in protecting the wearer from ripe tomatoes or from beer poured by sneering drunks over the heads of the Army girls who knelt to pray for sinners on the sawdust floors of Whitechapel saloons.

Since the Army was modeled after the British Army it was natural that William Booth, who was "General Superintendent" of The Christian Mission, should henceforth be given the title of "General" as the leader of the Army he created. And Booth looked like a leader. Tall and gaunt, he wore a long full beard which, as it whitened, gave him a startling resemblance to the great Moses as the latter is pictured in Biblical literature. Booth had a pale complexion and sad black eyes which one man said "seemed to look right into my soul."

Booth's adoption of uniforms and military titles evidently disturbed Queen Victoria. Her army was supposed to be the *only* army in England, and she was its royal commander. Although she took no direct action against Booth, she made it plain that she was opposed to his "generalship" and the military aspects of his organization, and this antagonism soon communicated itself to the middle and upper classes. Those who disliked Booth and his methods were pleased that the Queen was of their mind. Those who tolerated, or even might have encouraged Booth were now not inclined to incur Victoria's displeasure by giving any assistance to The Salvation Army. The mobs that attacked Booth and his followers felt that the Queen's attitude gave them a degree of immunity from any serious punishment, and it undoubtedly did tend to dull the concern of police and local authorities.

Although Queen Victoria ultimately recognized that The Salvation Army's aims and efforts were commendable, she never ceased to resent the fact that "General" Booth and his "officers" led an "Army" in her empire. Not until her son, Albert Edward, was crowned King Edward VII in 1901 did the royal attitude change for the better. King Edward was intensely interested in every cause and movement that would benefit his subjects, and he openly gave his blessing and generous support to The Salvation Army, a kingly move which later served to make General Booth welcome in the castles and courts of other nations.

General Booth's decision to carry his battle to the United States was motivated largely by 16-year-old Eliza Shirley, daughter of Amos and Anna Shirley, who were Salvation Army officers in Coventry, England, where Shirley worked as a silk weaver. The girl Eliza was also an officer in the Army.

When Amos Shirley decided to emigrate to America in 1879, Eliza went to General Booth.

"When we get to the United States, may we begin a corps?" she asked.

Booth stroked his beard. "Well, I don't think we're quite ready for that yet," he answered, "but whatever work you do, keep it along Salvation Army lines and perhaps we'll let you use the name."

The Shirleys settled in Philadelphia, where Eliza was soon holding open-air services which were so successful that she rented an old chair factory and began indoor Salvation Army meetings. People flocked to hear the teen-ager preach, and she soon sent a report and an appeal to General Booth: "Send us reinforcements!"

On February 14, 1880, Booth appointed his first commissioner, George Railton, to lead seven young women officers to broaden the work in America. They left England aboard the SS *Australia* and arrived in New York City on March 10, 1880.

Failing to find a church or hall for their first meeting, Railton and his "lassies" accepted an invitation from Harry Hill, owner of a notorious music hall, to open his Sunday night show. There they preached and sang amid jeers and cheers. As they left the hall they were joined by James Kemp, a Bowery character known as "Ashbarrel Jimmy" because he was a scavenger, constantly searching trash cans for food or junk. The next day Kemp became the first convert of The Salvation Army in America, later became a lieutenant, and was a captain when he died in 1895.

Chapter 2

THE BUM AND THE DRUM

The Salvation Army establishment in a Skid Row area is generally known as its Harbor Light Corps, and throughout the world it serves as a home and haven for those who are homeless, friendless and despondent.

Harbor Light work began in Canada some years ago when two retired Salvation Army officers in Vancouver, aroused by the plight of drunks and derelicts, held meetings in a store known as The Smoke Shop. The place accommodated a maximum of 25 people and was crowded every night, with several being turned away. Recognizing the need, The Salvation Army assigned Captain and Mrs. William Leslie to set up a Harbor Light Corps in larger quarters. They leased a combination cafe and rooming house with a disreputable history of illicit traffic in liquor, drugs and women.

No funds were available to renovate the place, but several converts who were skilled in carpentry, painting and other trades worked day and night to redecorate the building. The cafe became an auditorium seating 100 people, yet scores stood outside for lack of room.

Urgent appeals to the public brought in money which, combined with some of the Army's other funds, made possible the erection of a new building which was opened in 1956. Salvation meetings are held nightly, men are fed, and converts are helped to get jobs. The homeless can shave, get showers, fresh clothing, and polish and brushes to clean their shoes.

A medical clinic, manned by volunteer doctors, is available to all and includes a consulting room, a two-bed hospital room, and a dispensary. There are bedrooms to accommodate 42 men, a pleasant dining room and a modern kitchen. An auditorium seats 250 and at most of the nightly meetings there is standing room only.

Typical of the people helped is 47-year-old Ernest Welch, who became a compulsive drinker when he was 17, yet managed to earn a good living until he began to spike his liquor with codeine and barbiturates and finally hit the Vancouver skids in 1951. His wife left him, he lost his West Vancouver home, and sank lower and lower in the Skid Row muck.

Twice Ernie tried suicide without success. "I never made a third try," he says, "because I didn't have the guts or the strength."

His bedroom became a doorway, a park bench, or, on a cold night, the bathroom of a flophouse. One night in 1953 he sat in a saloon with another man and a woman, scheming to pick the pockets of a customer who looked prosperous. For some foggy reason that Ernie can't recall or explain he left the couple and wandered into the drizzly night.

Walking aimlessly he remembers squinting through the fogged window of a door. The door opened and a man's voice said in a kindly tone, "I'm sorry, but we're all filled up."

Ernie walked away, but a moment later the door opened again and the same voice called, "Hey! Come on in. Someone's leaving."

Ernie went back and found himself in the Harbor Light Corps where services were in progress. "I felt like cursing and mocking," he recalls, "but I went back the next night and the next, because I had an odd feeling that I would finally find peace."

On February 10, 1954, Ernie Welch accepted Christ as his Savior. With the Army's help and more courage than he thought he possessed, he fought off his craving for liquor and began to find satisfaction in bringing other derelicts back to decent living. Ernie became a Salvationist and within a few short years was Quartermaster of the Vancouver Harbor Light Corps, a post he held as this book was written.

Not all bottle-slaves are men. In Mexico City, Mrs. Irene de Moreno and her husband were once drunk most of the time, their children neglected and often hungry. One day their eldest son heard singing as he passed The Salvation Army building and stopped on the street to listen. An officer invited him in and took his name and address. A few days later the officer called at the Moreno home and was greeted by the boy's parents in their customary sodden condition.

Knowing that whatever he said would make little or no impression at that time, the officer left, but he returned the following day and began to make frequent visits to the home, talking to the Morenos about God and their need for salvation. It was Mr. Moreno who first decided to attend services at The Salvation Army's Temple Corps. He enjoyed the songs and the loud band music and even the preaching, and although he disliked the Salvationists' ban on the use of liquor and tobacco and other harmful habits he continued to go to their meetings.

Eight months later two women officers visited the Moreno home and found Mrs. Moreno cold sober. They read to her from the Bible and knelt in prayer. One of the women had tears in her eyes and although Mrs. Moreno did not completely understand everything that was said, she was impressed by the officers' fervor and promised to attend a meeting.

The following Thursday she not only kept her promise, but also became a convert. The conversion stuck, because she stopped her drinking, gave motherly love and attention to her family, and brought her children into the Army fold. Today she is secretary of the Salvation Army's Home League in the Mexico City Temple Corps, a member of the League of Mercy, and an ardent worker among Mexican youth.

Dramas of salvation such as these are enacted daily in London, Paris, Buenos Aires, Singapore, Capetown, New York, and scores of other cities where The Salvation Army lends its hand to man.

For a closer look at the Army's "bum-to-Bible" strategy I went to one of the world's skiddiest rows—the New York street called The Bowery. Although "Ashbarrel Jimmy," the Army's first convert in the United States, has long since been "promoted to glory," as General Booth would say, The Bowery where he once held sway is still a street of derelicts, abomination and vice which has its counterparts in practically every big city in the civilized world.

The Bowery was once a nameless trail used by Indians in hit-and-run raids on Nieuw Amsterdam. As the Dutch settlement grew, Governor Peter Stuyvesant built a fine home on its outskirts and the Indian trail became a road to the Stuyvesant *bouwerij*, meaning "farm." "Bowery" is simply an Anglicized version of the Dutch word.

Throughout the Civil War and for some years afterward The Bowery was the entertainment center of New York, studded with theaters of all kinds, the Great White Way of its day, where youthful unknowns won applause and encouragement for singing and dancing that sent them to the pinnacle of show business. In the house at No. 15 Bowery lived Stephen C. Foster, composer of *My Old Kentucky Home, Old Black Joe,* and other now-famous American folk songs and ballads.

The glitter of The Bowery began to tarnish in the 1870s when good theaters moved northward, giving way to cheap auction rooms, dirty saloons and dime museums. The Bowery degenerated more and more every year, taking with it a horde of deteriorating humans to whom Skid Row became the only familiar world, a place where men could do as they pleased—drinking, whoring, stealing, killing, begging, even dying—with little or no interference.

Only a few years ago the grimy steel pillars and tracks of the elevated railroad cast their shadows over The Bowery below, deepening the gloom and despair that pervaded the whole area. Today the elevated is no longer there, and in some spots there are new modern buildings where once stood

22

shabby taverns and shops, but the cheap saloons, the 25-cent flophouses (no charge for the lice), the uninviting restaurants with menus soaped on the street windows ("Pigs' ears and sauerkraut, 25¢") are much in evidence—and so are the bums and derelicts who patronize them.

In the greenish spotlight of a Bowery street lamp the shadowy figures of two men play out a real-life drama that has had more performances, with changing casts, than any Broadway smash hit. The time is Spring, 1960. One of the men is a thief with a thirst. The other is his drunken victim.

The victim, in such a stupor that he is completely oblivious to his surroundings or his plight, hugs the lamppost and mumbles incoherently while the thief unties the frayed rope-belt that holds up the victim's shabby pants.

The trousers slip to the sidewalk and the thief stoops to pull them free of the wearer's legs. He halts abruptly when he hears footsteps approaching. From the darkness a man's voice shouts, "Hey, there!" The footsteps quicken. The thief straightens up and runs down the street, vanishing in the countless shadows, not waiting to see who has thwarted his attempt at robbery.

The rescuer, who reaches the drunk in time to save him from collapsing into the gutter, wears a blue cap with a red band and a blue uniform with a high, clerical-like collar on which two silvery letters "S" catch the feeble rays from the overhead light and stand out boldly against the dark cloth. He is Brigadier Franklin W. Hoffman of the Bowery Corps of The Salvation Army. He pulls up and fastens the trousers; then, with one of the man's arms around his shoulders, he half drags, half carries him to the nearby Municipal Lodging House and gets him a bed for the night.

"The poor fellow had nothing of value except the clothes he wore," Hoffman says, in recalling the incident. "The thief undoubtedly wanted enough money to buy a bottle of cheap wine, and he would have sold the clothes for a quarter or fifty cents in one of the second-hand clothing stores along The Bowery. This isn't unusual in this neighborhood. Many times we see drunks lying on the sidewalks or in doorways without their pants, coats or shirts, wearing only shorts or union suits that haven't been washed in weeks or maybe months. Unfortunately it's an old, old story, and a sad one at that."

I prowled The Bowery in May, by day and by night. On a Saturday morning I watched a short, thin man in ill-fitting shabby clothes walk unsteadily in my direction, stop in the middle of the sidewalk and vomit. Not ten feet from him a disinterested sparrow pecked at a three-inch length of well-chewed corncob in the gutter. Two other men strolled past me and past the puker, giving him no more than a casual glance.

Across the street another man—or what once was a man—sat slumped in the boarded-up doorway of a vacant store, looking more like a pile of dirty wrinkled clothes than a human figure.

I passed a cubbyhole clothing store with clothes displayed in a small show window and hand-lettered signs: "Sport coat, $1.75. 2-pc. suit, $3.75. Shirt, 45¢." Another sign read, "Baggage checked—5¢ a day."

As I continued my walk I saw a girl wearing a yellow sweater and a tight blue skirt saunter up to a man leaning against a dirty brick wall next to a liquor store. The girl had wavy blonde hair, a rather voluptuous figure, and was quite pretty even with her blue eye-shadow and other heavy makeup. She was about 30 years old. The man wore a battered and stained gray felt hat, a well-wrinkled dark gray tweed jacket with one torn side pocket, and blue or black trousers that smothered his ankles with lumpy accordion folds because they were two or three inches too long. I judged him to be about 50, though it may be that the bristles of gray whiskers on his face made him look older than he was.

The girl spoke to the man, who grinned and pushed himself away from the brick wall, weaving slightly as he stood before her. A few moments later she stroked the back of his neck with one hand and he put both arms around her and pulled her toward him so that their bodies merged. She apparently asked him if he had money, because he fumbled in one pants pocket, then another, and dredged up some cash which he showed her. Evidently it was enough, because she took the man by the arm and they strolled down The Bowery, finally walking into a dilapidated building adjacent to a second-hand clothing store. The price of a session with the average Bowery prostitute, I learned later, is from fifty cents to two dollars, depending upon the customer's ability to pay.

On my way to the Bowery Corps of The Salvation Army I was approached by five drunken panhandlers within two blocks. Three asked me for nickels, two for dimes. One said he wanted a dime for coffee, adding that he hadn't had any breakfast. His breath was sour and nauseating.

"I won't give you the dime," I said, "but I'll buy breakfast for you if you're really hungry."

He blinked at me through glazed eyes and gave me a kind of indignant smile. "Whatsa matter?" he said. "You don't trust me, pal?"

"It isn't that," I said. "I just want to be sure you get enough to eat."

He nodded, and he kept nodding as he spoke. "Uh-huh. Uh-huh. So I'm a liar now. So I'm a goddamned liar. Hmmp. Hmmp." He stopped nodding. "Look, mister, you going to give me a dime or not?"

"No, I'm not. If I give you a dime you'll only spend it for more booze."

His eyebrows went up in mock surprise, then away down in a scowl, and we stared at each other for a moment without a word. Finally he rubbed a grimy finger back and forth under his coppery nose and said, "You're right, brother, you're absolutely right. *Thank* you. Thank *you!* You can keep your goddamned dime." He walked away, staggering and muttering.

Obviously, not all the people who frequent The Bowery are intoxicated and not all are beggars or bums. Many respectable folk live and work on the famous street, or use it as a thoroughfare to other neighborhoods. The casual visitor, however, is bound to take special notice of the drunks and panhandlers ("stemmers") and of the outcasts who stand or sit in doorways staring vacantly at passers-by and at the unceasing flow of motor traffic speeding north toward the incandescent glitter

25

of Times Square, or south toward the bricked-up gold fields of Wall Street.

In their own desolate and lonely realm, many find some degree of peace and always a friendly welcome in a fragment of the normal world erected especially for them and for others in need.

At No. 349 Bowery stands a neat tan-colored three-story brick building labeled "The Salvation Army." A red neon sign reads: "The Red Shield Club—Downstairs." This building is the Army's Bowery Corps, established in 1893—a "corps" being the Salvation Army equivalent for "church." In other cities the Bowery Corps has its counterpart in the Army's "Harbor Light" centers.

The officer in charge, Brigadier Franklin W. Hoffman, who was to take me through the place, said, "First let's step outside. I want to show you something."

Outside he pointed across The Bowery to a small store with a big sign, "Wines and Liquors." On the street corner near the store were several nondescript white men and Negroes, just standing around. A few doors away was another sign, "Blue Moon Bar."

"Liquor represents our biggest problem," Brigadier Hoffman said. "Most of the men on The Bowery steal, beg, roll drunks, do odd jobs or whatever else they can to get fifty cents or a dollar to buy cheap wine or whiskey." He told about the incident in which he prevented the theft of a drunkard's pants.

"Where do all the men come from?" I asked. "And what about the police? Don't they patrol the area?"

"The derelicts come from all parts of the country, even from foreign countries. Most of them are running from one thing or another, and a man who is running away can get lost easily on The Bowery. In other towns you can't drink yourself blind and lie around in the gutter as men do here. The police? Sure, the police patrol The Bowery and they do a good job under the circumstances. They break up groups on the street corners, and the groups re-form as soon as the police are out of sight. But what are the police going to do with ten thousand bums?

Who wants to clean up after them? Here they find others on their own low level—people they can talk to about the things they enjoy talking about—drinking, gambling, and women."

At the street corner a few feet away Hoffman pointed to a tall, grimy building in the next block and said, "That's the city's Municipal Lodging House. If a man is able to stagger up the steps to the entrance he can get a thirty-day ticket from the city and a place to eat and sleep. They feed up to six thousand men a day."

We went back into The Salvation Army building. In Brigadier Hoffman's office were a portable organ, a pulpit, and an amplifier. The organ is a fairly recent innovation. In the Bowery Corps it has partially replaced the famous Army bass drum and brass band, but these instruments are still used there and by the Army throughout the world, and they still play an important part in attracting sinners to hear how salvation may be theirs.

"We go out on the street every night at seven-thirty and hold a service on the sidewalk until seven fifty-five, then we move inside for a service in the chapel at eight o'clock," Hoffman said. "The street service is piped into the chapel and the chapel service is broadcast through the amplifier to the street."

The chapel accommodated 250 folding chairs. At one end was a raised platform and on the wall behind it, the only decoration, hung a reproduction of Warner Sallman's "Head of Christ."

Because I saw reproductions of this famous painting in all of The Salvation Army buildings I visited, and also in other religious institutions, I asked its creator, Warner Sallman, to tell me something of the picture's history.

Born in Chicago in 1892, Warner Sallman had early art instruction from his Swedish and Finnish parents, and as a boy he found great delight in the Bible pictures of Paul Gustave Doré, which he believes influenced his later work.

In 1924, when Sallman was art editor of a young people's church magazine, *The Covenant Companion*, he was in need of a cover illustration for the February issue. For years he had considered doing a picture of a virile, masculine Christ that would show Jesus' youthful maturity, His friendliness and loneliness, His courage and His humility. On the night before his magazine deadline, lying in bed wondering about the illustration, Sallman was startled by a visualization so vivid that it almost seemed to be on paper. While the image was fresh in his mind, he rushed to his attic studio and made a three-inch sketch of the picture, and in the morning he made an enlarged charcoal drawing which was published on the magazine cover.

Hundreds of requests came in for reproductions of the drawing, and some sixteen years later, in 1940, Warner Sallman painted the "Head of Christ" in oils. Reproductions were copyrighted and published by Kriebel & Bates, 4125 N. Keystone, Indianapolis 5, Indiana.

Says Mr. Sallman, "They informed me some time ago that the reproductions have run well over one hundred million copies since 1940."

He has since done a series of twenty other paintings of Christ in a variety of settings.

I asked Mr. Sallman whether or not he used a model for his famous painting. He did not. "Since my art school days and my early men's fashion commercial illustrating," he says, "I have not used models except when doing specific individual portraits, and very rarely have I used photographs of models for my paintings."

"I have had rather close association with The Salvation Army here in Chicago since the Century of Progress in 1932," he says. "I esteem them most highly."

In the Bowery Corps the Sallman "Head of Christ" looks across the chapel platform to a single row of wooden benches called "The Mercy Seat," or the "penitent form," where those who choose to may come in answer to an "altar call" to confess and repent of their sins and to accept Christ as their personal Savior, seeking His help and the help of The Salvation Army to find their way back to dignity and self-respect.

The room was spotlessly clean. "We can sit on these chairs and talk," Hoffman said. "All the chairs are sprayed and fumi-

28

gated every morning—otherwise they would probably be crawling with body lice, roaches and bedbugs. All of our bathrooms are disinfected thoroughly every day, and twice a month we have a professional exterminator come in to fumigate the whole place." He pointed toward vents near the ceiling. "See those openings? We have a blower system that changes the air in the whole building completely every six minutes, so there are no foul odors—except for body perspiration sometimes, which we can't help."

Body perspiration is almost perfume compared to other smells radiating from some men who come to Hoffman for help.

"Some of them sleep in doorways or on sidewalks for six months or more without a bath or a change of clothing," he explained. "They urinate and defecate in their pants. One man who came here recently had to walk with his legs wide apart because his inner thighs were actually raw from urine and fecal matter. We bathed him, coated his burns with ointment, gave him a change of clothing and a meal, and hope that he may come back to let us help him."

As we talked I noticed that Hoffman's shoes were not laced. "Your shoes are untied," I said.

He grinned and ran one hand over his thick graying hair. "They always are," he answered. "You see, I'm forever tramping up and down the streets, trying to do what I can to help these forgotten men. I get about four hours sleep every night —maybe five. But I do so much walking that if I lace my shoes my ankles get badly swollen."

As we talked a man about forty years old, wearing a short-sleeved blue shirt and blue trousers, walked through the room carrying a broom. He greeted Hoffman with a "Good morning," and went into a room on the other side of the chapel.

"See that man?" Hoffman asked. "One night he staggered up The Bowery, blind drunk, while we were holding our street service. When it ended and we came inside, he came along, but he was so stewed he didn't even know where he was. He just wanted some place to go. He was pretty ragged and very dirty. We fed him and got him a bed in the Municipal Lodging

House, and invited him to come back again. He came to another service when he was reasonably sober, and heard some of our converts give their witness and tell how they had been saved. The man grew pretty remorseful and told us what a great drunkard he had been and was, and pleaded for our help."

The man (we'll call him Marvin) told them his story. He was addicted to three evils—dope, drink, and gambling on the horses. Whenever he had money he would go to the race track, bet and usually lose every cent, then hitch-hike his way back to town. His vices made it impossible for him to hold any job longer than a few days, or past his first payday.

Marvin was made to bathe and shave, and was given a complete change of clothes from the Army's stock of used clothing. He was then sent to The Salvation Army Memorial Hotel, just a short distance from the Bowery Corps, on his promise to return.

He came back the next day, pale, shaky, and cold sober, and was asked routine questions about his personal history and background so that his answers could be recorded on a card kept in the file. The card carried such information as his name, birth date, birthplace, physical condition and description, occupation, last employer, Social Security number, names of relatives, education, marital status and other pertinent facts.

It was suggested that Marvin stay at the hotel for two days to get a complete rest. He did not take a drink during the two days, and when he again visited the Corps he was considered eligible to live in The Salvation Army Alcoholic Rehabilitation Center, an adjunct of the Bowery Corps.

The Center is actually a home for men who are sincerely seeking their way back to society. There are living quarters for twenty men. Except for a very few double rooms the men sleep in single bedrooms which are kept scrupulously clean. Each has a floor of light-colored vinyl tile (which is scrubbed every night), with walls of buff-colored ceramic tile. The single beds are covered with blue bedspreads and each room has a small bureau, a wardrobe, a comfortable chair and a big window.

30

There is a faint, clean and not unpleasant smell of disinfectant in halls and rooms.

An important part of the Center is an upstairs lounge where I saw an elevated television set, comfortable upholstered chairs, ashtrays, and a variety of magazines ranging from *The National Geographic* to *Time* and *Newsweek*. This lounge is used only by the men admitted to the Center to live. When the Center is full, as it usually is, others who have earned its privileges are housed in the Memorial Hotel and may use the Center's recreation facilities.

The residents have their own kitchen and dining room. A menu hangs on the wall and is changed daily. Sample entry: "Breakfast—two eggs and bacon, fried potatoes, buttered toast, coffee, 50¢." An aroma of boiling meat and onions heralds the news that beef stew is being prepared for dinner. If a man has no money he gets his meals and room free.

Marvin, like most of the men admitted to the Center, had no money when he moved in. The Salvation Army, as it does for many or all of its charges at the Center, sought a job for Marvin and found one in the stockroom of a New York department store.

One day Marvin came in and said, rather hesitantly, "You remember those questions you asked me a while back—the things you wrote down on that card? Well, some of those things weren't true. I'd like to give you the straight of it, if you want me to."

This, Hoffman told me, was not an uncommon occurrence. Many men were too ashamed to give their right names or to admit that somewhere they had wives and children, or parents, or brothers and sisters. Others might lie because they were being sought by police or for some other reason.

"Once we tried to identify them by their Social Security cards," Hoffman said, "but that wasn't reliable. Several of the men were pickpockets who could produce any one of six or eight Social Security cards they had stolen from different victims."

With frequent help from his Army friends, Marvin fought

31

off his craving for drink and dope, stopped gambling, and applied himself to his job so earnestly that he won a promotion.

When he began to earn a regular salary the Army asked him to pay for his room and meals at the Center. The charge: Fourteen dollars a week. He was not asked to pay for the quarters and food he was given before he became self-supporting. There is no limit on the duration of a man's residence at the Center. (Later I heard that one long-time resident at the Center made visits to his own home in another city "just long enough to make his wife pregnant!")

"Marvin came to the Bowery Corps three years ago," Hoffman recalled. "Today he is the head of his own department in the same store. He still attends our meetings regularly and in his spare time he comes here to help out any way he can. You just saw him carrying a broom. He's helping some of the men clean up the Red Shield Clubroom."

The Red Shield Clubroom is in the basement of the building and is open to the public. It has a television set, comfortable chairs, magazines, a snack bar, and tables where men play chess, checkers or dominoes. To become a card-carrying member of the Red Shield Club a man must be sober. There is no membership fee, but drunks are not eligible and a card-holder who is intoxicated will not be admitted.

Drunks are not kept from the evening chapel services, and probably more than half of the nightly congregations are bottle victims.

One night service I attended at the Bowery Corps with an old friend, Eddie Connors (a former Secret Service Agent) was conducted by Mrs. Brigadier Hoffman and her associate, Major Cora Nicholson, both of whom are Salvation Army veterans. Brigadier Hoffman played the piano for hymn-singing, and Major Nicholson spoke. The congregation consisted of about 140 men and one woman.

"But she's not an alcoholic," Brigadier Hoffman whispered to me. "She lives in the neighborhood and just likes to come to the services."

Women drunks are rather rare on The Bowery and the few who roam it are detested by the men.

Major Nicholson told us that the congregation was usually much larger, averaging about 250. "When it's cold outside a lot of the men come in just to get warm," she said. "Now warm weather is setting in, and they have favorite doorways where they sleep and which they don't want to give up, so they stay there. Also, a great many of the men take Summer jobs at pleasure resorts and camps—but they'll be back in the Fall. Some of these chaps have been on The Bowery for thirty or forty years."

The service began with the singing of a hymn, *Come, Every Soul*. The men didn't like it and wouldn't sing it.

"What do you want?" Major Nicholson asked.

Several shouted at once, but one loud voice boomed, "Two hundred and eight!" This hymn was *Wonderful Words of Life*, by P. P. Bliss, and the men sang two verses. Other favorites which they always sing with gusto are *Blessed Assurance, I Love to Tell the Story*, and *The Old Rugged Cross*, the latter a famous hymn composed in 1913 by Salvation Army Captain George Bennard in Kansas. It is said that Bennard could not read or write music, but played the guitar and strummed the tune which was written down by others.

After the hymns Brigadier Hoffman invited a group of nine men (including Ed Connors and me) to leave the front rows of the chapel and to sit on the raised platform facing the congregation. A few of the men were sound asleep, oblivious to everything. To the congregation she said, "Some of you who have not been here before may not know the significance of these men sitting here on the platform." She waved an arm in our direction. "All the men you see up here," she declared proudly, "have been saved for at least one month!"

In services at the Bowery Corps there is little "preaching," as such. The men are told, in down-to-earth language, about the forgiveness of sins and the chance they have to fight off the Devil. "It only takes two to do it—God and you yourself," sums up the fatherly or motherly content of most "sermons."

"We talk only about ten minutes," Brigadier Hoffman said. "The men get uneasy if the service is too long, so we try to keep it all within half an hour."

Connors and I looked out upon the strange congregation. From front row to back, from wall to wall, there were sad faces, faces that spoke silently of lost hope, despair, and a hunger for love, faces of failure and defeat, of cowardice, of frustration, of despondency and humiliation—the scratch-whiskered and clean-shaven pale or flushed or dark faces of human adversity.

Several of the converts on the platform were invited to come to the pulpit and read verses of their own selection from the Bible. A stocky Negro read from Matthew 9:13: "But go ye and learn what that meaneth, I will have mercy, and not sacrifice: for I am not come to call the righteous, but sinners to repentance."

A bald-headed white man of sixty or so, with a voice and accent like that of Maurice Chevalier, read Mark 6:12: "And they went out and preached that men should repent."

A short middle-aged man with thinning hair and a rich, thick Irish brogue, chose Luke 13:35: "Behold, your house is left unto you desolate: and verily I say unto you, Ye shall not see me until the time come when ye shall say, Blessed is he that cometh in the name of the Lord."

Throughout the service one wild-looking character, with a tangled mop of black hair and wearing thick-lensed horn-rimmed glasses, sat on an aisle seat arguing aloud with himself. He mumbled and shook a finger at the floor, then would glance at the ceiling and spout sentences. There were occasional cries of "Shut up!" and "Throw the bum out!", but the officers made no move to silence the man.

After the singing of another hymn, *I Have Found a Friend in Jesus*, the converts on the platform (excluding Connors and me!) were invited to give personal testimonies. They told how drinking had ruined their lives and how they had found the way back through repentance and through acceptance of Christ. Most had been sober for the past six or seven years.

Major Nicholson then made an "altar call," inviting anyone to come forward to the Mercy Seat to confess his sins and repent. For perhaps two minutes no one stirred. Then one man, sitting far back in the chapel, rose and came forward. He was about fifty, neatly dressed, and seemed to be on the verge of tears. Apparently he was not intoxicated. He knelt at the bench before the pulpit and one of the converts stepped from the platform to shake his hand, put an arm around his shoulders, and speak with him in a low voice.

Within five minutes four other men shuffled down the aisles to the penitent form and were received by four of the converts. The fifth man to answer the call had a sly smile on his face, and Connors whispered to me, "He looks like a phony."

After the meeting the entire congregation went downstairs to get coffee and doughnuts. (Every other night they are served soup, sandwiches and coffee.) While Mrs. Brigadier Hoffman and Major Nicholson worked in the stainless steel kitchen, we mentioned our suspicions about the "phony."

"Oh, that's quite possible," they said. "We get some men who are on the 'mission circuit.' They go from mission to mission, constantly 'repenting,' hoping for an extra handout or some special attention the sinners won't get. We know that many of the men who come to the Mercy Seat are putting on an act. Some come only for the food. Some won't or can't fight the terrific battle to straighten themselves out and to accept Christ—but if we can put just *one* out of a hundred on the right road, we feel that our efforts have been worth while."

Some who are saved become "backsliders," but may still find salvation. The 15-year-old son of one of Boston's old-line wealthy families ran away from home, served a year in the armed forces, worked for two years on a metropolitan newspaper, and finally joined the human roadblock of The Bowery, where he was on the bum for another two years. He returned to his Boston home and went to college for a year, then took a job in Texas, where he joined The Salvation Army and married one of its officers. He lost his wife, slid back to bumming and spent six terrible years wandering the Skid Rows of the country. On one Christmas Eve he was arrested for armed robbery and sentenced to prison for five to ten years. He was paroled, broke his parole and was recommitted. While in prison he found comfort in the counsel of Salvation Army officers who came to help him, and when he was finally released he became a highly responsible staff worker in The Salvation Army's $200,000 building on Skid Row in Chicago, where he now strives to break the stranglehold that alcohol has on other men as it once had on him.

Incidentally, Bowery and Skid Row converts cannot become full-fledged "soldiers" of The Salvation Army until they have been on their good behavior for an entire year. None is ever asked to join The Salvation Army—the request must originate with the man.

The dedication of Brigadier and Mrs. Hoffman and Major Nicholson in their struggle to restore these forgotten men to a long-forgotten world of decency stirs a warm and profound admiration for them, even in the hearts of those who visit with them only briefly. This feeling is one which radiated from every Salvation Army officer I met—and it was not a feeling that arose because I had never seen the seamy side of life. Both Ed Connors and I spent years together in the New York District of the United States Secret Service, coming into frequent contact with criminals of many types, seeing much of the sordid side of the underworld and observing big-time sinners through the eyes of the law-enforcement officer. Our visit with the Hoffmans and Major Nicholson was our first opportunity to meet and know Salvation Army people, and our impression was neatly summed up by Connors after we left the Bowery Corps.

"They really mean it," he said. "They're really wrapped up in what they're doing, and I guess they certainly have to be. I'm glad I had the chance to see how they work."

What induces a man like Franklin Hoffman to join The Salvation Army in the first place? His parents were staunch Methodists. He wanted to be a doctor. In Niles, Ohio, where he was born on October 28, 1903, he first saw a Salvation Army

36

group when he was seven years old. He was in the company of his father.

"Who are those funny-looking people?" the boy asked.

"They aren't funny-looking," his father said. "They're wearing special clothes they call uniforms, because they all belong and work together, like soldiers."

A little later they saw three Roman Catholic nuns. "Well, who are *those* funny-looking people?" young Hoffman said. "They don't have the same kind of clothes as the others."

"No, but in a way they are soldiers, too," his father said. "That's also a kind of uniform they wear. They're all fine people and they all work for God."

When Hoffman was in his 'teens he was in town one day with one of his brothers who was a professional boxer. "He was also what they called a 'drugstore cowboy,'" Hoffman added with a grin.

A Salvation Army group conducted a street service and was heckled by a gang of rowdy teen-agers. The Hoffman boys joined the Salvation Army captain, ready to help him if he needed them, but the gang wandered away. Franklin Hoffman went home, but his brother became interested in the Army, went to its meetings, and soon became a "soldier." Out of curiosity Franklin accompanied him to the Army services, which impressed him favorably. "For a long time," he recalls, "we went to the Methodist Church on Sunday mornings and The Salvation Army services in the afternoons."

Gradually the Army meetings took preference over the Methodist. "They say when you get Army fever you never get over it," Hoffman says. "I was working in a steel mill when I felt a definite call from God to become a Salvation Army officer." Today he has two brothers and a sister who are also officers.

Chapter 3

RULES AND SCHOOLS

"You will, if Salvation Army officers, without question wear uniform. If soldiers, we hope you will choose to do so. That means sacrificing the dazzling dream of a bridal dress, in its shimmering delight."

This suggestion comes from a Salvation Army "Handbook of Guidance" called *Married in the Salvation Army*, by Lt. Commissioner Alfred G. Gilliard.

"Soldiers" who prefer not to wear uniforms "will, we are sure, still wish to be married in the spirit of the Army, the bride foregoing the bridal dress of the conventional wedding for a simple unadorned suit, and the bridegroom choosing what we know as a business or lounge suit rather than the 'tuxedo,' which, by the way, is a 'uniform' indicating rigid social conventions. At the risk of appearing facetious or sarcastic we might ask, If you cannot wear Army uniform why, for this occasion, have the uniform of a night club waiter?"

The Handbook makes one concession, suggesting that this official "permission" from *Orders and Regulations for Officers of the Salvation Army* (1950 edition, Part 5, Chapter 6, Section 4) may be overlooked: "The bride may, if desired, appear without a head covering and wear a plain white or cream-colored sash, with a suitable motto worked in crimson."

Adds the Handbook: "You will not fall into the error of

38

thinking that the permitted sash was a touch of worldliness. It was, as a matter of fact, merely an extension of the hat band on the Army bonnet, a concession to the fundamental truth that most people are not good at recognizing the inner meaning of symbols."

Lighted candles at an Army wedding are considered out of place, except for use on tables at a reception following the ceremony.

One bridesmaid is considered enough to help the bride, although others are permissible.

Salvation Army tunes are preferable to so-called "wedding marches" which "have little in common with the spirit of a Salvation Army wedding." And sentimental ballads and love songs, "though they have a place in our lives, do not belong to the Salvation Army wedding service."

Regulations discourage the throwing of rice, confetti, shoes, or "any frivolous custom unworthy of the Army." Rice-throwing began as a pagan rite and has no place in a Christian ceremony, says the guide.

According to the Articles of Marriage, the Salvationist bride and groom wed not only each other, but also, in effect, they marry the Army itself. They declare that they have not sought the marriage for the sake of their own happiness only, "but because we believe that the union will enable us better to please and serve God and more earnestly and successfully to fight and work in The Salvation Army."

They promise to use their influence with each other to promote self-sacrifice in fighting for the salvation of the world and to regard and maintain their home as Salvation Army quarters. Among other vows they agree: "Should either of us from sickness, death or any other cause cease to be an efficient soldier, we engage that the remaining one shall continue to the best of his or her ability to fulfill all these promises."

The officer who joins them in wedlock says to the bride and groom, "My dear comrades, if you wish to be married upon these terms, and if, in the presence of God, who searches all hearts, you know of no just cause why you should not be joined in marriage, stand forward."

The bridegroom says, "I do solemnly declare that I know not of any lawful impediment why I, John Jones, may not be joined in matrimony to Mary Smith." The bride makes a similar declaration.

The minister (officer) then says to the bridegroom, "Will you have this woman to be your wedded wife, to live together after God's ordinance in the holy estate of matrimony? Will you love her, comfort, honor and keep her, in sickness and in health, and never seek to prevent her doing anything that is in her power to do, or giving anything that is within her power to give, to help The Salvation Army; and will you promise to use all your influence to promote her constant and entire self-sacrifice for the salvation of the world, and forsaking all others, keep you only unto her, so long as you both shall live?"

The same questions are asked of the bride.

The bridegroom and bride answer in turn, "I will."

The groom takes the bride's right hand and says, after the officer, "I call upon these persons here present to witness that I, John Jones, do take thee, Mary Smith, to be my lawful wedded wife and my continual comrade in the salvation war; to have and to hold from this day forward, for better, for worse, for richer, for poorer, in sickness and in health, to love and to cherish till death us do part, according to God's holy ordinance; and this I declare upon my honor as a true soldier of Jesus Christ."

The bride takes the groom's right hand and makes a similar declaration, and the groom places the wedding ring on the third finger of the bride's left hand, saying, "I put this ring upon your finger, as a continual sign that we are married under the solemn pledges we have this day given, to live for God and fight in the ranks of The Salvation Army."

The minister joins their right hands together and says, "In the name of God and The Salvation Army, I declare you to be man and wife together. Whom God hath joined together, let no man put asunder."

There is a final prayer, a suitable song, a short spiritual talk, and a wedding feast or reception.

Couples who are not Salvationists may be married by any licensed Salvation Army officer. The ceremony for non-Salvationist weddings is much the same as that in any Protestant church, and no references to The Salvation Army are made in any vows.

All Salvationists are expected to sign what Founder William Booth called the "Articles of War." Briefly these constitute (1) a statement of the member's personal experience of salvation, (2) his pledge to separate himself from the sinful world and be loyal to Jesus Christ, (3) his pledge of allegiance to the Army and of obedience to its officers, (4) his experience of faith in the possibility of holy living, (5) his pledge to refrain completely from using all intoxicating liquors "and baneful drugs," and (6) his promise to devote all of his spare time, energy, and money to promote progress of the salvation battle.

Children born of the union of Salvation Army officers frequently become officers themselves, and several now active represent the fourth generation of Salvation Army men and women.

There have been occasional divorces among Salvation Army officers. The only recognized reason for such divorces is adultery, and with a divorce both officers are compelled to resign. Within a few years the "innocent party" may apply for permission to rejoin the officer ranks. The case is then reviewed by top Army leaders, and if the individual has remained a good Salvationist soldier in the interim, he or she is generally reinstated and assigned to another part of the country.

Through the course of a marriage and a Salvation Army officer's career, family and personal problems are bound to arise, just as they do in any family. Generally these result from assignments which husband or wife may find difficult, or from discouragement about their work. If they take their problems to their superiors, efforts are made to solve them. It must be remembered that, unlike other Protestant clergy families, *both*

41

man and wife are ordained ministers, dedicated to their calling, and both have specific assignments in any appointment.

Salvation Army officers are released from their pledge to lifetime service at their own request. An officer may resign from any particular appointment. He or she is recorded as being "on furlough" for one year, during which time his situation is reviewed. If the officer has maintained a strong corps affiliation and demonstrates a continued dedication to the Army, he is generally offered a new appointment.

When an officer does resign from officership, he breaks a vow with the Army and with God, but this is considered a matter of his personal conscience. Actually, most former officers stay with the Army as Salvationist soldiers, and even in new employment don't get completely outside the fold, for they work for the Army as civilians, or for the Community Chest, the YMCA, or other service organizations.

There is a feeling among Salvation Army personnel that those officers afflicted with doubts are generally quite young, and that their immaturity creates their uncertainty as to whether or not they really have "the call" to a lifetime of service. It is not uncommon that a young officer's experiences in a first appointment are difficult, distasteful and frustrating, and fail to live up to his or her expectations. In such cases his superiors try to help the officer by reassigning him to other work, or by permitting him to resign and take a year to think things over. Instances in which an officer resigns, leaves in a huff, and completely rejects the Army are apparently rare, for none of the people with whom I talked knew of such cases.

Men and women who want to become Salvation Army officers may do so only if they complete the prescribed courses in a School for Officers' Training. The first such school was established by William Booth in London in the Spring of 1880 as the "Training Home for Women Officers," and was for women only, but it was so successful that he transformed his own home into a "Training Home for Men Officers" later that year and moved, with his family, to another house.

In those first schools many of the trainees had to be taught such unacademic subjects as the proper use of knives and forks, elementary table manners, and other social niceties which their earlier modes of living had never required. Eventually the sociological level of officer-candidates rose to a point where all emphasis was on intensive training in the conduct and promotion of Salvation Army principles aimed at the spreading of the Gospel.

In 1961 there were 30 Schools for Officers' Training throughout the world, including four in the United States—one in each of the Salvation Army "Territories":

Eastern Territory: New York   Central Territory: Chicago

Western Territory: San Francisco   Southern Territory: Atlanta

I visited the New York school, located at 1771 Andrews Avenue in the Bronx, and talked with its principal, Lt. Col. C. Emil Nelson, a rugged, handsome officer who, except for his Salvation Army uniform, would look at home in the chair of a bank president or a corporation executive.

The New York training school was once The Messiah Home (for children). "We still have occasional visitors who want to show wives or husbands the rooms they occupied when this was their childhood home," Colonel Nelson says.

The original building is a large Tudor mansion which was acquired by the Army on March 31, 1920. Entering the front door one is struck by the architecture of another day, with a long entrance hall and 14-foot ceiling, red tile floor, buff-colored walls and stout mahogany doors with frosted glass windows and transoms. On one wall are two bronze plaques listing "Doctrines of The Salvation Army." One room off the hall is a library, with well-stocked bookshelves and study tables, and a sign reading: "A generous bequest from Frederick W. Vanderbilt helps to maintain this institution." Another reads: "A memorial bequest for the betterment of humanity created in 1938 in the names of Emma W. and Jacob H. Schoonmaker, a substantial endowment fund to help train young people for Salvation Army service."

The Thomas J. Watson Hall, a new modern brick building behind the old one, should be completed and in use by the time this book reaches print.

The student body in 1960 totaled 72 men and women, called "Cadets," all living in the school building with the exception of six married couples residing in a house across the street.

For years the course of study in the school has covered a nine-month period, but with the opening of the new building the course will be extended to two years, with cadets spending 18 months in residence and the remaining six months in the field to gain practical experience in the application of their acquired knowledge. With the two-year course there will be about 150 cadets in residence, representing two classes.

Graduates are not from the "Class of 1962" or some other year, as in most colleges, but are identified by some chosen name such as "Pioneers," or "Ambassadors," or, as in the case of the 1960 class, "Great Hearts." The designation is the same for graduates of all Salvation Army officers' training schools, including the International (William Booth Memorial) Training College in London, England.

The nine-month course (extended to two years in 1960) is Bible-centered, with supplemental practical training. Subjects and approximate hours are:

BIBLE: Old Testament interpretation. Foundation course laying stress on the literature, revelation, history, poetry and prophecy of the Old Testament.

New Testament: Foundation course of the Life of Christ, the Pauline and General Epistles, and Hebrews and the Revelation. (Total, 120 hours.)

THEOLOGY: Basic Salvation Army doctrines and beliefs; understanding of other schools of belief and theology (55 hours).

CHURCH DISCIPLINE: Study of Salvation Army Government, regulations and instructions (65 hours).

HOMILETICS: Study of sermon-making (21 hours).

MUSIC: Participation in band and chorus. Private instruction on instrument of student's choice (150 hours).

44

PRE-FIELD TRAINING: Course in pastoral duties and methods (46 hours).

STUDY METHODS: Review course on study procedures (4 hours).

SERMON DELIVERY: Principles and methods of proper platform delivery (40 hours).

SOCIAL WORK: A survey course orienting students to terms and problems of the social work field (30 hours).

BOOKKEEPING: Survey of Salvation Army bookkeeping methods and procedures (22 hours).

CHURCH HISTORY: A study of the Christian church from apostolic days to the twentieth century (15 hours).

THE ART OF TEACHING: A course in various methods of teaching, particularly suited for work with children and young people (12 hours).

SALVATION ARMY LITERATURE: Supervised reading and reports of Salvation Army publications (9 hours).

LECTURES: Lectures on all types of Salvation Army procedures, policies, departments of work, including visiting leaders of The Salvation Army (International) who are occasional lecturers (75 hours).

INSTITUTES: Eight one-day institutes conducted by specialists in the several fields, geared to orient the student to Salvation Army programming and procedures in Young People's Work, Evangelism, Public Relations, League of Mercy, and Home League (40 hours).

FIELD PREPARATION: Supervised instruction for field work assignments (65 hours).

FIELD WORK: This includes the practical application of all methods and procedures peculiar to Salvation Army work which have been presented in the classroom. It includes conducting street meetings, evangelistic and worship services and children's meetings, observing operation of local community activities, and participating in financial efforts. The work is supervised by experienced Salvation Army officers who make observation reports to the school. The reports are passed on to the students with suggestions for improvement (635 hours).

Applicants for the officers' school must be members of The Salvation Army, preferably between 18 and 30 years old, who are high school graduates in good health. An applicant who did not finish high school may be permitted to take a "high school equivalency test" which will be acceptable if he passes it.

The boy or girl Salvationist in a local corps prepares for the training school by enrolling in a "Corps Cadet Course," which will educate him or her in basic Bible knowledge, in Salvation Army history and regulations, and teach him to work on corps projects in his own community. The course covers a six-year period, and is actually the equivalent of adult education courses in other churches. The youngster who completes the course receives a cash bonus ranging from $25 to $50, depending upon his grades, and is invited to join the Future Officers' Fellowship (FOF). He is not asked to make any commitments, but merely indicates his willingness to prepare for training as an officer.

In FOF he will get into group work in a Division. A Division is anywhere from 20 to 30 corps in a geographical area. Each Division has its FOF and there may be several in various communities. Each of the 20 or 30 corps may have 60 or 70 FOF members. FOF groups take part in week-end meetings, get special instruction in speaking, singing, playing musical instruments, and are taught to drive automobiles.

For the officers' training course the student pays only $127, which is less than its cost. This covers his tuition, room, meals and other expenses, including some books. He brings four books not furnished by the school: The Holy Bible, Cruden's Concordance, the American Collegiate Dictionary, and a Bible Dictionary.

College graduates are eligible to enroll, and several apply each year.

Before the youth is accepted at the training school he must pass a thorough physical examination and fill out a personal history form which is submitted along with recommendations and comments from his local superior officer, two lay members of his corps, his Divisional Commander and his Divisional Young People's Secretary. In the United States these papers are sent to the headquarters in each Territory for processing by the Candidates' Department and Candidates' Board, which may accept, decline, or defer approval of applications.

In the Candidates' Department in New York the papers are assembled and processed for the Board by Major Nellie Horwell, a soft-spoken, motherly Army veteran, and I talked with her about the types of young people who apply for officer training. I soon learned that each of Major Horwell's file folders is, to her, a proxy son or daughter whose personal history she knows like a mother.

She pulled out a folder at random, glanced at the name on it and said, "Oh, here's an interesting girl. She was born in Kiev, in the Ukraine, and when the Second World War broke out she and her family went to Germany, where the Nazis threw them into concentration camps. At the end of the war she lived in a camp for displaced persons in the British sector. She came to the United States in 1950, sponsored by the Church of the Brethren, joined The Salvation Army and wants to be an officer."

She grabbed another folder. "Here's a man who was born on the lower East Side of New York. His parents were Italian immigrants. As a child he went to the Salvation Army Sunday School in his neighborhood and joined our young people's groups. He learned to play a cornet and became a staff bandsman. He married a Salvation Army girl and they both went to officers' training school and are serving now as officers." She smiled proudly. "And they have three children and are as happy as all get-out."

A few years ago a Salvation Army captain needed a secretary. One applicant was a girl who belonged to the Russian Orthodox Church. She accepted the job, and when she mentioned it to her priest at the church he was quite upset. "It's bad enough that you should work there," he said. "Just remember that you must not go to any of The Salvation Army meetings or services."

The girl was so impressed by the spirit of the officers and soldiers with whom she associated on her job that she attended a meeting one night out of curiosity. She was so deeply touched that she was converted and became a soldier, complete with uniform and bonnet. Her parents and the priest were terribly upset and tried to persuade the girl to give up her job and the Army. Instead, she enrolled in the training school and is today an efficient and happy Salvation Army captain.

One couple, finally permitted to enroll as cadets in the training college, might not have met if it were not for the war in the Pacific. The girl was born in Peking, China, to Salvation Army officers who were missionaries there when World War II began. The entire family was imprisoned in a Japanese concentration camp for three years, when they were liberated by the Americans. Her parents were sent to the Philippines and it was there that the girl met and fell in love with the American GI who became her husband. Both are cadets in the training school as this is written.

At the training school Colonel Nelson explained that when a candidate is accepted he must take a specialized six-months home correspondence course, and if he has not completed it by the time he goes to the school he must devote his "free time" to finishing the course.

"It is actually a sort of preview of the work he will do on an intensive scale in the school," Nelson said. "It helps him in making what might be a difficult adjustment. Three years ago we had a cadet who had been a farmer. Every afternoon he would fall fast asleep in class. It took a long time for him to get used to sitting still for an hour or so at a time, all day long, after he had been pitching hay and plowing and doing all the other physical labor on a farm."

There are always more women than men in the training school. In 1960 there were 29 men and 43 women cadets. The school has a "Chief Side Officer" for men and a "Chief Side Officer" for women—the equivalents of the Dean of Men and Dean of Women in civilian colleges.

Some cadets decide that officership is not for them, and they resign. "Several of these, however, have reconsidered and returned," Nelson says.

A few find the studies too difficult and flunk out. Colonel Nelson tries to arrange matters so that any cadet who is to be flunked will remain until the Christmas holidays, when the entire student body goes home on leave. After Christmas the failure simply does not return to the school, so he is not embarrassed by having to quit under the sympathetic eyes of his fellow cadets.

Sometimes a poor student who is told bluntly that he faces failure reveals character traits that accent his strength or weakness.

"We had two women cadets, both rather dull and phlegmatic," Nelson recalls. "We told one, 'Your marks are consistently poor and we feel that you're wasting your time and ours.' She was quite lackadaisical about it and simply said, 'I guess you're right.' She left the school. However, when we said the same thing to the other girl, she huffed up and said, 'All right, then, I'll change. Don't make me leave. You let me work at it, and if I don't improve, okay, I'll go.' That girl really fought tooth and nail over her studies, and today she is an officer and doing very well."

Part of the training program is a ten-day campaign every Spring, when the cadets are sent into various communities in several States as guests of the local Corps. In telling about this part of the training Colonel Nelson made an important observation.

"Take seventy-two students in any other college and you will have seventy-two different ideas about what each will do when he graduates. With our cadets, however, you have seventy-two all thinking along one and the same line about the future."

Working in pairs (except that married couples do not work together at this time), the cadets take part in Sunday School activities, in open-air meetings, in regular adult services. Some go to morning services in prisons or reformatories, some visit the sick in hospitals, shut-ins at home, men and women in homes for the aged or at the Poor Farms. Some go to low-cost housing developments where scores of children may never have been inside a church, partly because there is no church in the area. They meet with teen-agers and other young people of the local corps in fellowship, and may conduct the adult evening services. Some go from house to house to meet people and to sell copies of *The War Cry*.

What do they learn from selling *The War Cry?* Says the colonel, "They develop confidence and resourcefulness and the ability to meet and mix with all kinds of people. Basically everything we in The Salvation Army do is selling to some degree. We are selling an idea, a way of life. If a cadet can knock on the door to the home of a person unknown and make a new friend, and if he can do it better every week, he develops a phase of his personality that he never dreamt he possessed."

When the cadets have successfully completed their courses of study at the training school they prepare to receive their commissions as probationary officers. The evening program includes a valedictory and suitable Salvation Army music, but this is all prologue to the most thrilling moment in the lives of these young people. A tremendous feeling of excitement surges through each cadet as he awaits the awarding of the commissions, when he will learn for the first time where he is to be sent for active duty. Assignments are closely guarded secrets until revealed during the graduation ceremonies.

At the climactic moment the Commissioner of The Salvation Army rises, steps forward and announces, "The time has come to give you your commissions and your appointments." Whispers waft through the group like the rustle of autumn oak leaves in a soft breeze, then the zephyr gives way to an eloquent hush of expectancy. The General Secretary calls out the name of each cadet. The cadet, whose footfalls seem extraordinarily loud in the stillness, marches forward to be greeted by the Commissioner. They exchange salutes.

The Commissioner says, "Candidate Robert Charles, I hereby promote you to the rank of Probationary Lieutenant." He pauses for a breathless few seconds before adding the big news, "You are appointed to be the assistant officer at the Harbor Light Corps in Detroit, Michigan."

No cadet objects to his assignment. He cannot apply for any specific post, but there is nothing to stop him from letting it be known in advance the type of work he prefers to do. Among all the officers with whom I talked, the universal impression I received was that their posts of duty were relatively unimportant to them; that they wanted to be wherever they were most needed and where they might best serve the downtrodden, and that they were happy in their work no matter where it took them.

It has taken them to many places. Since The Salvation Army operates like a military order, all officers must expect to go wherever they are sent. While most work in their native lands, many volunteer for service in other countries as missionaries or as corps leaders or in other positions, where they will gradually make new converts who will become self-sufficient and carry on the Army's work among their own people.

Salvationists from Western countries go as missionaries mainly to underdeveloped areas where they operate schools, hospitals, leper colonies, or other institutions. In Rhodesia, for instance, all commanding officers are Europeans or Americans, although members of their staffs may be Africans. India has a mixture of British and Indian officers. On the other hand, all commanding officers in Japan, an industrialized society, are Japanese. The principal reason is that less-developed countries do not have enough trained doctors, nurses and teachers among their own Salvationist population to man the Army's institutions and training schools. Japan is better off in this respect.

Certain foreign governments do not permit The Salvation Army to serve. Take China, for instance. Pioneer officers first arrived in Peking in 1916 and began an intensive study of the Chinese language in order to carry on a large-scale evangelistic program. Since that time more than 200 officers drawn from 12 overseas nations have served in North China, and almost the same number of Chinese Salvationists graduated from the School for Officers' Training in Peking and became officers.

Civil turmoil of the early years did not stop expansion, and steady progress was made. In 1927 a more serious crisis forced the withdrawal of many overseas Salvationists and placed new responsibilities on the Chinese officers. From 1937 onward, eight years of invasion and war sapped the vitality of the country and work was severely tested. For three years most of the overseas officers were interned, but under Chinese leadership the Army's work continued, especially its emergency relief work for the hungry and homeless.

At the end of 1951 there was a general exodus of missionaries ordered and all overseas Salvationists had to leave the country, handing over their work to a council of Chinese Salvation Army officers. There has since been no communication between these officers in Red China and International Headquarters in London.

In Czechoslovakia The Salvation Army began operations in 1919 in Prague, just after the country became an independent republic. The Army operated freely and effectively until June, 1950, when its activities were suppressed by the Communist government.

In Hungary serious restrictions were imposed upon the Army in 1949, but many Salvationists there continue "to maintain a faithful witness." No details of their activities have been received at International Headquarters.

In Italy under Mussolini's dictatorship Salvation Army officers were temporarily jailed, then banished, the Army was "disbanded" by government decree, and all of its institutions were closed. With the arrival of Allied forces in Rome in 1945 came Salvation Army Red Shield workers who reopened the corps. Salvationists took their uniforms out of hiding and began work again and today The Salvation Army in Italy is flourishing.

In Nazi Germany the activities of The Salvation Army were restricted but not completely suppressed during World War II. Publication of *The War Cry* was suspended, no collections were allowed, military ranks were forbidden, and social institutions confiscated. Many German Salvationists served in the German armies and some were confined to internment camps. Others, as civilians, continued to hold worship services and to minister to the needy as best they could. The Army has carried on its work in Germany continuously since 1886. In West Berlin the Army is recognized as a "Public Body with Legal Rights" and as a Public Corporation in the Land of Hesse. It is not permitted to work in East Berlin or other Communist-held territory, including the Soviet Union.

During World War II in Japan all Salvation Army installations were closed and there was a marked decline of interest in Christianity. Military titles and uniforms were forbidden, although Salvationists held meetings in civilian dress. When the atom bomb destroyed Hiroshima the Salvationists who survived were among those who pulled the wounded from the wreckage and gave them whatever help and comfort was possible. Since the end of the war many Salvation Army corps and outposts have been reopened and the Japanese people have taken a new and vigorous interest in Christian teachings. Japanese Salvation Army officers played an important part in organizing the evangelistic campaigns of Dr. Billy Graham in Tokyo and Osaka, and the Army's regular open-air meetings attract large crowds.

The School for Officers' Training in Tokyo has numbers of Japanese high school and college graduates who seek officership. The cadet program is similar to that in all of the Army's training schools.

After a cadet performs his one year of probationary service he becomes a full-fledged officer and an ordained minister. He gets a card which reads: "This will certify that Robert Charles is a duly accredited and ordained minister of religion in that branch of the Christian church known as The Salvation Army."

Most of the instructors at the New York School for Officers' Training are not college graduates, but are Salvation Army officers "trained in the crucible of experience."

The formal schooling of the graduates need not end when they leave the training college. After the young officer has had two years of basic training in the field he (or she) may apply for the privilege of attending local schools if the interference with his own work will not be too great. Where the studies are

53

related to the work of The Salvation Army, the Army will pay all of the tuition for the specialized education.

Suppose a young woman officer decides she wants to be a nurse. The Army arranges for an aptitude test. If it shows that she is fitted for this profession the Army will send her to school, pay her tuition and Army salary, requiring only that she render a specified number of years of service to the Army when her schooling is completed. If she fails to do so she must refund the tuition, but not the salary.

Many Salvation Army officers are qualified to hold lucrative jobs in civilian life, yet willingly prefer to devote themselves to salvation and service. Colonel Nelson himself is a good example. When he was 14 years old he and his brother were "floating around the streets in Union City, New Jersey." One day a Salvation Army captain invited the brother to play in the band. The brother went home and said to Nelson, "Hey! You want to blow a horn? If you go down to The Salvation Army they'll give you one and teach you how to play it."

As Colonel Nelson recalls it, "I went in one afternoon and walked out with a cornet under my arm. I didn't even know which end to put to my lips! I had taken violin and piano lessons for about six months, but that was considered sissy stuff, and a horn was good and noisy—much more to my liking. I took lessons from the corps officer and became tremendously interested. I played with The Salvation Army band, went to meetings, joined the Sunday School, and began taking Corps Cadet lessons. Of course I had to earn a living, and I finally worked my way up to a very good job in an export-import house. I became head of the traffic department, handling shipments of raw silk from Japan, shipping raw cattle bones from Argentina to China for making Mah Jongg sets, and handling rubber and coffee. I was an expert rubber and coffee sampler—not a coffee taster, but an expert on coffee beans. Then I was offered and took a job in the Finance Department of The Salvation Army, and after eighteen months there I decided to enter the training school. That was in 1925, and that's where I met the

54

girl who became Mrs. Nelson. We were married in 1929 and today we have two married daughters and a son, Karl."

Karl, a tall, slender and handsome boy, graduated from the University of Rochester in 1959. At the time of my visit he was a cadet in the training school headed by his father and expects to make The Salvation Army his career.

Chapter 4

UNDER THE CAPS AND BONNETS

Salvaging the downs-and-outs on Skid Row is trying enough for a man and especially difficult for a woman, yet many women officers work enthusiastically to restore derelicts to decency.

While attending a writers' conference in the Midwest I met Mrs. Major Margaret Troutt, a short, slender, brown-haired girl deeply interested in writing, and who has written several inspiring articles for *The War Cry* during her many years in The Salvation Army. She was kind enough to answer my questions about herself and her work.

When she was twelve years old, Margaret Troutt was one of four children living with their widowed mother in Evansville, Indiana. Her mother worked in a factory six days a week, and on Sundays she rested, too weary even to go to church. However, she insisted that her children attend a Presbyterian Sunday School, and eventually they became full-fledged church members.

One day a new family moved into the house next door. They were Salvationists and their children attended Salvation Army worship services. Soon they invited Margaret, her two sisters and her brother to accompany them, which they did.

"Mother permitted us to attend the meetings with the understanding that we must also go to the Presbyterian Sunday

School every week," she said. "That's what we did, but we'd rush home for a quick dinner, wash the dishes, then hurry to The Salvation Army for afternoon Sunday School."

Mother disapproved of this and insisted that her children stick to the Presbyterian Church. "You make it sound as though The Salvation Army couldn't get along without you," she said. "Well, they managed very well before you came along and they'll do all right if you're not around."

"I know that," Margaret answered, "but I enjoy helping them to help other people, and I want to work with them as long as they'll have me."

Margaret's sisters and brother felt as she did, especially her sister Babe, but it was three years before their mother let them enroll as soldiers. Meanwhile, Margaret had graduated from high school at the age of 15 with a four-year college scholarship.

"Mother had worked for us so many years I felt I owed it to her to help support the family," Margaret told me. "My conscience wouldn't let me go to college, even with the scholarship, because I'd have wanted to go from college to the Salvation Army's School for Officers' Training, and I wouldn't be helping the family financially. I just felt that the Lord wouldn't bless my life if I selfishly put first the things I wanted to do."

So Margaret went to work until her sister Babe graduated from high school and landed a job. Then, with her mother's reluctant permission, Margaret did enroll in the School for Officers' Training in Chicago. She was 19 years old.

The school was not quite the same as the meetings had been. "Contrary to my expectations I found that I had to pray just as much and sometimes more than I had done at home, in order to keep a sweet spirit at the officers' school," she told me. "I learned that sweetness of soul and contentment of spirit don't come from environment, but from the heart. My environment was all I could expect. We lived in a beautiful mansion on Chicago's North Side, given to the Army by a wealthy friend, yet I found that I sometimes rebelled against small disciplines and had constantly to remind myself that I was under orders that had to be obeyed."

In June she was commissioned a cadet-sergeant (a rank since discontinued) and was kept on the school staff, a disappointing assignment because she was eager to work in the field.

The next September a new group of cadets included her sister Babe. "I was so afraid the other cadets would think I was being partial to Babe that I went overboard to keep her at a distance," Margaret said. "I learned later that she cried herself to sleep many nights because I didn't treat her like a sister."

The following June Margaret was promoted to captain and placed in charge of the Army's Skid Row Corps in Chicago, with Babe as her lieutenant.

"That was a pretty rough assignment for two young girls, wasn't it?" I asked.

"Yes—but it was wonderful! We held meetings every night, with midnight open-air meetings in front of the burlesque houses in the district. Our hall was packed every night with men who often came in for a bed ticket or 'coffee and,' but many of them were led to the penitent form before the meeting ended. Later they testified in the service as to how they had been changed from drunkards to sober men, from gamblers, liars, thieves, even murderers, to men who loved the Lord and wanted to live uprightly."

That summer her brother Charles introduced Margaret to tall, rangy John Troutt, an engineer at Jackson Park Hospital.

"I wasn't anxious to meet him, in spite of the big buildup my brother gave him," she said. "We were so busy that we had little time for outside interests. John Troutt was an 'outside interest' because he wasn't an officer, and I knew the Army would frown upon any sentimental attachment that might develop."

Margaret and John did meet and liked each other right away, and John promptly took an interest in her work with the derelicts on Skid Row. "In fact he made generous contributions and soon became one of the 'money men' we depended upon to carry on our work."

Whatever romantic interest might have existed was interrupted after a year, for Margaret and Babe were sent to a different type of corps in DeKalb, Illinois, and John Troutt stayed in Chicago. Babe soon married Lieutenant Edward Jarvis and Margaret was transferred to Territorial Headquarters in Chicago, where she did secretarial work for almost five years.

During that time she saw John Troutt intermittently until one day he said to her, "I don't like this on-again-off-again business. How about it? Will you marry me or won't you?"

If Margaret married him she would have to resign as an officer. She loved The Salvation Army, and she loved John Troutt. Which to choose? It was a difficult decision and Margaret turned to prayer to help her make it.

"I finally decided that I'd get married and afterwards do as much volunteer service as I could," she recalled. "When I told my boss, Colonel Pugmire, he said he'd like to meet John."

When they met, the colonel said to John, "Have you ever thought about becoming an officer yourself?"

"I sure have," John said. "More than once."

"Well!" Margaret exclaimed. "That's a surprise to me."

"I never told you because I figured everyone would think I was joining the Army only so we could be married. Now that you've said you'll have me, I'll tell you that I've often wished I could be an officer and work with men who need help."

John entered the School for Officers' Training that Fall and was commissioned a probationary captain in June. He and Margaret were married the following November.

"That was twenty-six years ago," she told me, "and they have been the most exciting, the busiest, happiest years anyone could possibly have."

The Troutts have been in various fields of Army work. For several years they were corps officers in a Chicago neighborhood of low-income families, where they conducted an extensive youth program. At the beginning of World War II they served in the USO and went overseas to work with the Armed Forces in Salvation Army Red Shield Clubs. For a short time

John was Territorial Director of the Scout and Guard Department in Chicago. Margaret worked with the Girl Guards, spending most of her summers at a big Chicago Salvation Army camp where she was waterfront director and taught swimming and life-saving to the campers.

In 1947 they were both transferred to the Men's Social Service Department, in which they were still working at the time I talked with Margaret. Here they bring salvation to homeless men in ways described elsewhere in this book.

"We both feel that we're now doing the work we were especially called to do," Margaret said.

Despite Margaret's dedication to her work and her many responsibilities, she has managed to continue her formal education. In Chicago she attended night classes at Northwestern University, concentrating on journalism. In 1954 when John Troutt was appointed manager of the Men's Social Service Center at Waukegan, Illinois, he urged his wife to enroll in full-time day classes at Northwestern's Evanston campus. The Army gave its permission and Margaret started to earn the college degree for which she had prayed many years earlier.

After the first quarter she applied for and was given a scholarship.

"The next two years were demanding and strenuous," she recalled. "When you're forty-seven and competing against twenty-year-olds accustomed to class routine, it isn't easy, but I had such a wonderful sense of achievement and a grateful heart that God in his goodness helped me to see another dream come true."

In 1956 her education was interrupted by a transfer to Minneapolis, Minnesota, but she enrolled at the University of Minnesota, where she was initiated into Theta Sigma Phi (professional journalism society). The Army permitted her to return to Chicago for the Spring quarter so that she could get her bachelor's degree in Journalism from Northwestern University.

I asked Margaret if she and John had any children.

Rather wistfully she said, "No—and that's the only thing that could have enriched my life. Why it never happened we really don't know. We fretted about it often, but after the war when we returned from overseas, we decided there was no point in worrying about it. The Army would have permitted us to adopt one or two children if we had asked permission when we were under forty years old and if we had doctors' certificates showing that we would never have any of our own. However, we never had that definite word from the doctors. Even the Mayo Clinic thought it was only a matter of time before we had a family, and when time had finally run out for us we were past the age when we could adopt children. Maybe the Lord knew I couldn't stand any more happiness than I had. Maybe He wanted me to have more time to spend with other children, or with grown men and women who needed someone to look after them."

"What do you consider the most gratifying part of your work?" I asked.

She smiled and answered, "I think that's the question I've been asked more than any other. Without hesitation I can say that it's to know I have helped to lead a man to Jesus Christ."

"I know it isn't polite to ask a woman her age," I said, "but—"

"I don't mind at all. I'm fifty-three years old and I look forward to twelve more challenging years as an officer before I retire." She touched my arm gently. "For the Christian, you know, there's no such thing as retirement. He never stops facing new opportunities to witness for Christ and to work for the salvation of needy souls."

In cold print these words may seem cloying or even corny to some, but to me, coming as they did from a Salvation Army officer who has devoted her life to the service of others, they were truly and earnestly spoken from an unselfish heart. In talks with other men and women of The Salvation Army I was to be more than ever convinced that their own welfare and personal interests are subordinate to their chosen and often difficult ministry.

With the understanding that their names would not be revealed, nor certain towns identified, two officers furnished information that provides a graphic illustration of some of the personal conflicts that confront Salvation Army officers.

One of the two was a married officer in his sixties, with four children. The other was a widowed woman officer in her forties with two teen-age youngsters. For convenience we'll call the man Mark and the woman Ellen.

In the 1920s and early 1930s Mark and his family had been stationed in pleasant middle-class communities on the East coast, with thriving corps programs and good local financial support. In 1934 they were ordered to "farewell" and were sent to an Ohio town near the Kentucky border. Mark and his wife looked upon the new assignment as a challenge, but their four children were seriously disturbed by the change. The corps and living quarters were located on "the wrong side of the tracks." The town smelled of tobacco from a local factory. The congregation was made up of hill folk, illiterate and barefoot, a type of people wholly new and strange to Mark's children.

Mark's daughter, then ten years old, refused to go to Sunday School when she discovered on the first Sunday that her Sunday School teacher, a huge woman in a faded cotton dress and large starched sunbonnet, mispronounced simple words in reading from the Bible.

Mark's children attended public school, where they made new friends from other parts of town, with whom they spent most of their leisure time, but whenever anyone asked where they lived they gave their address reluctantly, with an apologetic air and a feeling of shame.

Mark and his wife, however, found great satisfaction in ministering to the underprivileged hillbillies, who were most enthusiastic about the Army's program. Sunday School attendance was built up, the Home League was especially useful to the mothers, and large numbers of children were attracted by the recreation programs.

This was the situation for some six years, then the family was again transferred to a modern, well-built corps in a clean small city on the eastern seaboard, with a thriving congregation. Parents and children were very happy with the change—

but it wasn't more than a year or so before they "farewelled" again, this time to a bleak Pennsylvania town where the Army's program was "on the skids." At this time Mark's children ranged in age from 10 to 18 years.

The older children were particularly bitter about this move. They were being uprooted from their good schools, pleasant home, and a small community with practically no slum areas, and ordered to a dying, depressed town. The youngsters themselves were depressed to the point of actual tears.

One of the teen-agers brought his resentment into the open. "This is a dirty deal," he said. "We've been through enough to deserve something better than what we're headed for. Are we being punished for something, or what, Dad?"

Mark had only one answer. "We have to go where we're needed, son. Anyway, it might not be as bad as you seem to think."

It wasn't. It was worse—much worse. Their new quarters, on a trash-littered street of sagging, weatherbeaten frame houses, were right in the middle of the town's red light district. It was literally so, for red lights glowed at night in the windows of whorehouses all about The Salvation Army family's home.

Even patient Mark was inwardly furious about this location, more in consideration of his children than himself and his wife, but he told the whole family, quite calmly, that none was to say a critical word publicly about their grievances.

On the first and second nights in the new "home," Mark was so upset that he couldn't sleep, and he walked the streets until dawn. On the third day he wrote a letter to his superiors protesting that the quarters were not fit for a family with children, and he obtained permission to break the lease and look for another residence. Within two months they moved into an old mansion, rented for $40 monthly, in another part of town.

The corps itself—the Salvation Army church—remained in the red light district. It had little resemblance to a real church or chapel. It was an old store with faded green curtains strung across the windows, stains on the walls and floors, and a leaky roof. There were 25 to 50 people in the congregation, mostly down-and-out barflies, unkempt, shabby, reeking of stale beer or whiskey, and a few prostitutes. In revolt, the two oldest children refused to join in the services and program.

Mark and his wife finally considered giving their Army superiors an ultimatum—either transfer the family to a better station or accept their resignations. Then Mark read an article in *The War Cry* about Colonel Mary Booth (now retired), granddaughter of founder William Booth. Mary was offered a chance to leave her post in Belgium and be evacuated when the Nazi invasion was imminent, but she declared that her place was with "her" people and that there she would remain.

Said Mark, "I decided that if Colonel Booth could stay on the Continent and face the Nazi occupation, I could stay in this town."

And stay he did. Within a year Mark and his family had made their place in the community. The two older children enrolled in a college in one part of the area, and a new military establishment opened up new fields of service for Mark and his wife among the American soldiers. They set up a center where draftees from the county could find overnight sleeping accommodations before being transported to basic training camp. They outfitted newly-constructed barracks for soldiers taking courses at the college. Mark received generous support from the town for these and other projects, and paid off the corps debts he had inherited.

Mark's children made a good adjustment in the town, but quite frankly told him that their bitter memories of and experiences in the slum neighborhoods in which they lived for so long made them lose all interest in The Salvation Army. Today not one of the children is a Salvationist.

Tomorrow Mark may "farewell" again for some other post.

In the other case, Ellen, the widowed officer, recalls a time when she was appointed to a small Ohio town. Her eldest daughter (now in her 'teens) was then 13 months old, and their living quarters and corps were flanked by saloons. One day Ellen's brother took the baby outdoors to play. When he went on an errand for his sister, she thought he had taken the baby with him, but he hadn't. He assumed the tot would be safe in the yard. When he returned the baby had disappeared.

Mother and uncle combed the nearby alleys frantically, to no avail. The distraught officer was about to call the police when a man came to the house holding the baby by one hand.

"She's been over in the saloon for an hour or so," he said. "Nobody knew who she was 'til the grocer came in and said the baby was your'n."

There were no playgrounds nearby, and it was in this atmosphere that Ellen's children, and others, had to grow up.

Both Mark and Ellen agree that times have changed considerably for Salvation Army officer families. Accommodations are more adequate than they were 20 years ago, and fewer officers have to live in bedraggled quarters and neighborhoods, especially if they have growing families. Some still do live in such places, however, since this brings them into closer contact with the very people they try to help.

Along with the stresses put on children by changing schools and moving from town to town, both officers indicated that there were times when their youngsters wanted them to be "ordinary" parents.

"For instance," Ellen says, "my sixteen-year-old daughter has asked me to please wear civilian clothes to Parent-Teacher meetings so that my uniform doesn't stand out."

None of the officers with whom I talked could remember hearing or knowing of any so-called juvenile delinquency among children of Salvation Army officers. They feel that if there are strains on their children, or if they do have periods of rebellion, their close family ties and very strong Christian training are bulwarks which keep them from delinquent behavior.

Chapter 5

FIND HER! FIND HIM!

Thousands of men and women, for thousands of reasons, have tried to abandon families and familiar worlds and to hide from their pasts. Some succeed. Some are found out. Some are traced by police. And many are located by a little-known branch of The Salvation Army, the Missing Persons and Inquiry Bureau.

The beginnings of the Bureau can be traced to General William Booth himself. In 1890 Booth published a book called *In Darkest England and The Way Out.* "The way out" was a proposal to alleviate some of the social ills in the overcrowded areas of Europe and to improve the situation of farmers and other workers. Briefly, the plan was to establish land and industrial colonies for the training of those who would be sent overseas, and later to found colonies and reception centers in Australia, Canada, the United States, and some South American countries.

Because of restrictions imposed by various national governments on immigrants, some of the plans had to be abandoned, but large contingents of migrants were transported by The Salvation Army to Canada, Australia, and some other countries.

As part of the "Darkest England Scheme" Booth provided for what he called "houses of help and inquiry." Many of those who had come to The Salvation Army for shelter were known to have left their families, and Booth wanted his inquiry bureau to reunite one with the other. As the great emigration of Salvationists from the British Isles spread to other parts of the world it was soon evident that the organization was well-equipped for this work. In 1888 a Missing Persons and Inquiry Bureau was officially established in London, and in 1910 an office was opened in New York City. Today a similar bureau operates in each of the other three Territories in the United States and in most Salvation Army establishments abroad.

Because of this and its many other international activities, The Salvation Army is classed as a non-governmental agency related to the Economic and Social Council of the United Nations.

How does the Missing Persons Bureau operate? Here are two actual advertisements from issues of *The War Cry*:

WHERE ARE YOU?

MULLER, MRS. FREDERICK—*Nee* Miss Muriel Batley; left England for U. S., 1941. Married Frederick Muller, 1950. Born July 28, 1920. Model; uses the name of Carol Vance. Mother ill, wishes to contact.

VALLEE, JOHN WILLIAM—Born Troy, N. Y., March 21, 1931. Social Security No. 124-22-6352. Disappeared April, 1960. Called mother on Christmas night from mission on Henry Street, New York City. Is short, medium height, brown eyes, curly black hair. Wife anxious over welfare.

A dozen or more similar notices appear in virtually every edition of *The War Cry*, inserted and paid for by relatives or friends of the missing people, and who cannot afford to pay the prices charged by other locating agencies.

The Salvation Army's customary charge for publication is only one dollar, to help defray expenses. If a photograph of the missing person is included there is an extra charge of $2.25, the cost of the necessary photoengraving. The cost is reasonable, but evidently seemed exorbitant to one woman who walked into the office of the Army's Missing Persons and Inquiry Bureau in New York City and spoke to Brigadier Alice Taylor, the officer in charge.

"I'm going to see an attorney to draw up a will for me," she said, "and there's someone I want to name in the will to inherit my estate. The trouble is I don't know where this person is and I want to insert a notice in *The War Cry* to try to find him."

Brigadier Taylor wrote down the woman's name and address and helped her to phrase the notice, giving the missing man's physical description and other pertinent details.

"We make a charge of one dollar for the advertisement," the officer said.

The woman frowned so that her eyebrows almost touched. "One dollar!" she exclaimed. "Well, I must say!"

"That really doesn't pay the cost, but it helps some," Brigadier Taylor explained.

The woman rose, grabbed the paper with the description from the desk and said indignantly, "You must think I'm made of money! I thought everything The Salvation Army did was free!" She walked out of the office before Brigadier Taylor could say anything more. Perhaps she made other plans for her "estate."

Occasionally a case takes an unusual twist. One man who asked for help later became the object of a fruitless search himself. Peter Hanson, a seaman in his early forties, asked the Missing Persons Bureau to find out if his mother was still alive and well in Sweden. Pete had left home twenty years before, after a serious argument with his parents. The Army's Stockholm headquarters located the mother, who was overjoyed to learn that Pete was alive and inquiring about her. Certain that he must be in dire need, she cabled The Salvation Army a thousand dollars to deliver to her boy, but when the Army went to find Pete he was nowhere to be found. The ship on which he was believed to be a crew member was contacted at half a dozen ports of call, but Pete was among the missing, and his mother's money was returned to her.

One woman from a rural area asked the Bureau to find her husband, who had left home some two months earlier and had failed to return. She was asked for the man's description and any facts that might be helpful in finding him and was told that the Bureau would do everything possible to locate her husband.

"Shucks," she said, "I don't 'specially care about that good-for-nothin'. The thing is, the huntin' season's comin' on, and when he lit out he took our only shotgun with him. I want to git the gun back!"

Today the information gathered and distributed by the network of Salvation Army centers throughout the world eventually leads to the successful conclusion of about one-third of the 1500 cases processed each year in the New York office alone.

In 1960 the Bureau in London traced 1979 missing persons. In Canada 506 of 996 investigations were successful. In all 86 countries where the Army is at work there were 12,028 missing persons sought and 6579 located. The search continues for the others.

How do people drift apart like this? Lt. Col. Tor Wahlström, Chief Secretary of The Salvation Army in Finland, explains it this way: "There are any number of answers. Adoption in early life, family quarrels, unsuccessful attempts at establishing one's self in new surroundings, illness in a strange country, alcoholism, vice, and a dozen other causes."

A Britisher was sought by his mother and wife, who had last heard of him in the Rhine district of Germany. Shortly after the first insertion of his description in *The War Cry* a town official in Germany sent The Salvation Army the man's correct address.

In Sweden, twin sisters named Greta and Julia were adopted by different families immediately after birth. Sixty years later Greta's son decided to learn something about his mother's people. He could discover nothing about her parents, but he and his mother were both startled when he found that Greta had a twin sister. They went to The Salvation Army, which agreed to investigate. An officer started at an infants' home, patiently traced the sister through parish records and finally located

69

Julia. She had known she was a twin and had been searching for Greta for years. The excitement of their meeting resulted in newspaper headlines throughout Sweden—and The Salvation Army was suddenly flooded with requests to find other long-lost relatives.

Once a Swiss bartender, picking up a copy of *The War Cry* left by a customer, found his own name and a message from his mother. They were reunited.

In one case a Swedish-born police officer working and living in Melbourne, Australia, was having lunch with a friend who carried sandwiches wrapped in pages of *The War Cry*. While eating, the officer glanced at the soiled paper, saw his own name, and learned that he was being sought by his sister in Sweden, whom he had thought dead. He wrote to her immediately and, says the Army report, "there was great joy for them both."

Are such accidents providential? Perhaps, says the Army, and points to another case in which a West London Corps ran out of copies of *The Young Soldier*, the Army's publication for children, and gave some of the kids copies of *The War Cry*. One little boy insisted that his mother read to him from the paper. As she glanced through it she noticed a "Missing" advertisement in which the description and Christian name tallied with her own, but the surname was different. Her curiosity aroused, she called at the Missing Persons Bureau and discovered that she was indeed the person they sought in behalf of her mother.

The woman took the next train to the town where her mother lived and today they see each other frequently. The strange part of this story is that the surname in the advertisement was that of a youth who had courted the woman many years before. She had run away from home, and her mother supposed that she and the boy had eloped.

Not all successful cases have happy endings. One old man close to death wanted to find his missing daughter before he died. The Salvation Army learned that the girl had been beaten to death by a drunken husband, who afterwards committed

70

suicide, but they deliberately kept this tragic story from the girl's dying father.

In Germany, where about every fifth person is a refugee, a successful tracing of missing persons brings new hope and new interest in life, and many are located.

In South Korea the war created problems with some ten million displaced persons. All Salvation Army institutions became clearing stations for information, at first to help lost children to be united with parents or relatives, then to help in the search for missing sons and husbands. News from behind the Bamboo Curtain of the 38th parallel was eagerly registered, but hundreds of thousands of cases are still open and may never be successfully closed.

Even the Iron Curtain has not proved altogether an impenetrable barrier. Recently a woman in Russia got a letter through to a friend in Finland to ask for news concerning her son, who had fought with the Finns against the Red Army. The boy was traced to Sweden, where a *War Cry* advertisement caught his attention. His address was sent to Finland and friends managed to forward it to his mother on the other side of the Curtain.

In New York, inquiries are received by the Missing Persons and Inquiry Bureau from International Social Service and other social service organizations, from government agencies, hospitals, family welfare organizations, the American Red Cross, broadcasting companies which get letters asking them to locate people, from relatives, friends, police departments, doctors and ministers.

"The purpose of our Bureau is to reunite families and friends, not to interfere with or assist law-enforcement agencies," says Brigadier Taylor. "If a man or woman comes to us to find a spouse and says there is an arrest warrant for him or her, we won't handle the case but refer the inquirer to the police. A lot of credit organizations come to us looking for missing debtors. We don't handle those cases, either."

In one instance a rough-and-ready deserted wife came in saying she was anxious to find her wandering husband.

71

"How old is he?" Brigadier Taylor asked.

"As old as I am," the woman answered.

"And how old are you?"

"I don't know. I was born during the flood."

"What flood?"

"I don't know. Just the flood."

"What did your husband do for a living?"

"I don't know."

"But you must understand that we need some specific information about him to try to identify and find him."

"Oh, you don't have to worry about that," the woman said confidently. She opened her purse and took out a small ragged piece of white cloth. "You see this? Well, when he flew out the door I grabbed him by his shirt sleeve and this hunk of his shirt tore away. All you have to do is find a man with a torn shirt that this piece will fit, and that'll be my husband!"

The missing man is still at large.

Even if he were located by the Bureau his whereabouts would not be revealed to his wife without his authorization. This is a condition which is agreed to in writing by every person who asks the Bureau to find someone, on the basis that a forced reunion might not be a happy one. In most cases the missing person, if found, is glad to return, knowing that someone cares enough about him or her to seek him out, but an estimated ten per cent refuse permission to make their location known.

One young woman, for example, came to the Bureau saying that she wanted to find her mother. The mother, it seems, had left the girl in an institution as a baby and had never seen her again, so the girl could furnish very little information about her mother.

"But she must be alive," the girl said. "I'm sure she's alive and I know she's been searching for me. I just *know* it!"

"Do you have any other known relatives?" she was asked.

"Yes, I have an aunt, but she doesn't know where my mother is. I've already asked her." She furnished the aunt's name and address.

The aunt was interviewed by an officer of The Salvation Army, and with considerable reluctance gave an address where the missing mother might be located. The mother was living in Chicago, where she had married a prominent attorney who knew nothing whatever of her past. When she was visited by a representative of the Bureau she was considerably upset.

"I don't know how you found me," she said, "but that's neither here nor there. The important thing is that I don't want my daughter to know where I am or anything about me."

The Salvation Army worker tried to persuade the mother that a reunion with her daughter might benefit both of them.

"No!" the mother said. "I might as well tell you the truth. That baby was illegitimate. An accident. A mistake. I took care of her until she was six months old, and then I got rid of her because I didn't want her. I never wanted her, I never tried to find her, and I don't want her now!"

Adhering to its policies, the Missing Persons Bureau refused to tell the girl where her mother was. The Army felt, however, that the girl ought to know that her mother was living and why she had rejected her daughter. Accordingly, an experienced and sympathetic social worker employed by the Army's Family Service Bureau was assigned to break the news as gently as possible.

"Of course the girl was heartbroken," Brigadier Taylor says, "and it was most difficult for us. Under the circumstances, however, we think it was the best solution."

Even though the Bureau may conceal the whereabouts of a person who asks that they do so, the Bureau sometimes acts as a liaison by delivering letters from searcher to searched-for without revealing the address of the latter.

Great care is taken to make a thorough investigation of the facts surrounding each case, and the Army considers both the seeker and the sought as its clients. Where advisable, facts are channeled through The Salvation Army's Family Service Bureau, where trained case workers, familiar with family problems, may consult with the clients to promote a well-rounded viewpoint of the whole situation.

73

Armed with all available information, representatives of the Bureau begin their search. They visit the last known address of the person sought and talk with neighbors. The local grocer or the newsboy on the corner may be of help. Former employers may provide important clues, or a moving company may guide the searcher to a more recent address. Churches, clubs, lodges and fraternities are visited. Outdated telephone books and city directories, Bureaus of Vital Statistics, or nationality groups, often provide useful leads. Much work is done by correspondence. A letter is always sent to the missing person's last known address saying that The Salvation Army has a message for the person. Sometimes the letter is returned marked "Address Unknown." Sometimes it is simply not answered, in which case another letter is sent by registered mail, return receipt requested. If the receipt comes back, a Bureau representative is assigned to make an investigation at the address of record.

Advertisements in *The War Cry* are often productive. This global voice of The Salvation Army provides a scope for inquiries that is unique, reaching as it does into the far corners of the world. Under the title, *The War Cry,* English editions of the publication circulate in:

> Great Britain
> Australia
> Canada
> United States (4 editions)
> Hong Kong
> India   (also in other languages)
> Pakistan   "   "   "   "
> Burma   "   "   "   "
> Ceylon   "   "   "   "
> Malaya
> New Zealand
> South Africa (also in Afrikaans)
> West Africa
> Central America and West Indies

Other nations publish the magazine in their own languages, with these titles:

Nsango na Kobikisa	(Congo)
Le Cri de Guerre (French) *Strijdkreet* (Flemish)	(Belgium)
O Brado de Guerra	(Brazil)
Yuddha Ghoshawa	(Ceylon)
Krigsrabet	(Denmark)
Sauti-ya-Vita (Swahili and English)	(East Africa)
Sotahuuto (Finnish) *Krigsropet* (Swedish)	(Finland)
En Avant	(France)
Der Kriegsruf	(Germany)
Yuddha Dhvani	(India—Madras and Andhra)
Nara-i-Jang	(India—Northeastern)
Pore Sattham	(India—Southern)
Mukti Samachar	(India—Western)
Berita Keselamatan	(Indonesia)
Il Grido di Guerra	(Italy)
Toki-no-Koe	(Japan)
Koo Sei Kong Baw	(Korea)
Strijdkreet	(The Netherlands)
Krigsropet	(Norway)
Nara-i-Jang	(Pakistan)
Die Strydkreet (Afrikaans and English)	(South Africa)
El Cruzado	(South America East)
El Grito de Guerra	(South America West)
Stridsropet	(Sweden)
Der Kriegsruf (German) *Le Cri de Guerre* (French)	(Switzerland)

Although The Salvation Army has scores of other publications of its own, it also advertises for missing persons in a non-Army paper, *News of the World,* published in London, England, which circulates among most of the free nations of the globe. If inquirers will pay for the advertising (about $7) the Army also places notices in daily newspapers or magazines where leads might be expected to turn up.

Once a police officer in New York asked the Missing Persons Bureau to find his brother, who had emigrated from Ireland to New York ahead of the rest of the family. The boy had written home several times, but when the family reached the United States they were unable to find him at his last known address and for several years they made fruitless attempts to locate him.

The Salvation Army began this case under somewhat of a handicap. The true name of the missing man was John Smith! In conducting an investigation in the neighborhood of the man's last known address, a Bureau representative learned that the man had set out to learn the baker's trade from a friend in New York. The friend was located and said the only clue he could furnish was that the boy had gone West after he learned the baking business.

The Bureau then advertised for the missing man in bakery trade journals. One day they received a letter from him saying that he had read the advertisement and giving his current address in Seattle, Washington. When a Bureau representative told him about his family he was happy to know how and where they were, and he immediately took a vacation to fly to New York for a joyful reunion.

Frequently the Consulates of foreign countries seek help from the Bureau in locating missing countrymen, and will arrange to publish notices for the Army in newspapers in the countries concerned.

About ten percent of the persons sought are seamen, and since The Salvation Army operates establishments on many waterfronts where seamen get mail or congregate when ashore, the officers in those centers are constantly on the alert for those who are being sought by the Bureau, and many are located in this way at ports far from home.

Alice Taylor's eyes shine as she tells about the cases with happy endings, and she sometimes sighs when she talks of those that are tinged with sadness. Like other Salvation Army officers, her dedication to her work is obvious and she approaches each case with a deep personal interest.

Brigadier Taylor was the child of Methodist parents living in Elmira, New York. As a high school student she was invited by several young friends to go on a Salvation Army ice-skating party, and it was this first contact with the organization that aroused her interest in its work and its people. She attended Army worship services, became an active soldier, and in 1921 entered the officers' training school. After service as a corps officer in Western New York until 1930 she was transferred to the Family Service Bureau in New York as District Secretary. Since 1952 she has headed the Missing Persons and Inquiry Bureau in the Eastern Territory, where she has only two assistants. She gets considerable help from eight active volunteers in various cities, none of whom are Salvationists, but who contribute their services for humanitarian reasons. One very wealthy New York woman reports to Brigadier Taylor one day each week to contribute a full day's service as a typist.

Chapter 6

DOUGHNUTS

The clouds were low and oppressive, hiding moon and stars, and the ominous quiet was broken only by the occasional *crack!* of a rifle in the cold hands of an American doughboy, then by an echoing shot from some unknown, unseen German soldier across a bleak strip of French earth called "No Man's Land."

It was another dreary night in what people in 1917 called "the World War."

In this sector, as in so many others, the Yanks had dug trenches in the protective ground, and with the dawn and the signal to go "over the top" hundreds of young men would scramble out of the ditches and cross "No Man's Land" to kill other young men, or perhaps to be killed or wounded themselves.

The trench was barely four feet deep. The earth was mucky from earlier rains, and here and there were small puddles with ragged fringes of ice. Through the mud, crouching low to keep her helmeted head below the trench top, a young woman carried a carton and stopped at each dark sleep-robbed figure leaning against the dirt wall or sitting with his back against it in the chilly muck.

Her clothes were streaked with mud, for she had been compelled to crawl across open ground to get to the trench, but in the blackness the dirt didn't show, and even if it did it wouldn't attract undue attention. Everybody was dirty all the time.

The girl was a Salvation Army "lassie," and the carton held a load of doughnuts and a big pot of hot coffee.

"Hi, soldier—have some coffee and sinkers," she would whisper. All talk was in whispers, because the enemy was so near that normal conversation would betray positions and attract gunfire.

She was greeted unfailingly by grins and whispered remarks such as "Man, oh, man, am I glad to see you!" Or, "Hey, now, whaddya know? If this is war, I'm for it!" Or, "Gee, thanks, sister. Now look—you keep your head down, see? We can't have nothin' happen to *you!*"

As she left each man she would pat his arm and say, "God bless and keep you, soldier. Say a prayer tonight."

Occasionally a boy would hand her a letter to be mailed home, or give her his home address and ask her to write to his mother or his wife or sweetheart to say he was all right—meaning "still alive."

Frequently she met men who were themselves Salvationists and who had either enlisted or been drafted, and whenever possible she and they would pray together in whispers.

When the doughnuts and coffee were gone she knelt in the mud near a few of the men and prayed softly. She smiled a farewell and slogged back through the ditch to return to her hut, not far from the front, where she and her companions would make more doughnuts and more coffee for other dough-boys, and where, more than a few times, they wept for the maimed and the dead.

What history calls "the First World War" ended in 1918, but thousands of American men who survived the fighting still have an affection for The Salvation Army because of its unselfish service, and for the coffee, pies and doughnuts made and served by its courageous members, often under enemy gunfire.

In St. Petersburg, Florida, a World War I veteran named L. J. Jones has a genuine Salvation Army doughnut which he keeps carefully wrapped in a piece of felt and stored in a small metal box for safe keeping, like great-grandfather's huge gold watch (and now just as hard!). This story symbolizes the feeling of most of the fighting men for the people in the other unique Army who tried to be where they were most needed:

On May 28, 1918, a young Salvation Army lassie, Captain Jessica Winter, made hundreds of doughnuts on the outskirts of Bertuele, a French village that served as headquarters for the American First Division. That was the day American troops entered their first major engagement—Cantigny—in which Yanks from the ranches of Texas and the streets of Chicago drove the till-then victorious Germans from their strong positions and fought off a fierce counterattack.

It was also the day when L. J. Jones drove an ammunition truck toward the front and was hailed by hitch-hiking Captain Winter, wearing the usual loose-fitting Army khaki and wash-basin helmet. She held a big pot of coffee and a basket of doughnuts and wanted a ride to the front-line trenches. Jones took her as far as he was going, and when she left the truck she gave him some coffee and several doughnuts.

Five months later Jones was ordered to turn in his battered ammunition truck for a new one. In cleaning out the old truck he found a lone doughnut behind the seat cushion, where it had obviously fallen from the basket carried by his Salvation Army hitch-hiker weeks before.

"It was then too old to eat, but I decided to keep it for good luck," Jones said later. The same doughnut, now a prized souvenir, survived the bloody Cantigny, the Aisne-Marne, St.-Mihiel and Meuse-Argonne campaigns.

"When I die I want to give it to The Salvation Army," Jones said. "It's just like The Salvation Army—something I'll never forget, and sturdy."

His attitude is typical, as indicated by a comment made to me by Albert F. Ceres, Jr., Special Assistant to the Commander in Chief of the Veterans of Foreign Wars. Said Mr. Ceres, "We all love The Salvation Army, the girls and the men who were always our friends when we most needed a friend."

The famous Salvation Army doughnuts were products of

necessity occasioned by shortages of materials. The lassies originally intended to bake pies, cakes and bread to give the doughboys home-cooked treats, but at the front no stoves and ovens were available for baking, and supplies were scarce. About all they could get was flour and lard.

"The only things we can make with this are doughnuts," one lassie said.

"Then let's make doughnuts!" another said.

The first doughnuts made by Salvation Army girls in France in World War I are believed to have been fried at Montiers. They built a wood fire under a small kettle of lard and patted out the dough by hand. They were able to fry only seven doughnuts at a time, and as soon as the aroma of the cooking wafted through the camp the soldiers flocked to the outdoor "kitchen" and lined up to get the food.

On the first day there were about 400 men in line and the lassies cooked 150 doughnuts before the flour ran out.

These first doughnuts were in cruller form, made of twisted strips of dough, because the girls had no cookie-cutters. The next day someone brought in an empty wine bottle and a spent shell-case to use as rolling pins. The top of a tin can was used as a doughnut cutter, and the second day's output totaled 300, but there were no holes in the center of the doughnuts until one morning when the top of a coffee percolator came loose and was used to cut the holes.

Gradually the lassies increased production until they were cooking about 5000 doughnuts daily. Later, when ovens became available, they made countless apple pies—but The Salvation Army's decision to fry doughnuts was made simply because the girls didn't have the supplies or facilities to cook anything else in quantity.

Moreover, the doughnuts were not the main reason for The Salvation Army's presence in the fighting zones. Its men and women were there primarily to give spiritual aid and comfort to the American soldier and his allies, to cheer him up as best they could, to be his link with home and family.

All in all there were 1507 men and women Salvation Army

officers serving on the French, Italian, and Russian fronts in World War I, and about 500 of these were from the United States. They became substitute parents or sisters or brothers to thousands of appreciative doughboys for whom they cooked, sewed, wrote letters, read, sang, smiled, dressed wounds, prayed, and often cried.

Many people think that Salvation Army service to members of the armed forces dates from World War I. Actually this tradition of service to military personnel began at least as far back as 1880, when England and the Transvaal were at war, for Salvationists were there behind the lines bringing comfort and cheer to the fighting men.

Thanks to Miss Marian F. Tuthill of The Salvation Army's National Headquarters in New York, I was privileged to have an interesting visit with Colonel Florence Turkington, R.N. (retired), who was one of the first Salvation Army lassies to be sent overseas from the United States in World War I.

Colonel Turkington, who speaks both softly and forthrightly and with a delightful sense of humor, is short and slender and has graying hair and facial features similar to those of Actress Helen Hayes. She also has traces of a wispy shyness that has been with her since childhood. To her close friends and to many of the doughboys who became her friends she is and was affectionately known as "Little Turk."

Little Turk entered The Salvation Army's training school for officers in September, 1917, when she was 18 years old, but before her cadet training was completed she and three other girls were asked if they would be willing to serve overseas if they were chosen to do so. They agreed.

"I'll never forget the day when [National Commander] Evangeline Booth assembled the four of us on the roof of the headquarters building," Colonel Turkington says. "She told us that if we went overseas we were taking great risks; that it might mean death to all of us, and that The Salvation Army was not ordering us to go. It was a terrific challenge to a young girl who had never been away from home. It made me feel a part of something that was more than just service."

82

GENERAL WILLIAM BOOTH, FOUNDER OF THE SALVATION ARMY

*(All photographs courtesy of the Salvation Army Public Relations
Department)*

Six of the first seven official Salvation Army lassies who came to the United
States in 1880.

Salvation Army lassies at the turn of the century invaded poverty- and vice-ridden areas. (Courtesy, Bettman Archive)

Sketch of a Salvation Army open air meeting on the steps of City Hall, Brooklyn (as published in *Leslie's Illustrated Newspaper*, August 19, 1882).

A typical Bowery habitué, whom the Salvation Army strives to rehabilitate.

A Night Meeting outside the Salvation Army's Bowery Corps in New York City.

Inside the recreation room of the Bowery Corps in New York City. Here homeless men are encouraged to rehabilitate themselves. (*Photo by Sidney B. Bloch.*)

Cadets at the School for Officers' Training attend a lecture on social service work.

A Cadet receiving her commission at the School for Officers' Training.

As part of his training, a young Cadet leads an open-air meeting.

Brigadier Gladys Phillips chatting with a resident of the New York Women's Lodge. The famous Warner Sallman "Head of Christ" hangs over the fireplace.

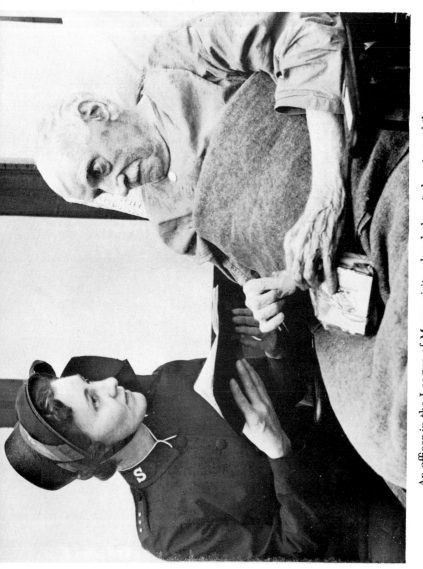

An officer in the League of Mercy visits a lonely hospital patient while . . . .

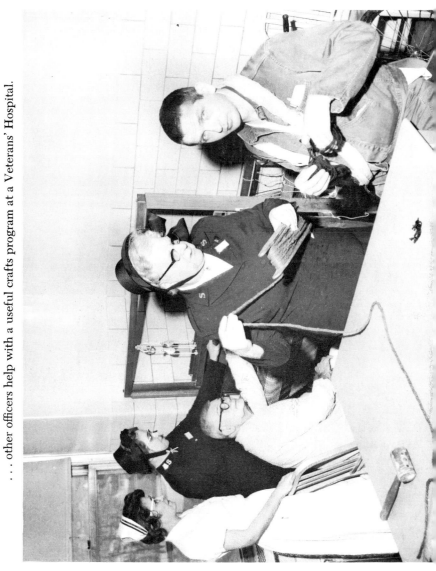

. . . other officers help with a useful crafts program at a Veterans' Hospital.

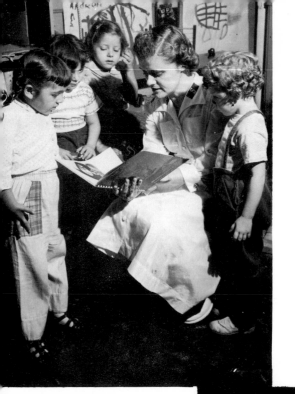

(*Left*) Children of many nationalities are cared for in Salvation Army day nurseries.

(*Right*) Many nationalities are members of a Junior Songster Brigade in the Manhattan Citadel.

(*Above*) The Salvation Army feeds children of impoverished families in Chile.

(*Below*) A happy ending in the Salvation Army's Missing Persons Bureau.

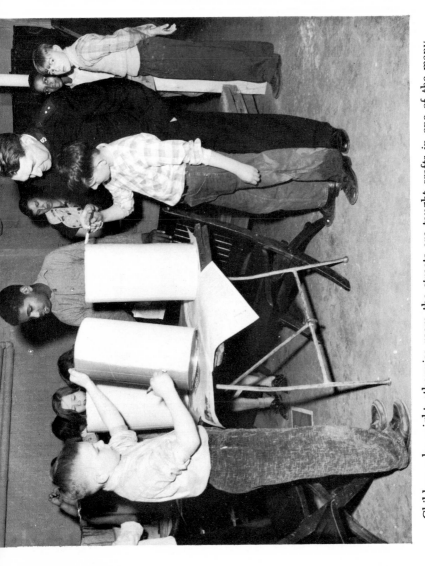

Children who might otherwise roam the streets are taught crafts in one of the many Salvation Army neighborhood centers.

In December the four girl cadets sailed aboard a French ship to Bordeaux, where they were met by Colonel William S. Barker of The Salvation Army and taken to the Normandie Hotel in Paris. "Everything was top secret," Little Turk recalls. "We didn't know where we were going."

A Salvation Army group from England was with the British Army. Little Turk and another cadet, Louise Young, were sent to Ligney-en-Barrois, where General John J. Pershing's First Division was in training. There they met three other Salvationists and established Salvation Army headquarters within about one mile of the front-line trenches. Salvation Army trucks and drivers hauled supplies from the headquarters to Salvation Army "huts" closer to the fighting.

"Sometimes at night we were routed out and sent back to dugouts on orders of the military," Little Turk says. "Next morning we would hitch-hike back, diving into ditches and ducking shells until a truck picked us up."

Little Turk's service took her to the 16th, 18th and 26th Regiments of the First Division and into the thick of the battle zones. Most of her "hut" experience was at Menil-le-Tour, near Bar-le-Duc, where she served with Captain Mary Bishop—and a strange experience it was.

"We had no manuals, no rules or regulations," she recalls. "You had to play everything by ear. We were dumped in a hut on the side of the road with a bag of flour, a can of cocoa, some lard, and our suitcases. We had to find our own billets—sometimes there was a place to sleep, sometimes not. Sometimes we could find part of a barn with a heavy clay floor where we could put up a field range or build a fire to heat lard."

Little Turk was one of those who crawled under enemy fire through muddy trenches, carrying a can of coffee and some doughnuts which she gave to the men in the front lines.

"One night the U. S. Army Band was billeted across the street from our hut in Pannes," she remembers. "That was near the Verdun sector and the Argonne. We got barrages from the Germans every night and we learned to live with the shelling every night. The shells would whistle and get heavier and

83

heavier, landing all around us. The building we were in was thick and pretty safe, except from direct hits. We always had the feeling that the shells wouldn't touch us. They were for somebody else. I guess most soldiers feel that way, too. The windows of our building were blown out and the explosions came awfully close, but we didn't have one casualty. Unfortunately, though, one barrage shot up the building where the band kept its instruments, and there was a lot of wailing from the men who had grown attached to their music-makers."

As the doughboys became better acquainted with The Salvation Army lassies, they made all sorts of unusual requests.

One boy came in with a helmet full of eggs. "I just bought a dozen eggs from a farmer," he said. "Would you please fry 'em for me, sunny side up?" He ate all twelve within five minutes!

Two others brought in a tin can filled with wild strawberries, and a bottle of heavy cream which they bought from another farmer. "We'd appreciate it, ma'am, if you would make us up an old-fashioned strawberry shortcake," they said.

Some of the requests carried notes of sadness, for several of the men would bring prized personal belongings to the lassies with requests that the girls forward them to homes and families if the boys went "over the top" and didn't make it.

Occasionally American aviators flew from bases miles away to take back a load of Salvation Army doughnuts. In one case a flier dropped a note in front of the Salvation Army hut and circled until he was sure it was picked up: "I will be back tomorrow afternoon to get about a hundred doughnuts for a bunch of hungry guys. Don't disappoint me." He returned as promised and the doughnuts were ready for him.

"Ordinarily we don't think of doughnuts as a feast," Little Turk says, "but if you were living in muddy trenches, being shot at, eating hardtack, and came out of the lines dead tired, needing sleep and a bath and a shave, and if you suddenly hit a spot where someone offered you steaming hot coffee and doughnuts, it would seem like heaven. Everything is indeed relative."

Every morning Little Turk and her friends would make 1500 or more doughnuts, with more to come if and when the first batch gave out. As supplies became more plentiful the lassies also made pies, cookies and bread.

Cooking was only one of their jobs. They wrote letters home for the boys, prayed with those who wanted them to, mended torn and tattered uniforms, played checkers or dominoes, and operated a canteen where the men could get toothbrushes, shaving materials, chocolate and other items.

"We also visited the boys in the field hospitals," Little Turk told me. "We were billeted near the front line, where an outfit would come in for a short stay. We would wake up in the morning in a dead calm and discover that everybody had moved up in the middle of the night. We could hear heavy barrages and we would worry about those boys. Then, one night we would wake up and hear hobnail boots on the cobblestone roads—the boys were coming back. We'd jump out of bed and start the coffee and do what we could to cheer up the men. We'd look for Joe, or Bill, or Tom, only to find that they were never coming back."

Little Turk and the other lassies had to get cold water from a pump in the village square for bathing. There was no heat of any kind except for cooking. The soldiers brought in a couple of pot-bellied stoves and some precious wood for fuel. "We never asked them where they got it," she says with a grin. When they had trouble lighting the fire, one big old Southern boy named Jonah said, "Lootie [for Lieutenant], if you'll jist get outa here for a few minutes, I'll talk this here fire into goin'. I got a language all my own, but with you around I cain't use it the right way."

"I remember many boys from the deep South who were lazy and sweet, and many who were brisk," Little Turk says. "And with the Eighty-second and Eighty-ninth headquarters units there were some wonderful men from the Midwest. Some could play the piano, some could sing, and we had them entertain. I still remember one boy, Rex, who said, 'Lootie, some day I'll come back and sing you *Rose in the Bud*.' He never did."

One man came to the hut just to sit and watch the girls.

"Can we help you?" they asked.

"No, thanks," he said. "I was watching you because you remind me of my wife and baby back home. Tomorrow I'm going over the top, and—" His voice trailed off. "I hope you don't mind," he added.

Little Turk was deeply impressed by the great respect shown by American soldiers to her and other American women serving overseas. "We met all kinds of men from all walks of life," she says, "but I can honestly say that I never once heard a single expression of any kind that was improper. Often there were only two of us women, but we felt protected and completely safe every minute."

After the war Colonel Turkington was assigned to The Salvation Army's Home and Hospital in Boston, where she received training in child care for 18 months. She was released for nurse's training for three years, became a registered nurse, and was subsequently appointed administrator of a Salvation Army hospital in Covington, Kentucky.

Little Turk played an important role in the designing and building of Booth Memorial Hospital in Flushing, New York, and although she retired in 1958 at the age of 60 (which is the Army's official retirement age for women officers), in 1961 she was actively working with architects and others in planning a Home for the Aged as an adjunct to Booth Hospital.

That, in brief, is the story of Florence Turkington, one of the many Salvation Army lassies who won countless friends and more than a few converts in the First World War.

There is one more fact that might be added to Little Turk's story. Her salary during World War I was five dollars a week.

In World War II The Salvation Army was one of the agencies invited to form the United Service Organizations (USO). This is separate and apart from the USO Camp Shows, a unit established to provide entertainment for men in the armed forces.

The USO in World War II included some 3000 Salvation Army Red Shield Centers, manned by several thousands of men and women officers, offering a home away from home to the allied troops on 26 different fighting fronts.

Some of The Salvation Army USO services: Social and recreational facilities; food for troops on the move and for civilians fleeing danger zones; food, clothes and helmets for soldiers and for civilians on defense duty; medical care, hospitalization and evacuation of civilians; homes for children orphaned by battle; medical care for expectant mothers; day nurseries for children of defense workers; knitted goods, toilet kits and gift boxes for soldiers, sailors and marines throughout the world; comfort for those hiding in bomb shelters; ambulance service— and countless other activities, including sock-darning and the sewing on of buttons for fighting men.

More than a thousand Salvation Army mobile units rolled up to sectors where men were under bombardment, to serve food and coffee and to bring what cheer they could.

In major Allied amphibious landings Salvation Army mobile "invasion canteens" rolled down the ramps of LST's along with jeeps, trucks and tanks. They set up shop along shell-pocked roads leading to the front and they advanced with the invading armies. In France alone, 23 Salvation Army mobile units were attached to the invading forces. In some cases they even preceded the fighting men, often operating only a few hundred yards from enemy lines.

Red Shield canteens took part in the tragic retreat at Dunkerque, when the British were driven into the sea. Only two of twenty canteens returned to England, and it was at Dunkerque that The Salvation Army had its first casualties in World War II.

In the Pacific, Salvation Army workers landed on beaches with the first assault waves. On Labuan Island, four Salvation Army men went ashore with invasion troops and set up a Red Shield canteen in a Japanese hut within half an hour after hitting the beach.

In Iraq, Salvation Army workers set up two tents on the desert in a sandstorm, and in less than two hours cooked 400 eggs and made 500 sandwiches to feed weary troops who had just finished a 380-mile trek across the desert.

The Salvation Army also had its own "lend-lease" plan. When thousands of Czechs, Poles, Belgians, Hollanders and Norwegians in ragged uniforms poured into neutral ports, hungry and tired, they found shelter, food, beds and medical care in hundreds of Salvation Army homes. In turn, in their ravaged lands, other Salvation Army people were helping men and women of many nationalities. In each country The Salvation Army said, "We will share what we have with your people, you share what you have with ours."

In New Guinea the first Red Shield clubs were sheets of canvas stretched between trees along a jungle trail. Supplies carried in by plane were picked up miles away and carried piggy-back along narrow paths into the jungle. "They don't register distances in miles in these parts," one foot-soldier said. "Even the maps record distance in terms of walking time. It took me half an hour to go a hundred yards. Salt sweat dripped down my forehead, stinging my eyes. My mouth was parched, my lips cracked. In a valley near a crude mule track was a Salvation Army canteen where every man could get hot coffee and food. I blessed The Salvation Army as I dropped on a rustic bench that seemed as restful as a feather bed."

Everywhere the fighting soldier blessed The Salvation Army —in Africa, Australia, New Zealand, Hawaii, Iraq, Canada, Sicily—in Sicily nine Salvation Army officers landed with the assault troops and set up dressing stations to care for the wounded. Many of the soldiers in the landing forces had also been "soldiers" in The Salvation Army.

Said one weary dogface to one Salvation Army officer, "What are you doing in this God-forsaken place? Me, now, I gotta be here, but you ain't. You crazy or somethin', boy?"

The officer smiled at him. "God hasn't forsaken this place, son, nor you and me. This is where I want to be. This is what I want to do."

In addition to canteens, hospitals, shelters and other services,

The Salvation Army sent chaplains to serve with allied troops on every fighting front.

With the other USO agencies (YMCA, YWCA, National Jewish Welfare Board, National Catholic Community Service, and National Travelers' Aid Association), The Salvation Army continues to provide relaxation, recreation and comfort for men and women in uniform, and to help them with their personal problems. Worship services are held regularly and religious counseling is available upon request, but no effort is made to effect conversions.

In 1961 in the continental United States The Salvation Army operated 31 Salvation Army-USO units in 17 communities, and 19 Red Shield Clubs and lounges for military personnel. Under the international administration of The Salvation Army there were 24 hostels for servicemen and seamen and 231 other centers for members of the armed forces in various countries, all designed to provide a home away from home for the soldiers and sailors on foreign soil.

Chapter 7

WOMEN IN TROUBLE—AND OUT

One of the least known and most tragic of Salvation Army services involves its homes and hospitals for unwed mothers (usually called Booth Memorial Hospitals), where scores of young unmarried girls give birth to babies they generally don't want, and get not only the best of hospital care but also the love and understanding that an ostracizing society has denied them.

Forerunner of these unusual institutions was the private home of the Cottrills, a baker and his wife, in London's East End. The Cottrills were Salvationist soldiers, dedicated to the objectives of the Army. Late in 1883 or early in 1884 Mrs. Cottrill, on her own, set out to befriend the prostitutes who roamed the London streets. She invited girl after girl into her home, and although many pushed her aside as a meddler, some accepted her invitation, were fed and housed under her roof, and a few were motivated by her advice and kindness to abandon the oldest profession for one less ancient and more honorable, such as sewing or cooking.

As the word spread, more streetwalkers beat a path to Mrs. Cottrill's door as an entrance to a new and decent life, but many were turned away because her house was crowded to capacity. The baker's wife then appealed to General Booth to inaugurate an official Salvation Army program in behalf of the prostitutes, and the sympathetic General founded the Army's first "Rescue Home" in Whitechapel, London, in May, 1884, naming his daughter-in-law, Mrs. Bramwell Booth, as its director.

When news of the London Rescue Home reached The Salvation Army in Australia a similar Home was established there in 1884. In 1961 such Homes, or some facilities for helping pregnant unmarried women, were available in the 86 nations in which The Salvation Army operates.

One example also illustrates the nature of work done by Salvation Army missionaries abroad. In Capetown, South Africa, a "Rescue Home and Laundry" was established in the early 1900s to care for "social casualties." Today it is a maternity hospital for paying patients and unwed mothers, supervised by Captain Donnelly, a Matron who is a Salvation Army missionary.

All patients are "non-European," meaning "not white." They include Malays, Indians and Africans. Brigadier Bernard McCarthy, reporting on a visit he made to the institution, had this to say: "Many of the unmarried mothers are scarcely out of their childhood. Some have no known parents. Cast off by relatives they have cohabited with casual acquaintances. Others, in reasonably good employment, have got into bad company or have been trapped by vicious men. When one knows the slum conditions in which many of these poorer types of coloreds live, one is surprised at nothing. Quickly excited and as speedily depressed, they turn to drinking and gambling as an escape from their misery. Sexual morality means little to these unfortunates."

According to the Matron the girls come in a state of apathy and acute depression, or of sheer indifference. Some are brought by their employers who know about the Army's social welfare work. Others come because they have been told they will find a kindly welcome. One girl arrived shoeless and in rags after walking from a town 80 miles away. Another was left at the Capetown railroad station with her luggage when it was discovered she was pregnant. Her employer had simply ditched her. The girl found her way to the Army's hospital and stood outside for more than an hour trying to pluck up courage to ring the bell.

In the Army's early days, as now, many girls had been innocents who were seduced under promises of marriage, or who were otherwise duped and betrayed by boy friends, employers, or even by lecherous relatives. The stories of many of the young women victimized by deceit in 1884 are strikingly similar to those unfolding in 1961.

Consider the case of Lucy, for example. Lucy was one of four children living with their parents in a crowded tenement in Brooklyn, New York. One night her own father began to teach her the facts of life by compelling her to submit to his advances and to be his partner in sexual intercourse, with the result that Lucy became pregnant. With little money available the family could not pay normal fees for a doctor and hospital bills, and a social worker who learned of Lucy's predicament arranged for her admittance to the Salvation Army's Home for Unwed Mothers at Flushing, New York, adjoining Booth Memorial Hospital. There she will get the best of medical attention and hospital care—and a doll.

Lucy still likes to play with dolls. She is eleven years old.

Another young patient at the Home has a different kind of story. Kathy is only fourteen years old—a child who is going to have a child. When her baby is born it will be labeled by Kathy's friends and neighbors as "illegitimate," and Kathy will be called names even worse.

Kathy is an only child who comes from a comfortable home in a middle-class Long Island community. Her father works for the City of New York, her mother is a sales clerk in a department store. Upon her admittance to the Home, Kathy was interviewed by Major A. Louise Richardson, the officer in charge, and by Miss Incoronata ("Cora") Mattia, an experienced social worker employed by The Salvation Army.

Questioned by Major Richardson, Kathy identified the father of her unborn baby as a 16-year-old boy who lived in her neighborhood.

"How did it happen?" the Major asked.

Kathy shrugged. "We were just left alone too much."

"Couldn't you have your friends come to your house?"

"Oh, sure—but not all the time."

"Just what do you mean by being 'alone too much'?"

"Well," Kathy said, "you and a boy go to the bowling alley, or to the movies or someplace, see? And then you run out of money and you can't go anywhere else, so you go home and sit on the couch and look at television. But, gosh, you don't want to watch it all night, so you start talking and pretty soon you start mushing or something, and the next thing you know you're in trouble."

"What about your parents? Weren't they at home most of the time?"

"Well, some of the time. But they both work all day, and at night they often go out to a movie or to play bridge or something. Anyway, if they were home and I wanted to go out someplace I'd just go."

"They wouldn't ask you where you were going, or try to stop you?"

"Oh, they prob'ly would. But that wouldn't matter, because if I made any kind of a fuss they'd give in quick enough. That's the trouble. If I had been living with my grandmother I wouldn't be in this fix now."

"What do you mean by that?" Miss Mattia asked.

"Well, my grandmother is strict, see? Real strict. And when I used to spend week-ends at her house she kept tabs on everything I did. I had to be in bed by eleven o'clock, and I couldn't go out at night by myself, and all that sort of stuff. But we had fun, too, because she used to take me to the beach, or the movies, or we'd play cards or something. I guess she really cared about what happened to me. I used to think that it was awful, her being so strict, but now I wish I'd been living with her all the time. Then—then I wouldn't be here."

"Suppose your mother and father had told you to stop seeing this boy? Would you have obeyed them?"

Kathy shook her head. "I guess not, because if I wanted to

93

keep on seeing him I'd just keep arguing with my parents and they'd finally give in. They always do."

In telling me about Kathy, Major Richardson commented, "Here was a child saying, 'Please put limits on my activities. Even though I fight about it, don't let me do things I shouldn't.'"

Ironically, Kathy's parents are puzzled and hurt by their daughter's wayward action. "We can't possibly understand how she could do such a thing," they say. "We both work hard all day so that she can have nice clothes and the right kind of home life and a good education. We've given her everything she wanted."

Everything but the right kind of parental control.

Kathy's case is not unique. It provides a significant commentary on modern family life and reveals a facet of teen-age introspection that not only is kept hidden, but also would probably be denied vigorously by any youngsters questioned about it. And it may be that they themselves are not aware of this paradox unless or until they are faced with a serious problem as Kathy was and is.

When Kathy's baby is born it will be one of nearly 200,000 infants born out of wedlock in the United States annually. In a typical year more than 12,000 unmarried mothers of these babies were helped by The Salvation Army, and of that number more than 7600 were cared for in 36 maternity homes and hospitals owned and operated by The Salvation Army (which has a total of 90 such institutions throughout the world).

The Booth Memorial Hospital in Flushing is a completely modern general community hospital with the very latest medical and research equipment, 425 employees, plus 240 physicians representing every medical specialty. Attached to it is the home for unwed mothers. Members of the hospital staff examine all of the girls admitted to the home, and each girl will get the best of hospital care until after her baby is delivered.

Not all of the unmarrieds are "too young to know better." Mary Ann, for example, is 21 years old and was in training at a New York City hospital for a career as a registered nurse. She had been pregnant for five months when she came to the Home and offered to work in the adjoining hospital to earn her food, lodging and maternity care. Her family, living in the far West, knows nothing of her pregnancy and was told simply that she was living and working at Booth Memorial Hospital as part of her nurse's training.

Paul, the father of Mary Ann's baby, is a Jewish boy and a medical resident in the hospital where she was first in training. He and Mary Ann had been going together for about six months when she became pregnant. Paul visited her regularly at the Home, and at first he told her that they would be married as soon as he finished his residency. Gradually his attitude changed and he finally told her that his parents strongly opposed the marriage on religious grounds and would never accept her because she was a Protestant.

Mary Ann, looking to a respectable future for her baby, told Paul that she would convert to Judaism, which should make her acceptable to his mother and father, but Paul sputtered and muttered about his inability to support a family and about the difficulties of setting up a profitable medical practice. Only then did Mary Ann realize that Paul was planning to pull out of his promise to marry her. There was no wedding, and in desperation Mary Ann put up her baby for adoption.

As she herself put it, "I had to sacrifice my baby."

This is a decision that confronts virtually every one of the unwed mothers—shall she keep her child or give it up for adoption?

The Salvation Army does not actually place babies in adoption homes, but it does work closely with licensed adoption agencies in making plans for the children.

"Some of the mothers do not want to see their babies at all," Major Richardson says, "and this alone is a painful experience, once the baby is born. One girl kept insisting that her baby be taken away quickly when it was delivered, so that she would not have even a swift look at it, because it was to be made available for adoption. After it came, however, she said, 'Maybe I ought to see it for a minute, just once.' She saw it and immediately had the urge to keep it. Eventually, and with great reluctance, she gave it up."

One 22-year-old German refugee girl, Bertha, came to the United States to work as a governess. Her employer introduced her to one of his personal friends, with whom Bertha fell so much in love that she willingly gave herself to him, believing his promises of marriage. When she became pregnant she was discharged and her "lover" severed all association with her, leaving her practically destitute.

At the home for unwed mothers, Bertha declared that she had no desire to keep her baby and would give it up for adoption, but when the child was born and she saw it, her intentions went out the window. Even though the baby had a defect in its vocal cords, Bertha insisted she would keep it. The doctors were able to remedy the vocal defect and Bertha and her newborn went out into an unsympathetic world. She had no relatives in the United States, and only a few friends, with whom she went to live. At last reports Bertha was working at a part-time job and finding it difficult to support herself and her infant son, so she had applied for public assistance.

Some of the girls are cold-blooded about their babies. One, for instance, refused to see her child and said she didn't care who took it or what happened to it. "As far as I'm concerned," she said, "it's just the same as delivering a bundle of laundry."

Quite different is the story of Grace, a 35-year-old secretary who lived at home with her parents. Lonely and concerned about her spinsterhood, Grace one day met a handsome truck driver who seemed more attentive than any man had ever been, and she welcomed his attentions. Even when the man confessed that he was married, Grace refused to end their relationship and they continued their clandestine meetings and intimacies for some six years. Then Grace became pregnant.

Panicky, she pleaded with her family doctor to help her in keeping the news from her parents, who had no suspicions about her truck-driver sweetheart. The doctor told her father and mother that Grace was on the verge of a nervous breakdown and needed complete relaxation in a rest home operated by her employer in another State, and he then arranged for her admission to the home for unwed mothers.

The truck driver readily admitted paternity of Grace's baby and was perfectly willing to give the baby his name on its birth certificate.

"But what about us?" Grace wanted to know.

"I'll have to divorce my wife before I can marry you," he said. "If you ask me to do that, I'll do it, but in all honesty I have to tell you that I still love my wife and I don't want a divorce if there's any other way."

Under the circumstances Grace decided that his divorce might make three people unhappy, and that she would let matters stand as they were—but with an understanding that she and the truck driver would continue their covert romance as before.

Ironically, the wife of the truck driver is unable to bear children and the man is happy to be the father, even of an illegitimate child. As for Grace, "Of course I feel guilty about the baby," she says, "but maybe I just needed to prove that I could be a wife and mother."

Oddly enough, Grace never became a wife, and her mothering was of brief duration. She had gone to great lengths to keep her secret and had no wish to proclaim her motherhood to her parents and the world. To do so she would have to involve her lover, thus disgracing them both and bringing only heartaches to her mother and father. The result was that she put up the baby for adoption, despite mixed feelings on her own part and on the part of the errant truck driver.

While most of the girls appreciate the kindness and care they get at the Home, there are occasional fault-finders who are at odds with the world and who are thoroughly disagreeable. One of these, a crippled woman in her thirties, complained about the beds, the food, the other girls, and was antagonistic towards the staff. A hypochondriac, she imagined all sorts of aches and pains, accusing the doctors of not knowing their business when they insisted her ailments were mythi-

cal. Her most frequent complaint was about her "headaches."
At first she was given two white tablets.

"What's this stuff?" she asked.

"It's aspirin," she was told.

"Hmpf! Aspirin! All the aspirin in the world couldn't cure
my headaches. I found that out a long time ago. I don't want
any aspirin."

She took it anyway, upon Major Richardson's insistence, but
grumbled that it had no effect whatever upon her pains. Subsequently the Major, with the doctors' approval, gave her Buf-
ferin, but the woman squawked that this was no better than
aspirin. Finally Major Richardson gave her another well-known
headache tablet, available without prescription, but passed
the word that the woman was not to be told the name of the
product. Its principal ingredient was aspirin!

"What is it this time?" she asked.

"This is something that was made just for your headaches,"
she was told. "This will fix you up just fine."

She took two of the tablets and later came to the Major.
"That new special medicine is good stuff," she said. "It sure
chased away my headaches."

"That's fine," the Major said. "We thought it would."

"I noticed that the pills had a big letter 'S' stamped on them,"
the woman went on. "What's the 'S' stand for?"

The "S" stood for the name of the manufacturer, but the
Major said simply, "Oh, that stands for 'Salvation.'" The woman
was satisfied.

This woman, incidentally, lived in a cheap rooming house
where she had met a chronic alcoholic who fathered her baby.
To her, pregnancy was merely an inconvenience, and she willingly gave up her child for adoption.

Unlike this patient, who was a public welfare recipient when
she came to the Home, most of the girls are from families in
the middle-income brackets and a few have parents who are
wealthy.

The girls' identities are carefully protected, and newcomers
to the Home Department for unmarried mothers may decide

98

for themselves whether or not they want their last names known to those already there. Mail can be routed through another address which has no connection with the Home. After a girl is discharged, if she were in the company of other people on the street and should meet one of The Salvation Army officers who knew her at the Home, the officer would avoid speaking to her or making any other sign of recognition unless the girl herself spoke first.

Two of the girls in the Home at the time of my visit were themselves born out of wedlock, although they do not know it —and this fact and their identities will remain among the countless other secrets in the archives of the Home.

Sometimes a young woman who is married, divorced or separated and is made pregnant by someone other than her husband, needs the same kind of help and understanding as the young unmarried woman. Frequently the father of the expected child also needs help, and counseling is available to him on a confidential basis. Parents of a boy or girl in trouble often turn to The Salvation Army for advice. Whether the request comes from the expectant mother, the man in the case, a parent, a friend or a relative, The Salvation Army offers understanding and skilled help in strictest confidence.

The home for unwed mothers at the Booth Memorial Hospital in Flushing can accommodate forty guests and is generally filled to capacity. If room is available, any girl who is pregnant out of wedlock, not too greatly disturbed mentally, and free of venereal disease, can be admitted. Girls are referred by about 30 different sources, including welfare agencies, ministers, teachers, doctors, lawyers, and various employers.

One pregnant girl riding on a bus was told about the Home by her seat companion, a total stranger. Another landed in a New York bus depot and began a casual conversation at the luncheonette counter with a girl who told her about the Home. The newcomer went there directly and was admitted.

The Home is open to members of all races and religions. There is no age limit, and ages have ranged from 11 to 37 years. Although a girl may be admitted at any time in pregnancy as her need requires, it is preferred that she arrange an appointment for a personal interview and begin care six to eight weeks before her time. Written reports on venereal tests (a Wassermann, Kahn, or Massini, and a vaginal smear) are necessary before admission, and these may be done at the hospital when the girl comes for her first interview. Delinquent girls referred by the courts are accepted only after it has been made clear to the court that this is an open shelter and that The Salvation Army cannot be held responsible for the custody of such girls.

The facilities of the whole hospital are available to meet all health needs, and when a girl begins labor she is transferred to the Maternity Floor of the hospital for delivery and convalescent care, usually five days. If she is in a Home not adjacent to a hospital, she will be placed in a hospital when her time comes and will return to the Home to convalesce.

In a typical day at the Home the girls are awakened at 7:30 A. M. and have breakfast from 8:00 to 8:30. At 8:35 there is a five-minute family prayer, followed at 8:45 by a "clinic call," in which those girls receiving medicine on prescription get their regular dosage. Anyone with a specific complaint also gets expert treatment.

Once a week at 9:00 A. M. there is a Health Class in which the girls see films and hear talks on biological changes in pregnancy, diet instruction, see a demonstration of and practice special exercises, all taught by registered nurses.

At 10:00 A. M. comes Housework. Each girl is responsible for cleaning and keeping neat her share of the room she occupies. In addition she gets a general housework assignment, such as table-setting or helping to keep lounges and craft rooms in order.

One of several craft classes is held at 11:00 A. M. daily, with attendance optional. Candle-making, shellcraft, copper enameling, knitting and sewing are alternated.

Luncheon is served from 12:30 to 1:00 P. M.

From 1:00 to 3:30 P. M. school is in session, and the girls

may take any course offered in the regular high school curriculum except laboratory courses. Two teachers from the Home Bound Instruction Division of the Board of Education of New York City are assigned to the Home so that girls of school age may continue their studies, receive marks on City report cards, take Regents examinations, and receive certificates or diplomas. In this way schoolgirls may keep up their classes and return to the school from which they came or go to another, as seems best for the individual girl. Those past school age may spend the afternoon as they choose, and with permission of the staff they may go shopping or to the movies or wherever else they wish. After 3:30 the girls attending school are free to do as they please.

Dinner is served at 5:30 P. M.

Evenings are spent watching television, listening to records, reading, working on sewing projects such as maternity smocks, layettes and general wardrobe items, or attending a class in ceramics. Once a week there is a Bible Class. Once a month there is a recent movie and a birthday party at which the guests of honor are all the girls whose birthdays fall in that month. On occasion there are travel slide-talks.

Psychiatric consultation and legal advice are available.

Within the Home there is a Salvation Army worship service at 11:00 o'clock each Sunday morning. There is a Catholic church nearby to which Catholic girls may go if they wish, and Jewish girls go to a synagogue in the vicinity of the Home.

The Home has its own nursery for new babies.

All rooms are homey, bright and clean, and most have two or three beds. Community bathrooms, with green tile walls, have five shower stalls and two bathtubs. There is a modern laundry with set tubs, automatic washers and ironing boards, where the girls may do their own washing and ironing.

Most of the girls enjoy talking with each other about their own cases. "They're all 'junior psychiatrists,'" Major Richardson says with a smile. "They love to analyze each other's problems, but they have no solutions. They have learned one thing, though—that money and prestige don't bar a body from having

101

serious problems."

Sometimes a girl who has been at the Home wants to come back and help others who are there. One girl now writing for a popular magazine wants to use her writing skills to keep other girls from getting into trouble. An expert photographer, she is teaching several of them how to use a camera and how to develop and print their pictures.

Girls stay at the Home for an average of eight to ten weeks, although some have lived there only two weeks and others as long as ten months.

Costs of care at the Home—without profit—total $8.42 a day for the mother, $8.47 a day for the baby. The average total *cost* to the Army is about $800, but the average *charge* is only about $300. Most of the girls pay these fees or a substantial part of them, but The Salvation Army would not refuse admission to a girl because she could not pay, and they have had many free cases, with the Army footing the bills. In some cases where a girl is penniless the Army asks her permission to appeal to the city or county for financial aid for her, but if the girl refuses such permission the request will not be made.

Major Richardson and her officer-staff, with Miss Mattia, are deeply concerned about the girls. If one gets a stomach ache or has a nightmare the Major or one of the officers rushes to the girl's side to comfort her as a mother would do. When a girl is discharged from the Home she is asked to return after six weeks for a physical examination. Almost without exception there is one comment the Major hears over and over from those who come back: "I certainly miss you and this wonderful place."

"Many cry when it's time to leave," Major Richardson says, "because this is the only place where they have known any inner security."

Louise Richardson's first memory of The Salvation Army goes back to her home in Reading, Massachusetts, where her parents were active Methodists. "My father couldn't stand to wear mended socks," she recalls, "so whenever his socks needed darning he would give them to The Salvation Army. But my mother always mended them first anyway! I remember the trucks that used to come to our house to get the socks and other things."

When she was thirteen her family went to St. Petersburg, Florida, where they planned to seek out a Methodist church. However, Louise and her sister made friends at school with two girls who attended The Salvation Army Sunday School and who invited the Richardson girls to go with them. Their parents approved, and Louise became so interested that she never did get to the Methodist church.

Returning to Reading, Louise felt that The Salvation Army "was the place the Lord would have me work." When she discussed this with her father he was quite unhappy about it, and suggested that she first complete her education. She went to normal school, but in her bureau drawer she had an application for Salvation Army officer training.

"Well, Lord," she said, "I'm not sure whether I should teach or go to the School for Officers' Training. If I get an appointment before July I'll teach school. Otherwise I'll go into training."

In June she got an appointment, so she became a school teacher, but by the middle of the second year she knew she had made the wrong choice. She told her mother she was going to become a Salvation Army officer.

Smiling, her mother said, "I wondered how long it would be before you'd make that decision. I think I've known all along that you'd do it."

So Louise Richardson became a cadet, completed her officer training, was assigned to Ivy House, a children's home in Philadelphia, and in 1953 was placed in charge of the home for unwed mothers, where she devotes herself completely to the welfare of the unhappy girls and women who bring their troubles to her doorstep in a never-ending stream.

Practically all of the new mothers return to their families or to work when they leave the Home, though occasionally a girl may prefer to avoid relatives and old haunts, and may seek a future in new surroundings.

Chapter 8

WHEN DISASTER STRIKES

A violent earthquake, to one who experiences it, terrifies and shatters the nerves, not only by the death and destruction it inflicts but also because it generates in man a feeling of utter helplessness to combat the upheaval of his world. When the earth cracks open, or rises up, or falls away at your feet, where can you go? Nowhere. What can you do? Not much except pray and wait.

In the South American winter of May, 1960, a series of the greatest cataclysms in history tore apart great chunks of Chile, the long, thin nation between Peru and Cape Horn, marking the western edge of South America.

Early on the Saturday morning of May 21, Senior Major Edmundo Allemand, commanding The Salvation Army in the Chilean capital city of Santiago, was shaken awake by a strong earth tremor.

"We are used to earthquakes in Chile," Major Allemand says. "In this long strip of land there is an average of an earthquake a day, although most are so minor that they are detected only by the seismographs. But that Saturday morning I could tell that there was a violent upheaval somewhere."

The news came by radio. The epicenter of the quake was in Concepción, some 320 miles south of Santiago and third largest city in the country, with a population of 150,000.

When disaster strikes, The Salvation Army needs no push to act. Major Allemand and Major Helmuth Huhner immediately met with representatives of Church World Service in Santiago and obtained from them a truckload of food, clothing, blankets and emergency supplies. Next step was to get official authority to travel into the disaster area. Permission was granted and the two Salvation Army majors, with three men cadets and a young helper, drove toward Concepción. Nearing the city they drove cautiously in the darkness, for parts of the highway were twisted and broken, and it was not until 4:30 A. M. that they reached Salvation Army headquarters.

Actually they reached what had been headquarters. The walls had been pulled apart and one wall had collapsed. Although the staff had been celebrating its second anniversary in the new building when the quake hit, no one had been injured. Major Allemand and his associates went to the city authorities to offer their help. The city fathers were most grateful.

"You are the first people outside the city to come to our aid," they said.

It was agreed that the authorities would send to The Salvation Army all people who had lost their homes and that the Army would provide them with food, clothing and blankets.

The distribution began at two o'clock Sunday afternoon, May 22. At ten minutes before three there was an ominous rumble, like muffled thunder, and a "short earthquake that put us on our guard." Twenty minutes later the earth shook again, this time more violently. The Salvation Army people and the others rushed out the back of the building, where the wall had collapsed, and into a small wooden shack in a neighbor's yard.

"One has to experience an earthquake to understand what it is like," Major Allemand says. "It is most difficult to explain in words. The floor beneath us rose and fell in great waves, and we held on to each other so we would not fall down. The buildings and trees started a hideous dance. The women cried, and so did the children. The men were pale. Some people fell to their knees and asked God for mercy. The underground growling, the cracking of the wood, the crash of walls and the clouds of dust they raised made a frightening and unforgettable picture."

When the earth subsided, not one of the circle of Salvationists had been injured.

"By battery radio we learned that the epicenter of this latest earthquake was in Valdivia, 320 miles further south, the most important city of Southern Chile," the Major said.

More tremors came, and with them great tidal waves. Eleven volcanoes erupted, and a new volcano was born. "A whole third of our country was damaged," the Major declares. "The disaster was the biggest of its kind in the history of the world, so far as the area covered is concerned. Hills fell down, burying whole villages. Other hills sprang up. Tidal waves wiped out a number of small ports and caused terrific damage to the big ones, sinking ships and taking a heavy toll of victims. The volcanoes added to the terror and killed many country people who had climbed the slopes seeking safety. Railroads were destroyed, roads were impassable. The temperature was below freezing, and heavy rains brought threats of floods."

In this atmosphere The Salvation Army did its relief work. The pastor of the Methodist church, a strong concrete structure, invited them to make his building their center of operations, which they did.

Says Major Allemand, "For four days we were the only ones in the whole city to give out food, clothing and blankets. We helped more than seven thousand sad, hungry, shivering people. We had no water except rain water with which everybody cooked and made tea. We had no electricity, no gas, no telephone or other communication except our battery-operated radio. Nearly everybody slept outdoors in the cold, for fear of new tremors. Some slept in cars or trucks, some used scraps of wood for a roof. Even beds were hauled out of houses and put in the streets. After long hours of standing in queues for food, women fainted and had to be brought into a house, but we had no water even to give them an aspirin. Finally the national army came in to carry on with supplies gathered from other cities, so we prepared to go to Valdivia, where we had

106

a corps and Men's Center, but no news as to what had happened to them."

Once again Church World Service furnished The Salvation Army with a truckload of supplies, which they took to Valdivia.

"Valdivia was worse than Concepión," the Major recalls. "Even strong concrete houses, schools and factories came completely down. The whole ground of the city sank from five to ten feet. Trees and telephone poles showed their tops from the middle of the river. Luckily our own hall had suffered minor damage, and we held a cottage meeting with fifty of our comrades."

Major Allemand and his staff met the pastors of ten evangelical churches and arranged to give each a part of the goods they had brought from Concepción. The ministers furnished lists giving ages and sexes of children, so that the clothing could be apportioned accordingly, and distribution began the next day.

"There were many unforgettable episodes," Major Allemand says. "I think perhaps the one that moved me most concerned a twelve-year-old boy who was badly injured in the town and climbed a hill for safety. He had seen his father, mother, brothers and sisters killed by the earthquake, and he himself soon died on the hillside. In his pockets, however, we found a note with these words: 'Oh God, why have You done this? Why have You killed my Mother and Father, brothers and sisters? Now I am alone, I am hungry, I am cold, I have nowhere to go. To the people I say, come now and help us, give us to eat. We are hungry. To the children I want to say, be good to Father and Mother while you have them. Now I have not got them any more.'"

When the earthquake struck on Sunday, services were being held in two churches. In one the pastor said, "Do not leave the church. Nothing will happen here. Let us pray to God." And as they prayed the walls crashed down upon them and killed a number of children and teachers.

In the other church the minister told his congregation of 400, "The hand of God shakes the earth. Let us show that we fear

His wrath, leaving this place and seeking safety." They fled. No one was injured and the church was not damaged in any way.

In the Pacific port of Corral, where the populace knew earthquakes might fling a tidal wave over their town, they had sought to save their church by lashing the building to surrounding trees with steel cables. They climbed the hills and watched the ocean drown the town. So great was the force of the water that the big trees around the church were torn up by the roots, and church, trees, cables and all were swept away.

Some of the townsfolk fled for their lives in trucks, cars, even on horseback, but the tidal wave came surging through the streets with the fury of a raging torrent, engulfing the refugees and turning the town into a watery grave. Even 30 miles inland the salt sea flowed over farms and grazing lands.

In New York City, Lt. Col. Roy Barber, National Coordinator of Disaster Services, used the Men's Social Service Center as the collection depot for critical supplies for earthquake victims and for money to buy materials. Americans responded quickly to appeals for Chilean relief, and in a short time The Salvation Army in the United States shipped several tons of winter clothing, a thousand blankets, and hundreds of dollars to the disaster areas through the cooperation of Pan American Grace Airways. Colonel Barber himself soon flew into the distress zone for a personal inspection.

The Salvation Army stands ready to lend practical help as well as spiritual comfort to victims of any disaster. At Springhill, Nova Scotia, The Salvation Army furnished soup which they piped down a mine shaft to provide the first nourishment in days for a group of entombed miners. The Salvationists also visited the families of miners who were dead or missing, to bring such solace as they could.

In New Jersey, when a railroad commuter train plunged from an open bridge into Newark Bay, a fully-stocked canteen manned by Salvation Army workers was set up on the trestle; and by order of railroad police, Salvation Army workers were the only people outside of rescue crews permitted on the bridge.

In a series of articles in 1960 the New York *Post* revealed that unemployed West Virginia coal miners and their families were in dire need of food and clothing. Readers in New York City wanted to know how they could make donations. The publishers sought the cooperation of The Salvation Army, which arranged for eight of its Social Service Centers in New York, New Jersey, Long Island and Westchester County to collect contributions.

Within 12 days The Salvation Army had picked up more than 20,000 pounds of clothing, food and vitamins for the miners. Trucks were then donated by the Hudson Transportation Company of New York to haul the goods to Welch, West Virginia, where they were delivered to Captain and Mrs. Harold Brinson, in charge of The Salvation Army Corps there. The Brinsons distributed the supplies to the needy families.

It is no accident that The Salvation Army is often the first relief organization on the scene of disaster. The relief program is no helter-skelter affair in which its officers simply appear as if by magic and hand out coffee and doughnuts. They act in accordance with detailed and specific orders set out in a *Manual for Emergency Disaster Service,* which establishes a Director of Operations, an Assistant Director, and officers in charge of Communications, Food Service, Transport, Clothing, Shelter, Casework Service, Public Information, Religious Service, and Identifications.

A first-hand account of some of the Army's problems was given to me by Colonel Barber, who led a relief squad into flooded areas of Connecticut in 1955, when torrential rains sent the Naugatuck River on a rampage, swamping homes and streets in the city of Waterbury.

Thousands of men, women and children fled from the rising waters, congregating in and around the parish hall of a Polish Catholic Church. Many women were on the verge of hysteria, frightened children were crying, and even the men were dazed, trying to realize that they were victims of a disaster which they always thought happened to other people, but not to them.

Gas and electricity were turned off in the city. The only bright light came from a floodlight on a mobile canteen of The Salvation Army, where Army workers served hot soup and hot coffee throughout the direful night. Women and men holding babies in their arms, or comforting older children, stood patiently in a long line to get food for themselves and their families.

Amid the babble of voices, the sobs, the shouts from the darkness, one middle-aged man sidled up to Colonel Barber, who was ladling out the hot soup.

"Can I talk to you a minute?" the man said.

"What is it, mister?" Colonel Barber asked. "We're terribly busy here."

"This will only take a minute. It's important."

Colonel Barber stepped away from the soup cauldron and leaned down in response to the beckoning finger of the man, who said in a low voice, "Listen. I have a wife and little girl out there. If we have to stand in this line we'll be all night getting something to eat, or else the food will be all gone. Now I'm pretty well-to-do. I have money." His voice became a hoarse whisper. "How much do you want for enough soup and coffee for the three of us so we won't have to wait our turn?"

Barber stared at the man for a few seconds, then shook his head. "As I told you, mister," he said coldly, "we're very busy. I'll be glad to give you food for your family, but you'll have to stand in line to get it like everybody else." He went back to ladling the soup.

Roy Barber recalls this incident as perhaps the most distasteful in the Waterbury episode. His other recollections show how the Emergency Disaster Service of The Salvation Army goes into action without red tape and with a disregard for danger, to serve those in need. We see their people at work, but few of us are aware of the problems and obstacles they encounter to do their jobs.

One of the first pleas for help in Waterbury came to the

Director of Civil Defense in New York on a Friday night. The Salvation Army is one of only two welfare agencies named in "The National Plan for Civil Defense and Defense Mobilization" (the other is the American Red Cross). The Civil Defense Director called upon both to respond to the appeal.

Summoning other officers, Barber sped to the Army's giant mobile canteen, purchased and equipped by the Loewenstein Memorial Fund. The canteen is a self-contained feeding unit 32 feet long, weighing about 20 tons. It has its own power generator and can also work from a 12-volt storage battery. Using propane (bottled) gas, it has three 6-burner and three 2-burner units, along with a gas heating plant for winter use. There are two separate burners, each with a 10-gallon tank, to heat water. The canteen is completely equipped, even to its own toilet facilities and a two-way radio. The Army now has two of the giant canteens and several smaller mobile units for similar use.

One of Barber's first acts was to recruit volunteers from the throng of evacuees. "That's our policy in disaster work," Barber explains. "Victims who stand around doing nothing are much better off if they work."

He provided Salvation Army armbands for the volunteers and assigned them to tasks. Within a half hour he was deluged by other people wanting to volunteer, but Barber soon discovered that most of them only wanted the armbands, which would permit them to roam through all restricted areas searching for friends and relatives.

"Since there was no electric power, all refrigerators and freezers were out of operation, and householders, store and restaurant owners were asking what to do about their stored food," Barber says. "They were told to bring it to our canteen. Our chef was from the Loewenstein Cafeteria, and the local health officer designated him as the man to decide whether or not such food was fit to eat. One night later in the week we cooked seven hundred pounds of steak from a restaurant because it would soon go bad." Powdered milk was furnished for children, and hot milk for baby formulas.

Throughout the night Barber and his companions fed some 4000 weary homeless people, and continued to do so for the next two weeks. The morning after the canteen arrived, a Saturday, the Connecticut National Guard arrived to protect the town. Hundreds of sightseers from other communities streamed into Waterbury, creating traffic jams and interfering with the operations of the relief workers.

Refrigeration and water were two of the biggest problems. One was solved when a huge refrigerator truck rumbled in and parked beside the canteen, providing a refrigerator "as big as a boxcar." Next, a Mutrie tank truck, customarily used for hauling milk, came in with 15,000 gallons of water; the local Coca-Cola bottling plant contributed water in huge Coke bottles used for counter displays; and the Fire Department brought muddy water pumped from farm wells. All water was boiled before use.

"We kept running short of bread," Barber remembers. "I went out on a scouting trip to see if I could scare up some, and I found the driver of a big truck unloading loaves intended for the National Guard. I told the driver how desperately we needed bread."

"Yeah?" the driver said. "Well, that's tough, Mac, but you'll have to stand out of my way. Just stand over there, huh? Right there, near the corner of the truck."

Barber backed away. A moment later the truck driver quickly passed him a carton of loaves and continued to unload more, putting them on the ground. For every three or four he stacked up, he gave one to Barber, who began his own stockpile which he then took to the canteen.

"After that first morning there was no problem of supply," Barber says.

On the first Saturday afternoon The Salvation Army served bouillon as part of a meal. As each person came to the canteen a server would ask, "Bouillon?" Most of the people shook their heads and took the other food.

"I don't understand it," Barber told one of the officers. "How come these hungry people don't want our soup?"

"Beats me," the other said.

A little girl about eight years old who overheard this conversation pulled Barber's sleeve. "Is that soup, mister?" she asked.

"Yes, honey, that's right. You want some?" Barber asked.

"Yes, please. And I'll tell my Daddy. He didn't know what the big word was."

"The big word? You mean 'bouillon'?"

"That's it. My Daddy doesn't know many big words, I guess."

Barber was suddenly aware that many of the people in the line spoke with an accent (he later found they were Lithuanians). He promptly instructed his servers to stop saying "Bouillon" and to say "Soup" instead. The soup rapidly disappeared.

The flood waters had swept away not only homes and belongings, but human lives as well. Corpses in soggy clothing were brought to the relief area, where anxious and terrified survivors crowded to gaze at each still, pale face. Throughout the night and in the week ahead the agonizing screams of women who looked down upon lost loved ones were as the tolling of bells. Some women fainted. Many grew hysterical. Some, with their menfolk, sat together simply rocking back and forth, staring blankly, numbed by shock.

Sergeant Frank S. Duren of the Bethany Division of the Connecticut State Police, himself a Salvationist, recalls the flood tragedy. His wife, a professional cook and Home League Secretary of the Waterbury Salvation Army Corps, did the daytime cooking at the canteen with her assistant, Mrs. Ann Yavecchia, under the supervision of Major Vernon Post, now of Bristol, Connecticut.

Sergeant Duren told me about Corps Sergeant Charles Rietdyke, a member of the management staff of the Scovill Brass Company in Waterbury, and a young man wearing a sweatshirt who was watching the rescue activities.

"Is there anything I can do for you, Mac?" Sergeant Rietdyke asked.

113

"I might ask the same thing of you," the young man said. "Can I lend you a hand in any way?"

"Well, as you can see, the street is pretty well cluttered up with debris. How about pushing a broom and getting it cleaned up?"

"Fine!" the man said. "Just get me the broom."

The sergeant gave him the broom and said, "Thanks, Mac."

Each morning young "Mac" appeared and asked for work assignments, gladly doing whatever was suggested. One day while "Mac" was moving some heavy boxes, Sergeant Rietdyke saw a nun come out of the church and look at the crowd. Young "Mac" waved at the nun and shouted, "You looking for me, Sister?"

She smiled and went toward him. "Yes, Father, I am," she said.

Sergeant Rietdyke felt a sinking sensation in his stomach. A few minutes later he approached the young man. "Father, I'm terribly sorry I've been calling you 'Mac,'" he said. "If I'd known who you were I certainly wouldn't have asked you to do these cleaning-up jobs."

The priest laughed. "Think nothing of it, my friend," he said. "I've enjoyed helping out, and you can still call me 'Mac' if you want to. I don't mind a bit."

On another occasion Sergeant Rietdyke and Major Post were in a serious discussion about the lack of sugar. An elderly man overheard part of their talk and came up to them.

"I hear what you say," he said. "I help you, I think. You come."

He led them to the rear of a building, unlocked a door and invited them in. They found themselves in a warehouse in which were several sacks of sugar.

"You take what you need," he said.

"This is yours?" the sergeant asked.

"Mine, sure. I have bakery."

"But if we take this we should pay you for it," Major Post said. "How much for a sack?"

The man frowned and shook his head vigorously. "I no take

money for help all those people. What kind fellow you think I am?"

In Ansonia, Connecticut, another Salvation Army officer, Captain Allan Cranford, stationed in that town, saw his own building washed away with all of his personal belongings. He established headquarters in the Armory to feed others who had lost their homes, and when the National Guard arrived he moved to Falcon Hall, a Polish lodge, which was the center of relief operations in that area for several weeks. Captain Cranford's greatest assistance and labor supply came from the Veterans of Foreign Wars, which acted as part of The Salvation Army disaster organization.

With the food situation under control, Colonel Barber returned to New York to prepare shipments of shovels, rubber boots, disinfectants and other clean-up materials. Arriving at New York headquarters he learned that messages were being received from a mysterious "Mr. Wood" in Naugatuck, Connecticut, asking for food and equipment. The Salvation Army had no corps in Naugatuck and no one in Barber's office had ever heard of "Mr. Wood," but they sent him what he asked for.

Later the colonel learned that Wood was vice president of the local bank and had set up a relief depot in the bank lobby in the name of The Salvation Army. Barber also found that Wood was a member of a Salvation Army Service Extension Unit and thus had a right to act in the Army's name.

There are thousands of other members of the Service Extension Program who are not actually Salvationists, but who perform volunteer work in behalf of The Salvation Army and use its funds.

The Service Extension Program began about 1930 in Burlington, Vermont, where a group of Salvation Army volunteer workers collected money for the Army. The treasurer of this group suggested that a portion of the funds be set aside to be used for indigents during the year. Arbitrarily they decided to leave 20 percent of their collection in Burlington for this purpose, to be administered by a local "Service Unit."

This was the beginning of the Army's Service Unit Welfare Program, which extends the helping hand of the Army into small communities and other areas where there are no resident Salvation Army officers. The program spread rather quickly across New England and there are now about 6000 extension committees throughout the United States. Each is supplied with a detailed printed guide and a "Service Unit Manual" telling them exactly how to proceed in the handling of needy cases and in responding to disasters.

According to the guide, "The Salvation Army is a religious and charitable movement, finding its expression in a desire to alleviate human distress wherever found. It is not primarily a disaster relief organization, but by tradition and inclination usually finds itself serving at the point of greatest need during the emergency period of a disaster."

If a disaster emergency is "beyond local ability to handle," the committee is instructed to communicate with The Salvation Army, which will send trained people if necessary. In any event, the guide sets out, step by step, the procedure to be followed by the local Service Unit so that there will be no needless delay in providing immediate help. Cooperation is sought from local authorities and from members of Rotary, Kiwanis, Lions and other civic clubs.

In preparation for emergencies such as the Waterbury flood, the guide provides a "Disaster Equipment Check List" with instructions to each committee to maintain an "Emergency Cupboard," including such items as two 5-gallon insulated beverage containers, 2000 paper cups, paper or wooden spoons, food containers with covers, serving spoons, instant coffee in sealed containers, canned and powdered milk, sugar, canned meats and spreads, a gasoline pressure stove, a foam-type fire extinguisher, official armbands, a first-aid kit, Bibles, stretchers, folding cots and blankets, and other emergency materials.

In the State of New York there are 380 local Service Extension committees, of which 132 are in the counties of Suffolk, Nassau and Queens, supervised by Mr. Ellis Heglund. Heglund, by profession an engineer, was approached in his own

116

community to become chairman of a committee there. He accepted and later joined The Salvation Army as a soldier, then became an employee assigned to help promote the Service Extension Program. He has designed various brochures, written publicity, and developed the printed guide, and has helped to increase the program's funds in his area from $30,000 to $262,-000. Much of the money is spent for eyeglasses, crutches, wheelchairs and other aids for sick or handicapped people who cannot themselves afford to buy such equipment.

"Recruiting volunteers for this work isn't too difficult," Heglund says. "Somewhere along the line maybe a grandfather or grandmother got free coffee and doughnuts from some Salvation Army officer. This made a favorable impression and they told their youngsters about it. Now the youngsters are willing to serve."

The committees are not intended to supplant existing public welfare agencies. Often, in fact, the committees refer cases to other agencies for help. Occasionally they get unusual requests which are handled by The Salvation Army. In one case, for instance, a Long Island youth serving in the armed forces and stationed in the West was carrying a can of gasoline into a tent to fill a gasoline stove used for heating. The can was leaking. Another soldier accidentally flipped a lighted cigarette butt into the trickle of gasoline.

The blaze flashed to the can, which exploded, burning the boy from head to toe. The victim's mother worked in a factory on Long Island and an effort was made to telephone her collect. She was too poor to pay for the call, but knowing that it came from the area where her son was on duty she appealed to the Service Extension unit for help. They placed a return call and learned that the boy was expected to die very soon. The story was relayed to The Salvation Army which instructed one of its officers in the military area to go to the boy's bedside to pray with him and to keep the mother informed of his condition. The final call made to the mother was from The Salvation Army officer, who told her that her son had died in his arms.

117

As Ellis Heglund and others have pointed out, a "disaster" need not always involve scores of people in catastrophes of nature. One jobless family man might constitute a disaster of another kind, and Heglund told me about such a case.

A jobless World War II veteran, 29, and his 22-year-old wife, who was expecting their first child within a month, were evicted from their small apartment for non-payment of rent. In desperation the couple appealed to their local Service Unit of The Salvation Army, whose welfare secretary learned that the wife had had no medical care since the inception of her pregnancy.

The Service Unit quickly located a furnished room with cooking privileges and paid one week's rent in advance. A Unit member with a station wagon helped them move their meager belongings, while the Service Extension Bureau arranged with the Department of Welfare for the wife to have maternity care at Meadowbrook Hospital.

Next the Service Extension Bureau lined up a job interview which resulted in employment of the husband at $50 a week. A few weeks later the welfare secretary learned that a local religious organization sought a young married couple to act as caretakers for its property and to live in a rent-free house. The husband could also hold a regular job. The secretary arranged an interview with the couple and they were hired. They are now safely settled and successfully managing their own affairs—and their own new child.

Chapter 9

TRUCKS, TRASH, AND TRIUMPHS

In the 1890s a familiar vehicle on the streets of New York was the pushcart wheeled from house to house by a Salvation Army "Salvage Brigade" to collect paper, rags, and miscellaneous junk, all aimed at the Army's slogan, "Work for the Workless." Many of the goods were repaired and sold in Army thrift stores, as they still are. The men who pushed the carts were paid a small wage, derived from the sale of the goods they collected, and as part of their pay they were given food and lodging by the Army. Horses and wagons later supplanted the pushcarts and were in turn made obsolete by the now-familiar Salvation Army red motor trucks.

By 1902 there were salvage centers in 22 American cities. Today The Salvation Army operates 118 Centers from coast to coast in the United States alone, and scores more in other lands, all designed to help homeless and discouraged men to regain their self-respect through self-help. By putting in a full day's work on the sorting and repair of donated merchandise, the men at the Army's Social Service Centers regain sound work habits lost through dissipation and aimless wandering. At the same time they are encouraged to feel that they are returning value for the care and service they receive. The Centers in the United States care for more than 56,000 men in need of help.

Two floors of the Center's seven-story brick building at 536

119

West 46th Street in New York City are jammed with second-hand furniture, clothing, lamps, radios, vacuum cleaners, clocks, record-players, bedsprings, mattresses, attic fans, electric heaters, shoes, women's hats, tablecloths, pocketbooks and other usable merchandise cast off by thousands of people and donated to The Salvation Army for sale to the general public.

One day a telephone call was received at the Center from a Mrs. Miller, who said she would give the Army some chairs, tables, a desk, a bed, women's clothing, and certain bric-a-brac if they would pick it up. The truck driver who called for the goods was quite excited when he returned to the Center.

"Hey! You know who this Mrs. Miller really is?" he asked.

"Never heard of her," was the answer.

"You've heard of her, all right, and you've seen her, too—in the movies."

"Yeah? Who is she?"

"She's Marilyn Monroe, that's who! Miller's her married name. Mrs. Arthur Miller. Boy! Is she something!"

The mysterious communication system known as "the grapevine" spread the news so swiftly that scores of people descended upon the store within the week. "Where's the stuff you got from Marilyn Monroe?" they asked. Or, from girls and women, "I want to see the clothes you picked up from Marilyn Monroe."

Major Edwy Hinkle, the Director of the Center, issued strict instructions to his staff and workers to maintain The Salvation Army's policy of keeping such information confidential, but once again the grapevine twined through the buyers and within a short time they had purchased virtually all of the goods donated by Mrs. Miller, including her discarded clothing, which was snapped up by would-be glamour girls.

Merchandise for sale at the Center store is frequently donated by famous people such as Eleanor Roosevelt, Helen Hayes, TV star Steve Allen, and band-leader Xavier Cugat, but for the most part it represents the generosity of thousands of housewives and others who have no claim to fame.

How does The Salvation Army process these old clothes, the
120

broken chairs, the old newspapers and magazines that you and I and hosts of other people donate (meaning "throw out")? Newspapers and magazines are baled and sold to paper manufacturers.

All rags are graded, including clothing so worn that it is not salable. Such clothing is graded "No. 1" and is sold to overseas markets where it is made usable. Grade No. 2 consists of rags that go into the making of roofing material, and No. 3 rags go to mills which clean and bale them for sale to engineering and shipping companies for wiping engines and for similar purposes.

Scrap iron is sold to dealers in junk or scrap metals.

Usable clothing for men, women and children is put on racks in the Center store (or in other Salvation Army "thrift stores") for sale to the public, along with shoes, furniture and other household items. Some of the clothing is repaired and cleaned, as is some of the furniture.

Unfortunately, tons of goods are given to the Army every year which are obviously beyond further use. Many people who accumulate bulky trash, such as armless and legless chairs with broken springs and shredded upholstery, or shoes so "holey" that they look as though they had been through a Swiss cheese factory, are under the false impression that the Army wants such useless merchandise. It doesn't. It wants materials that are at least capable of being mended or repaired, but its people continue to accept the dross and litter because they want to be helpful and to maintain the good will of the public. If you want to dispose of worthless trash, give it to your trash collector!

In the cellar at the 46th Street Center I saw miniature mountains of broken furniture, worn-out footwear and other non-salvageable rubbish awaiting disposition. Since The Salvation Army strains to make the most of every contribution and every dollar it collects, the unusable debris is piled near the furnaces and is burned instead of coal to heat the building in winter. Even then there are sometimes such great quantities of the trash that some must be hauled to the city dumps.

The types of clothing donated to the Army provide clues to

121

the fashions that are becoming obsolete. For example, when the "trapeze" dress suddenly showed up in quantity, the employees at the Center knew that it had met the fate of the bustle and the sack dress.

The salvaged clothing that comes to the Center is sorted and graded by women, some of whom are on parole from prisons, seeking to rejoin a respectable society. In most cases the women were paroled only because The Salvation Army agreed to give them jobs that would make them self-supporting.

In the clothing processing section I stood engulfed by a strong camphory smell of mothballs and surrounded by stacks and racks of men's suits and overcoats, and watched a man pressing clothes to be offered for sale. I looked at a dark gray flannel suit which had just been ticketed. It was a Hart, Schaffner & Marx suit in new condition, showing no sign of wear whatever. The price tag read "$5.50." Another nearly new blue suit carrying the Roger Kent label was tagged at $5.00. Prices are figured on the basis of past experience and the laws of supply and demand.

Women's and children's clothing was marked anywhere from 50¢ to $5.00. One woman, the wife of a milkman and the mother of twelve children, comes to the Center store almost every week to buy clothing for her husband, herself and her brood. "With all these hungry mouths to feed," she says, "and with prices being what they are, I don't know what we'd do about clothing ourselves if it wasn't for this store."

In Spring and Summer the Center gets Fall and Winter clothing, and in cold weather they get Spring and Summer apparel, so that storage is always necessary for seasonal use.

The store is a favorite shopping place for many young newlyweds who can't afford new furniture. It is also a good hunting ground for antique collectors, and I saw one couple inspecting a pine chest of drawers. The woman, about forty, wore a well-tailored brown suit, a mink stole, a string of pearls, and diamond engagement and wedding rings. The man wore a black Homburg, an expensive blue suit and a huge sapphire ring on his right hand. Apparently they decided not to buy the chest, and when I left they were still roaming around the big room seeking treasures in the trash.

Thousands of books, most in excellent condition, are stacked in rows of bookcases and priced from 25¢ to $1.00. In the cellar at the Center I saw a mound of books about eight feet high and perhaps fifteen feet in diameter, waiting to be sorted and sold.

Theatrical producers often visit the Center looking for clothing, furniture, books or bric-a-brac to be used for "props" in a stage production. A scene in one play called for the use of scores of shoes of all kinds. The producers bought a load of shoes from The Salvation Army, and when the play ended its run they brought back the shoes and permitted the Army to keep the purchase price. Occasionally the producers obtain props on a rental basis.

The Salvation Army has about 80 regular employees at the Center, many of whom came there originally to seek help. They work as bookkeepers, stenographers, telephone operators, storekeepers and supervisors, carpenters, sorters and in other jobs. There is a printed sign near the exit on the first floor, reading: "THANK YOU FOR YOUR PATRONAGE. THE MONEY YOU HAVE SPENT HERE WILL ASSIST US IN CARRYING ON OUR REHABILITATION PROGRAM FOR MEN."

Another building at 535 West 48th Street is an important part of the Center. Here are sleeping quarters, a kitchen and dining room, a chapel, a canteen, recreation rooms, a medical examination room, a library, and a work area where the men renovate the household items collected from the public. The building itself is one of the oldest Salvation Army structures in the United States and is located in the section of New York known as "Hell's Kitchen," once the hangout of gangs, cutthroats, and purveyors of every form of crime and vice. At one time no police officer would venture into the Kitchen alone and its streets were patrolled by policemen in pairs. Today the neighborhood is reasonably tame and respectable.

The Center has beds for 192 men and is usually filled to

capacity during the Winter, slacking off somewhat in the Summer when several men leave New York to work at Summer hotels and resorts. Some have lived at the Center for only a few days. Others have made it their home for several years. No man lives at the Center and works for private employers, although some who work at the Center do live elsewhere. Most of them eat, sleep and work on the premises. Once known as "inmates," then as "clients," the men are now designated by the Army as "beneficiaries."

Says Major Hinkle, "Each man has a problem. It may be mental, physical or spiritual, or perhaps all three. Probably the biggest problem is that of alcoholism, which hits about eighty percent of the men."

To help the chronic drinker fight the bottle, the Center sponsors two Alcoholics Anonymous groups which meet there weekly, and the AA program of help-one-another has been highly effective in the battle against John Barleycorn. Always it is strengthened by the Army's own program of spiritual counseling, work, medical care and recreation, all designed to rehabilitate both soul and body.

"Most of the men don't know how to hold jobs or how to handle their money when they get paid," Major Hinkle says. "Payday here is on Saturday, and Saturday night is a very crucial time to the man with an alcohol problem, because it's a night when many people are celebrating and he has money with which he could buy liquor. Times Square and the bright lights are but a few blocks away and offer a terrific temptation. For this reason we make a special effort to stage Saturday programs that will keep the men interested enough to stay at the Center."

The "Saturday Night Jamboree" includes volunteer professional talent such as tap dancers, barber-shop quartettes, pianists, violinists, and other entertainers who put on a one-hour show. There is an intermission for refreshments—coffee and soft drinks with doughnuts or cookies—followed by the showing of a recent feature movie until eleven o'clock, when most of the men are ready to retire.

The Center has pool tables, chess and checker sets, dominoes and shuffleboard, and arranges tournaments and elimination contests for these games. Many men have been away from social life so long that they shy away from participation, but they are required to take part and many thus develop new interests or renew old ones. Others backslide and return to the streets, lacking the will-power, moral strength and desire to stay on the straight road.

Those to whom the Center is home seem happy and comfortable. Dormitories are on the fourth, sixth and seventh floors, the fifth floor being reserved for members of the staff. A newcomer is assigned to the sixth floor, which has the oldest beds and equipment. As the man progresses he is moved to the seventh floor, which is better, and finally to the fourth, which is "best." There are a few private rooms off the dormitories, occupied by rehabilitated men who have lived at the Center for years.

There is a chapel with an electronic organ, a piano and a pulpit, and worship services are held at eleven every Sunday morning. Bibles were donated by the New York Bible Society. Each man attending services must wear a necktie, and for this purpose an assortment of ties is kept on a coat-hanger in a room adjoining the chapel, so that any man arriving tieless may select one before he enters. In some cases this is the only time during the week when a man "dresses up."

The Center's library has paneled wood walls donated by an estate, and comfortable upholstered chairs. A plaque sets out the "Twelve Steps" of Alcoholics Anonymous. Shelves are filled with books of all kinds, ranging from *Confessions of St. Augustine* to *Peyton Place*, and current newspapers and magazines are available.

There are two television rooms set up like little theaters, with the TV sets elevated so the screens may be seen by everyone. One room has its set tuned to baseball games or other sporting events, the other to dramatic programs, to avoid dissension in program selection.

The men do their own laundry in automatic washers and

gas dryers in the basement, use flatirons and ironing boards, and are given clean sheets, towels and pillowcases once a week.

They have their own dining room and get three substantial meals a day. As a do-it-yourself project they built a formica-topped snack counter with a ceramic tile front and ten blue plastic-covered stools, where they can buy candy, sandwiches and coffee. All recreation equipment and supplies are paid for with funds derived from the snack stand. The money the men spend there must be used for their benefit and cannot be spent for other purposes.

The entire Social Service Center, in fact, is operated completely with money received from the sale of the used clothing, rags, furniture and other discarded material collected by the Army. No funds contributed to the Army in Community Fund or other campaigns, or collected from other sources, are used to finance the Center.

The men at the Center range in age from 22 to 50 years, though the average is about 48. Youths under 21 are not eligible for residence, although a homeless boy might be given food and lodging over night while the Army arranged for his care by some other welfare agency.

No man is excluded because of his race, religion or color, but the Center will not accept a man who is intoxicated, because he upsets the other men. Each resident must be "dry," and if he brings in liquor or gets drunk during his residence, or if he fights with other men, he will be ordered to leave.

The Center is open twenty-four hours a day and an "intake clerk" is always on duty. If a new man arrives seeking help, the intake clerk gets his name and Social Security number and looks in the files to see whether or not he has been at the Center before and has caused any trouble. In the latter event, he won't be taken back. If his record is satisfactory he is given a bed for the night (provided one is available) and is told to report at the desk in the morning.

In the morning he is interviewed by a counselor, and if it develops that he is interested merely in finding a job, the Army won't accept him as a resident at the Center, but if he has a problem and seeks help he will be welcome. During his first week he will get a thorough medical examination and attend an orientation meeting where the rules and purposes of the Center are explained.

The man will be put to work sorting clothes or on other jobs utilizing his best abilities. In addition to his food and lodging he will be paid a cash gratuity ranging from $1 to $12 weekly, based upon his progress, attitude, cooperation and behavior. Eventually he may be hired as a regular employee at a salary of $40 a week or more, with increases depending upon his responsibilities and years of service.

One job of the beneficiary may be as a helper on the collection trucks. The truck driver is a regular employee. The red Salvation Army trucks, incidentally, are somewhat unusual. When a truck (usually a Ford or Chevrolet) is three years old its chassis and motor are replaced by new ones, but the truck body continues in service. The Lindsay bodies are specially constructed of steel and aluminum in such a way that any one section which becomes damaged or worn may be removed and replaced, and some of the bodies remain in use as long as 20 years.

"Unfortunately," says Major Hinkle, "we can't do the same thing with people. We have to rebuild the whole man."

Mr. Joseph J. Timmons, Counselor at the Center, is an AA member and a tall, slender testimonial for the Center's benefits. Quiet, efficient and well-educated, Joe Timmons takes a personal interest in every man, especially the alcoholic. "I know what they go through," he says. "I had a good home, a good job and a wonderful family in California. I lost them all because of my drinking." Thanks to The Salvation Army and AA, he has regained his self-respect and dignity and for some six years has tried to help others do the same—but this is not always easy or even possible.

One man at the Center smuggled in a bottle of liquor, drank it, then sneaked up behind Timmons and hit him on the back of the head with the bottle. Timmons didn't strike back, but the man was evicted.

Timmons ticks off various cases as they come to mind. "We had one man who had been drinking for years," he says. "He had been away from his wife for more than three years. We helped him to straighten out and gave him a job as a chauffeur. Just recently he went back to live with his wife and they're getting along just fine."

One alcoholic had been arrested for check forgery and came to the Center as a parolee to live and work. The parole officer, however, was unhappy about this arrangement, although he had never been inside the place. His conception was similar to that of many other uninformed people.

"That place is filled with bums like those on The Bowery," the parole officer complained. "I don't want this parolee associating with crumbs like that. He'll only get into trouble again."

When Timmons heard about this objection he telephoned the officer and invited him to visit the Center. The officer accepted and was shown through the entire building, introduced to several of the men, and told in detail about the rehabilitation program. At the end of his visit his entire attitude changed and he admitted that he would be glad to have the parolee remain there. The ex-forger, now 56 years old, a widower with eight children, all married, has conquered his craving for alcohol, works steadily, and is happy and contented.

The fight against alcoholism is waged by The Salvation Army around the world. One of its more unusual installations is The Salvation Army Inebriates' Sanatorium on the 300-acre island of Rota Roa, 25 miles from Auckland, New Zealand. Since 1908 so many men have conquered their craving for alcohol with the help of The Salvation Army at this place that Rota Roa has been called "The Island of Begin Again."

A typical case described by Captain John C. Waite began when a bleary-eyed, unshaven derelict, dressed in dirty wrinkled clothes, staggered up to the door of Salvation Army headquarters in Auckland and was greeted by Captain Eric Bridle. When the drunk reached out to shake hands he would have fallen down if Captain Bridle had not grabbed him just in time.

Captain Bridle poured cup after cup of hot tea into his visitor, put him to bed, and a few hours later listened to his story. His wife, disgusted with his constant drinking, had locked him out of their house and tearfully declared that she never wanted to see him again. Shock, remorse and self-pity sent the man to another bout with the bottle, and with no home to go to he had zigzagged his way to The Salvation Army for food and shelter.

The story was all too familiar to Captain Bridle, even that part of it where the man insisted that he wanted to stop drinking. Many other men had expressed the same desire but lacked the will-power to bring it to reality.

Before taking any action the captain visited the man's wife, who told him how her husband's affliction had wrecked their home life, lost him his job, and brought constant shame and embarrassment to the family. The final blow came when he had staggered into the house one night and smashed lamps, chairs and dishes. Yes, she said, she meant it when she told him she never wanted to see him again. She was convinced that he could never break away from heavy drinking.

When the man sobered up he was both ashamed and repentant, and pleaded with the captain to arrange a meeting with his wife. He swore he would do anything to get away from alcohol.

"Anything?" the captain asked. "Would you permit the Court to commit you to The Salvation Army's sanatorium on Rota Roa?"

"What is it?" the man asked. The captain explained.

The man rose and paced up and down, stroking his hair. Finally he faced the officer and said with some hesitation, "All right. If that's the only way, I'll do it."

The man and wife were brought together and the plan was unfolded to the woman. Her husband went to Rota Roa, where he found himself among men of many trades and professions,

129

including chemists, physicians, salesmen, sailors and laborers, all having in common the desire to quit drinking.

In the year that he spent on the island the man from Auckland found strength from the others and also did what he could to help them control their terrific craving. In his final weeks he became interested in The Salvation Army itself, and at one of many worship services he accepted the invitation to approach the Mercy Seat and accept Christ as his Savior. He left the island completely cured and went back to his work and family.

Says Captain Waite, "Of course there have been failures. There are men who leave the island and once again become slaves to drink. There are some who return to Rota Roa. But The Salvation Army never loses faith, and there is always hope, even for the worst."

One of the most important and most unusual activities of the Center in New York is the Loewenstein Memorial Cafeteria on the street level of the 48th Street building. The story is that Wilhelm Loewenstein, a Russian immigrant, landed in the United States years ago penniless and alone. Unable to find work, suffering from hunger, he roamed the city streets seeking a helping hand and finding it in the city's social welfare agencies—but only after answering endless questions about his personal history, so that the information could be neatly listed on forms and buried in a filing cabinet.

At the time of his death in 1938, Wilhelm Loewenstein was a millionaire leather merchant. In his will he left more than $900,000 with the New York Community Trust Company to establish an effective program to provide food for hungry men and women down on their luck, as he had once been. His instructions called for setting up "one or more places in the nature of a cafeteria where cooked food may be obtained by, and will be served free or for a nominal charge, to all orderly persons applying for it, regardless of their race, color, or creed."

The Community Trust, charged with transforming this dream into a reality, rejected the idea of setting up an independent restaurant on a philanthropic basis, and preferred to work with an agency engaged in providing food for needy people. A survey of such agencies in New York led directly to The Salvation Army.

The Army agreed to make its facilities and personnel available and to establish a daily feeding program for a nominal charge—except in cases where a patron was unable to pay any fee. The Loewenstein Memorial Cafeteria was opened in 1940 as part of The Salvation Army Men's Social Center, and at the dedication ceremonies more than a hundred hungry men sat down to the first dinner provided by Wilhelm Loewenstein's generosity.

The charge for meals was indeed "nominal." For several years breakfast cost a nickel, dinner a dime. Under today's inflationary pressures, the prices have been raised. Breakfast is now fifteen cents, dinner is twenty!

A typical 15-cent breakfast consists of corn flakes or other dry cereal with milk, scrambled eggs, dry toast, and coffee or tea.

When I visited the cafeteria at dinner time there was an appetizing cookery smell like that of an outdoor barbecue. The menu was chili con carne over rice, two frankfurters, bread without butter, excellent cake (donated by Schrafft's), and coffee or tea.

The average cost of the 20-cent meal is 36 cents, the difference being paid from the Loewenstein fund. The restaurant is kept scrupulously clean, the stainless steel kitchen equipment is completely modern, the employees are dressed in white, and the food is wholesome and well-prepared.

The cafeteria seats 72 diners at red formica-topped tables, and in an average day it serves some 400 meals. As a patron enters he buys a ticket from the cashier near the door, which he hands to the server at the food counter. Other welfare agencies in New York often purchase Loewenstein meal tickets which they give to clients who need food. Any person who is without funds may eat free. On the day of my visit the counterman told me that they had served 104 meals in 50 minutes, including 88 paid for and 16 without charge. On an average week

131

night they feed from 250 to 300 diners. On Sunday there is only one meal, served between 10:00 A. M. and 1:00 P. M. to an average of 400 to 500 people, some 25 or 30 of whom are not able to pay.

On the cafeteria wall is a plaque reading: "If you are hungry and in need of help, this cafeteria will assist you to secure a nourishing meal for less than cost. But if you are able to pay commercial rates for food, please let us serve others who are in greater need. — Wilhelm Loewenstein."

Major Hinkle points out that food and shelter are the two most important material needs in the lives of the hungry and homeless men that come to the Center. "Our first task with them is to feed them, give them a place to sleep, and give them something constructive to do. After that, we can talk about saving their souls."

Hinkle was born on a farm at Kingsville, Ohio, on the shores of Lake Erie, the son of Salvation Army officers. He has been in the Army for 22 years, all spent in men's social service work, and has been at the Center in New York since 1957.

His is a tough job, trying to live within a budget that is dependent upon other people's castoffs and discards, but like all other Salvation Army officers he is both dedicated to his work and enthusiastic about it. "It's really very satisfying, especially when I watch men stagger up out of the dregs, beaten and discouraged, and then see them walk down the street with their heads high and smiles on their faces," he says.

When I left the Center after my last visit I was impressed by the irony of a whiskey advertisement I saw in the window of a liquor store about three blocks away. It read: "Time to join the society for better drinks—never a shortage of volunteers."

Chapter 10

FRIENDS OF THE FAMILY

The tall, thin woman walked slowly past the entrance of the building at 546 Avenue of the Americas (formerly Sixth Avenue) in New York City. She turned and walked in the opposite direction, then she stopped in the middle of the sidewalk and stared at the doorway for perhaps two minutes, obviously engaged in a silent debate with herself. Her decision made, she straightened her shoulders and went into the building, taking the elevator to the third floor offices of The Salvation Army's Family Service Bureau.

At her request she was escorted to the office of Brigadier Ruth Kimball,* Director of the Bureau, and introduced herself as Janet Brown (which is not her real name).

"I'm here at the suggestion of a friend," she said. "I feel funny about all this, though, because I don't see how The Salvation Army can be of any help to me."

"We can try," Brigadier Kimball said. "Do you want to tell me about your problem?"

"Well, it's my husband. He's—well, he's changed. He isn't like he used to be when we were first married."

"When was that?"

"Almost ten years ago."

---

*Brigadier Kimball was "promoted to glory" soon after the research for this book was completed.

"You say he's changed. Just how do you mean?"

"Well, he handles our money, our bank account, our bills and things, and I never know how much money we have or anything. He gives me what I need to buy groceries and run the house, but he never tells me anything and if I ask him about our financial situation he says for me not to worry about it."

"Perhaps that's why he does it—to keep you from worrying."

"It isn't only the money situation. He never talks to me any more about his work. We don't discuss things as we used to. If he gets a day off he goes away somewhere by himself and doesn't even tell me where he's going or what he's going to to. And he never takes me out to a movie any more."

"Do you go by yourself, then?"

"Sometimes. Sometimes I go with friends."

"Do you talk with your husband about your own activities— what you do during the day, and so on?"

"What for? He wouldn't be interested. Anyway, there's not much to talk about. I do the washing and ironing and house-cleaning, and go to a bridge party now and then. Nothing exciting."

"Does your husband know you were coming here?"

"Good heavens, no!"

"If we're going to help you, we'd like to talk with him. Would you give me his office telephone number so that I might call and make an appointment?"

The woman was startled. "Oh, I don't believe you should. Suppose he thinks you're just meddling on my behalf? Then things will be worse than ever between us."

"I don't think you should worry about that—not yet. Why don't you let us see what we can do?"

The woman finally agreed, and an appointment was made for a representative of Brigadier Kimball to see the husband. Although polite, he seemed surprised and somewhat resentful when he learned the nature of the mission, but he listened quietly while the Bureau worker explained the situation.

"You know why I don't discuss our affairs with her like I

134

used to?" he asked. "Because she's always complaining. If I talk to her about money she'll find fault with something or other. If I don't talk to her, she gets sore about that. And she never says anything to me about taking her to the movies—she always goes with one of the neighbors or some friend from her bridge club. As for my days off, sometimes I go fishing, which Janet doesn't like to do, and sometimes I go to the ball game or maybe to the beach. After all, I have to relax once in a while."

At intervals for a period of six months the Family Service Bureau representative talked with Janet and with her husband, at first in separate visits and later bringing them together for a frank discussion of their differences. Gradually they conceded that they had both contributed to a real lack of communication and that both had been at fault. The result was that they talked out their problem, each recognizing the other's viewpoint, and today they are sharing a harmonious and happy life once again.

From its inception The Salvation Army has been concerned with the maintenance of a strong family life as basically healthy for the various levels of society in which it carries on its work. In the Army's first years, devoted women armed with brooms and buckets visited private homes in the slums of the larger cities—dirty homes cluttered with rubbish, where they scoured floors and walls, bathed children, dressed wounds which were often hidden by grime, and gave helpful household hints to wives and mothers, along with Scripture readings and prayers. These were the original "Slum Sisters," and others follow in their footsteps today, helping to remove the causes of bad housing and improve patterns of family living.

In the larger cities Salvation Army officers, although experienced in social welfare work, are generally assisted by well-trained professional social caseworkers who are paid employees of the Army and who get expert advice, when necessary, from psychiatrists, psychologists, home economists and other specialists on a consultant basis. In most smaller communities the officers have no outside help and are equipped by training and experience to carry on the tasks of the Family Service Bureau themselves, also seeking guidance from others when needed.

In New York City The Salvation Army has its own Psychiatric Service, which was established because working with psychiatrists in private practice, on a case-by-case basis, was not satisfactory. These doctors were often booked with patients for weeks in advance and were not available to the Army when needed, so the Army employed a psychiatrist to keep office hours daily at Army headquarters.

The psychiatrist helps workers determine the underlying reasons for difficulties in individual cases and thus find the most helpful line of treatment. Occasionally he interviews clients and diagnoses their symptoms, deciding whether emotional disturbances are of a kind that can be treated or whether they involve mental abnormality which a case worker cannot touch safely. He will arrange for proper hospitalization when needed. He conducts seminars for the staff to show how case work can best incorporate the skills and concepts which psychiatry offers.

The case worker gets valuable help from the home economist, who is able to furnish the worker with expert know-how when faced with problems in home-making. She analyzes faults in a client's home situation, the potential abilities and physical strength of the home-maker, and the community resources available to ease home responsibilities. The home economist is able to prepare and interpret budget standards and allowances to help the family get the most desirable living from available income.

One case cited by Miss C. Elizabeth Chichester, Supervisor of Professional Services for the Family Service Bureau, provides a graphic portrayal of the program in action.

The Tom Price family, consisting of Tom, his wife Lucy, and their five children ranging in age from 18 months to 14 years, lived in a public housing project in New York. Tom, a disabled war veteran, drew a government pension but was not employed. Lucy found it impossible to get enough day work to support the family. They applied for assistance to the Department of Welfare of the city, but their application had to be investigated and processed, and they needed financial help quickly, so they went to The Salvation Army. The Army provided funds to straighten out their immediate situation and offered to help with their other problems, but Tom and Lucy declined this offer with thanks.

Within the next two or three years Tom and Lucy returned to the Army on several occasions, always asking for immediate financial help. They had been on and off the public welfare rolls. Tom had been in and out of hospitals. Lucy worked when she could, but the trouble was that the money she earned, together with Tom's pension, was never spent planfully. In desperation Tom and Lucy finally went to the Family Service Bureau and pleaded for help and advice.

Slowly, carefully, the Army explored the family's problems and needs. Lucy became ill. Tom proved to be irresponsible, had fought with a neighbor and was brought into court. The oldest boy in the family was a truant. The oldest girl was ashamed of her father and paid no attention whatever to her mother's restrictions. The younger boys got into trouble for throwing stones through windows. One was arrested for stealing from a store. All in all, the family was on the verge of disintegration as a unit.

"First we tried to help them work out their financial situation," Miss Chichester says. "The father was irresponsible about handling money and was in and out of the home, so we encouraged the mother to take over the planning of family expenses."

This was a new field for Lucy, but she was quick to see the value of planning, and when the financial crisis gradually began to lessen, she became proud of her ability to manage the money. She also found more time to devote to control of her children.

The school-age youngsters were not doing well with their studies. The oldest boy showed the most serious problems, so the Army brought him to the psychiatric consultant and arranged for psychological and vocational tests, which showed

137

that the boy had been so disturbed by the family situation and had lived so long under tension that he should have concentrated assistance and residential treatment.

"It was impossible for us to find residential treatment for him," Miss Chichester says. "This, unfortunately, is a resource in which there is a shortage and a great need. However, we did the next best thing. We assigned a case worker to help the boy, and within a few months he began to respond. Today he is exploring various fields to learn what he wants to do vocationally."

The disturbed boy was only one of the family problems. Tom and Lucy were threatened with eviction for non-payment of rent. The Salvation Army intervened with the Housing Authority, which canceled the eviction notice because of the Army's efforts to help.

The boy who had stolen from the store was brought to Boy Scout meetings and to the Community Center, where he became interested in sports and organized a swimming club.

The Army worked with this family for some six years. The older children graduated from school and found jobs, and with the added income the Army helped the family to move to a better apartment which seemed to give them all a new and brighter outlook on the world. Tom is still hospitalized frequently, but the family is together and happier than it has been in years.

"One of the things you see in a family like this is not that there is any miraculous change, but a certain kind of stability," Miss Chichester points out. "We were able to work through the family pattern of one crisis after another and help them to move toward constructive experiences. Too many families go from one crisis to another and only ask for help at the point of crisis, rather than seek help with the *causes* of their troubles."

She made one other point. "Sometimes a family like this has a great deal of strength as a family group, and you don't realize what that strength may be until you assess the strengths and weaknesses of the family as a whole in society. Along with

138

other social agencies, The Salvation Army has great interest and concern about the total family group."

In one Family Service Bureau case the social workers learned that conflict between husband and wife grew from the fact that the husband expected a great deal of attention from his wife, but refused to take care of their two children if she wanted to visit friends or relatives. He made little effort to help around the house, leaving his wife to attend even to small tasks, such as repairing a leaky faucet.

The social worker had four interviews with the wife alone, one with the husband alone, and finally brought the two together for a frank discussion. The husband seemed quite surprised to know of his wife's attitude and admitted that she was undoubtedly right.

"It was obvious that they were really very fond of each other," the social worker recalls, "and once their differences were brought into the open the remedy was not long in coming. The man became a willing baby-sitter whenever the woman wanted to go out, which wasn't very often, and he also became a rather ardent do-it-yourselfer around the house."

It is a curious fact, almost an anomaly, that The Salvation Army officer with a wife and children faces serious difficulties in maintaining his own family life while he seeks to mend or promote that of others. His meals are generally irregular, his hours long, he frequently has to make trips away from home, yet most officers manage to keep their family attachments strong and to bring up their children to be worthy men and women. Not all are perfect and some families do break up, but few groups in the United States have a smaller divorce ratio and less difficulty with behavior problems in children than do officers of The Salvation Army.

Behavior problems motivate many school authorities to refer cases to The Salvation Army. One such instance involved a teen-age girl named Dorothy, who appeared not only to have difficulties at home, but also to be unhappy in associating with other young people in school.

139

The Family Service Bureau learned that Dorothy and her brother lived with their mother, who had been deserted by her husband about five years earlier. The husband's whereabouts were unknown and he had never communicated with his family. Dorothy's mother had a daily job which, coupled with her efforts to take care of her two children, was quite overwhelming.

The Army case worker discovered that both Dorothy and her brother were extremely sensitive and unhappy about being deserted by their father.

"All men are the same," Dorothy said. "None of 'em are any good, none of 'em!"

"What about your brother?" the worker asked.

"My brother? Hah! That's a laugh. He's worse than the rest. Talking with girls, going out on dates and all that stuff. You wait—some girl's going to be sorry, that's all I've got to say. You'll see. He'll turn out just like my father."

"Do you have any boy friends, Dorothy?"

Dorothy glared at the visitor. "I should say not! I hate boys! I absolutely despise them."

When Dorothy's mother became friendly with a man and occasionally invited him to their home for dinner or a social evening, Dorothy spoke curtly to him and made it clear that she resented his presence and his interest in her mother, failing to realize that this companionship meant a great deal to her mother.

Little by little the Army case worker drew out Dorothy, inducing her to talk at length about her feelings and her relationship with other people, and at the same time the worker planted suggestions in the girl's impressionable mind about the values and dividends to be gained from friendship and understanding.

After weeks of this subtle therapy, one day during their conversation Dorothy said, "You know something? A boy in school asked me to help him with his homework yesterday. Imagine! A boy asking *me* to help *him!*"

"And did you?"

140

"Well, yes, I did." Defensively she added, "Anyway, that shows I'm smarter than he is."

"I'm sure the boy knew that, or he wouldn't have asked you."

"I suppose."

"Didn't it give you a rather pleasant feeling to know that somebody needed you and that you were able to help?"

Dorothy seemed reluctant to answer. "Well, I guess it did."

"Of course it did," the worker said. "And I think it was wonderful of you to help the boy. After all, there are times in life when each of us needs someone—just as your mother, for instance, needs love and understanding from you and your brother, and just as you both need hers."

From that time Dorothy's school work improved and she made special efforts to make her mother happy and to be friendly with her brother. Dorothy is continuing her studies to become a school teacher and has so whittled down her antagonism towards men that she may even become a bride before this book reaches print.

In the minds of many people the term "family welfare" means "charity," and case work is something "done to" people who must submit as the price of receiving financial or other assistance. Gradually the taint of charity is fading, and agencies such as the Family Service Bureau are getting applications for help from people who not only do not need money, but who are also able and willing to pay a fee.

Although The Salvation Army will not refuse to meet a human need for economic reasons, it does charge fees in several of its programs, and for good reason. First, the payment of a fee, however small, makes a client feel that he is not a charity case but is paying for the help he gets. Second, the fee system removes the objection that people in middle- and high-income brackets should not be given, free, a service which the general public contributes funds to maintain. Third, it does cost money to provide this service and the Army facilities and personnel. Actually the number of clients who pay fees is relatively small and, says the Army, will probably never be large.

The minimum weekly fee, based upon the number of persons in the family and their total take-home pay after deductions for income taxes, old age and survivors' insurance, and union dues, is one dollar. The maximum weekly fee is ten dollars. The same degree of assistance is given to the family that can't afford any fee as is rendered to the family earning enough to pay the maximum.

The Director of the Family Service Bureau in New York emphasizes the fact that its activities are based on recognition of the worth and dignity of human personality and the right of the individual to the respect and consideration this demands. Also, as a dedicated Salvation Army veteran she says with deep feeling, "We realize that the spirit of man is of Divine origin but is subject to influences that strengthen or weaken the measure of his self-respect and courage. The influences most helpful are those which include the spiritual elements."

An unusual field for family help deals with the *braceros*, Mexican migrant workers who flock into the United States every year to work on cotton plantations and to harvest fruits and vegetables in several States.

When Salvation Army officers in Arkansas and Louisiana proposed that officers of the Mexican Division be assigned to work among the *braceros*, Captain George Gan and Captain Miguel Saldivar, both of Mexico City, were chosen for the task. Captain Gan was one of the first ten national officers trained in Mexico City. Captain Saldivar was supervisor of 56 boys in a children's home in Tetelpan and, as a youth, had himself worked as a *bracero* for two seasons in California.

With American officers the Mexican Salvationists traveled in five mobile canteens through Louisiana and Arkansas, stopping in fields wherever *braceros* were seen at work, and through amplifiers inviting them to attend evening meetings. Every highway stop was concluded with The Lord's Prayer, as the *braceros* paused in their work to stand with heads bowed and sombreros in their hands.

In the evening the officers would talk to the assembled workers, listen to their family problems, and sometimes show colored slides about the life of Christ. When they were paid

142

their wages many of the *braceros* rushed into the nearest town, where their pay often went to buy liquor, flashy clothes, or was lost in card and crap games. The Salvation Army teams held open-air meetings in the towns to attract the migrants, and were able to induce a number of them to send money to their homes in Mexico or to refrain from spending it foolishly after working so hard to earn it.

Captain Philip E. Collier, of the Southern Territory of The Salvation Army, points out that there is still much room for improvement in the living and working conditions of the Mexican migrant workers. Where the *braceros* are concerned, Captain Collier says, "the fields indeed are white unto harvest, but the laborers are few."

Salvation Army service to families extends around the world. In a recent year in a tenement in Glasgow, Scotland, a Salvation Army officer making a room-to-room visit found five or more families on one floor, each in a single room, all using a common sink and toilet. One bed held two naked children. Their father was ill and unemployed, their mother walking the floor with a baby in her arms, and two other children had been taken to the hospital that morning. Promptly The Salvation Army provided clothes for the whole family, more bedding, food and medicine, and arranged to find work for the father when he recovered from his illness.

One of the world's great problem areas for family service is Hong Kong, the British Crown Colony known as "The Pearl of the Orient." Lt. Col. Fred Jewkes, commanding The Salvation Army there, points out that in certain areas there are more than 2000 persons to the acre, with an influx of nearly 1400 a week crowding in from Red China. The housing shortage is acute. Squeezed into cubicles in dark tenements, ten or more families may use one kitchen. Some build squatters' huts of mud, wood, bamboo, scrap metal and cardboard, but have no water supply, no sewers, no lighting. Hundreds live in improvised shelters on the sidewalks.

The government has erected new apartment buildings in some areas to house the refugees, and The Salvation Army,

143

using funds provided by its United States Central Territory, has built a number of small cottages and a community youth center where it conducts a day school and vocational classes in dressmaking and carpentry so that families may learn trades to earn money to keep themselves together.

In the "bush" country of the West Indies a mother died giving birth to her fifth baby, but could not be buried until authorities fixed the cause of death. A Salvation Army captain, a woman, alone on her regular trek, came to the bamboo hut four days after the mother's death. The body, already corrupt, was covered with flies. The newborn baby, still unwashed, wailed for food. The dead woman's husband had done his best to keep the child alive but knew little about baby care or feeding.

The captain communicated with the authorities and arranged for the immediate burial of the mother. She cleaned the hut, washed and fed the new baby, took the widower's other young children to his relatives, and arranged for them to see that the man and his new child were cared for. When she came to him to say goodbye he handed her a short note, scrawled in his own unsteady hand.

"I cannot tell you thanks because I do not know what thanks to give," he had written. "My wife died from heart. May God keep you with same good mind for evermore. Amen."

Chapter 11

WAYSIDE

When a new family recently moved into a house on Long Island, a boy named Mark already living in the neighborhood came to watch the movers unload their van and to talk with young Jimmy, who belonged to the new arrivals.

During their conversation Mark said, "Where do you go to church?"

"The Salvation Army," Jimmy answered.

"The Salvation Army!" Mark's face showed his surprise. "Gosh, I don't think my mother will let me play with you."

"Why not?"

"Well, you know—The Salvation Army. I guess that means you're always in trouble, or something."

Here again is the false image.

The truth is that The Salvation Army does fight delinquency and crime in much the same way that any other Christian church does, through Bible lessons, Sunday Schools, character-building organizations for boys and girls, summer camps, and similar activities. The Army, however, also makes direct and concerted efforts to rehabilitate "delinquent, neglected or dependent girls" in an unusual institution known as the Wayside Home School at Valley Stream, Long Island, New York.

Founded originally by Brooklyn churchwomen in 1898 as a home for unwed mothers and girls on parole, Wayside moved to Valley Stream in 1917. In 1935 The Salvation Army took over operation of the school and in 1942, when the Army's work on behalf of unwed mothers was shifted elsewhere, the Wayside Home School became a residence for girls whose delinquency, because of neglect, did not warrant their imprisonment.

The officer who has headed Wayside since 1946 is Major Emily Eastwood, a tall, gray-haired lady with down-to-earth philosophies, a forthright manner and a sweet face, who mothers her charges with genuine affection and also contends with more personality problems than an overworked psychiatrist tries to treat. No real mother ever had a tougher, more trying, more discouraging—or more satisfying job.

The satisfaction comes from cases like that of 14-year-old Mary, who was abandoned a few days after she was born. Her parents were arrested and imprisoned. Her mother escaped from a reformatory and her father served his time and was later sought by the FBI as a fugitive on another charge. Mary was placed with her grandparents, who never lost an opportunity to remind her what no-good people her parents were.

"And you're no good, either," her grandfather would tell the child.

"It's in the blood," her grandmother echoed. "You'll grow up to be trash, just like your worthless father and mother. Trash, that's what!"

Mary was placed in a foster home when her grandparents died, and although she was then only six years old, she had developed an invisible armor molded of fear, suspicion, hatred, and mistrust of all adult humans.

To a child who had never in her brief life known love, love was merely a word without meaning. When her first set of foster parents told her they loved her, Mary's six-year-old mind conceived "tests" that were more like the plottings of an adolescent. Playing in the bathtub, she deliberately let water overflow to the bathroom floor. For that she was spanked, deprived of dinner, and locked in her room.

146

(*Above*) Unwed mothers in the Home Department of Booth Memorial Hospital, Flushing, N. Y., have their own Christmas celebration.

(*Below*) Family counseling is one of the many Salvation Army services.

(*Above*) The Salvation Army's Women's Residence in Paris, France.

(*Below*) Booth Memorial Hospital, Flushing, N. Y., a Salvation Army institution. (*Photo by Paul Parker.*)

Salvation Army Christmas kettle on the Ginza, Tokyo, Japan.

Cadets in Tokyo set out to sell *The War Cry*.

Japanese girls at a Music Camp in Japan learning to play the tambourine.

(*Above*) In Africa a Salvation Army officer visits a native family.

(*Below*) A protesting patient at an African dispensary is comforted by Mrs. Captain Vingerhoedt.

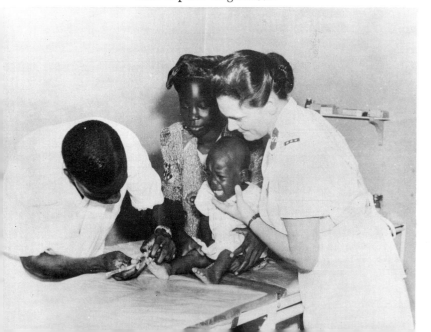

"Somewhere in France" during World War I:
the birth of a Salvation Army doughnut.

Salvation Army doughnuts were equally popular in World War II.

Salvation Army lassies mended soldiers' uniforms in World War I . . .

. . . and sewed on their stripes during World War II.

(*Above*) Outside the Men's Social Service Center in New York City.

(*Below*) Inside a Salvation Army store.

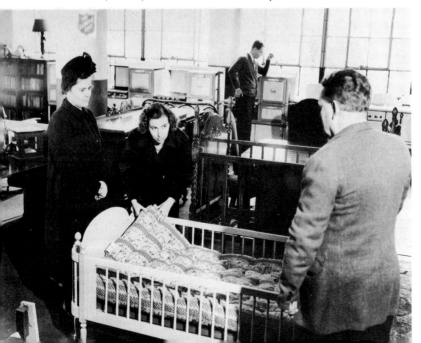

(*Above*) Salvation Army Emergency Services lend assistance when fire strikes a small community.

(*Below*) In 1955 the Salvation Army mobile canteen helped feed flood victims at Naugatuck, Conn.

(*Above*) Clothing collected by the Salvation Army being loaded for shipment to victims of the earthquake in Chile. (*Photo by Jim Holmes.*)

(*Below*) The New York Staff Band led by Bandmaster Major Richard E. Holz. (*Photo by Paul Parker.*)

EVOLUTION OF THE

(*Above, left*) The original Quaker-type bonnet worn by Salvation Army women.

(*Above, right*) The 1887 bonnet was known as the "Hallelujah Bonnet."

(*Below*) In the 1900's, this large, heavy bonnet, worn here by Evangeline Booth, daughter of the Founder, was known as "the coal scuttle."

Evangeline Booth here shows the smaller bonnet worn by the 1920's.

SALVATION ARMY BONNET

The smaller, distinctive bonnet worn today.

THE
SALVATION ARMY
FLAG

For taking a toy fire-truck away from the family's own four-year-old son, she again was scolded and spanked, and when she refused an order to say she was sorry, her foster-father seized her by the shoulders and shook her until she screamed.

By such devices did Mary decide that there was no such thing as love. One after another, foster parents refused to keep the girl in their homes.

"I remember one place," Mary said later, "where my foster parents punished me by pushing my face into a pillow until I couldn't breathe. I almost suffocated. And sometimes they held my head under water in the bathtub or the wash-basin. I ran away from that place, and I got picked up by the police, but I begged them not to send me back. When I told how I had been treated they checked up and learned I was telling the truth, so I was given a new foster home."

At that time she was seven years old.

When she was fourteen and came to The Salvation Army's Wayside Home School, Mary had been in and out of *thirty-five* foster homes!

"She had absolutely no use for any adult," Major Eastwood told me. "If we asked her to do some little chore she'd sneer at us and say, 'Ahh, do it yourself!' And she had a vocabulary that would match any truck driver's. If I had five cents for every time she told me to go to hell, I could retire in comfort tomorrow."

Even Major Eastwood, with her genuine love for girls in her care, almost gave up on Mary. Almost. "At staff meetings I kept reminding everybody about the great damage that had been done to this child, but she really tried our patience," the Major says. "She fought with all the other kids, she argued constantly with the staff, and resisted and questioned any kind of authority every step of the way. We went for nine months before we could see even the slightest change in her."

The change manifested itself at a birthday party for Major Eastwood at the Home. The girls had made a birthday cake and brought little gifts which they themselves had made. Almost shyly, yet with a touch of belligerence, Mary handed the Major a small package.

This in itself was highly significant, but when Emily Eastwood opened the package she felt her throat tighten so that she had to force a swallow. She wanted to cry, though not in sorrow, and she held back joyful tears, admitting only that perhaps her first view of Mary's gift was a little blurry.

"There, in that wonderful package, was a really beautiful present—a wrinkled, dirty little doily," she remembers. "Mary had reluctantly attended our craft classes and had learned to crochet, and in the secrecy of her room she had made the doily with her own hands, especially for me. It was the first present she had ever given to any other person—except lip. It was one of my prized possessions, and when the child saw how pleased I was, she was happy, too, probably for the first time in her life. In all those childish years she had really wanted to love and to be loved, but she just didn't know how to give of herself."

The "dirty little doily" was given to the Major in 1949. Later Mary graduated from high school and then left the Home to take a good job with an insurance firm. In 1959, ten years after the historic birthday party, she came to see Major Eastwood with her husband and two lovely children, so that he and they might see the place where she divested herself of her armor and learned that love is indeed more than a meaningless word.

None of the 45 girls in residence has been guilty of a crime. Each has come to Wayside through the courts because of chronic truancy, frequent disobedience, or running away from impossible home situations. All have been referred to the institution by local judiciary or welfare agencies. In age they range from 12 to 18 years, averaging 14 to 15. Less than 40 per cent of the costs are paid from public funds. The balance is met by The Salvation Army's annual public appeals.

"Don't get the idea that our girls are all from poverty-stricken homes," Major Eastwood told me. "We have a lot of over-indulged children whose parents are wealthy. Parents with money often send their kids to boarding schools to get

148

them out of the way. This is plain and simple rejection, and the youngsters know it."

As an example she told about a 16-year-old we'll call Sally, who has a Protestant mother and a Jewish stepfather, living in a swanky apartment house in New York City. When her mother remarried, Sally was sent to a private school against her wishes and was brought up in the Jewish faith, which she resents so much that she wears a small gold cross on a neck chain, merely to irritate her mother. The stepfather, says Major Eastwood, is a wonderful man and obviously loves Sally a great deal, but the mother is a "fashion plate" more interested in her personal appearance and in her social status than in her daughter.

Sally has a younger half-brother on whom her mother lavishes everything. He was babied since birth, always had new clothes, and was given a regular money allowance, while Sally had to beg her mother for every dollar.

At one time her mother had Sally's room redecorated and refurnished without consulting Sally at all. Instead of a regular bed she had two sofa-beds put in so that she could better accommodate frequent overnight guests. Sally resented the fact that her room was also the guest room—why not use her brother's? And why couldn't she have some voice in the decorations?

"Because I know more about such things than you do," her mother said.

In rebellion against her mother, Sally made friends with a group of teen-age beatniks and hoodlums, white and Negro, and made sure that her mother met these undesirables, for Sally was well aware that her mother, always reaching for the top social strata, would be considerably upset by these low-level companions. She was right. When the mother censured Sally and insisted that she sever her relationship with the embryo gangsters, the girl boldly refused, satisfied that she was punishing her mother by the refusal.

One day when Sally's mother was out of the city, Sally invited her whole crowd to the apartment for a party. The celebration was wild and loud, and when it finally ended the place was a shambles. Silken upholstery was ripped, deep scratches zig-zagged across polished mahogany tables, cigarette burns scarred the grand piano, expensive vases lay in fragments on the floor, and remnants of food left grease marks on the Oriental rugs. Repairs and replacements cost Sally's parents more than three thousand dollars.

Angered and frustrated, the mother brought Sally to court, where a judge decided that the girl would be better off in the Wayside Home School and ordered her sent there.

An embittered Sally was not at first cooperative. At home a full-time maid had cleaned Sally's room, picked up and cared for her clothes, and performed other household tasks. At the school, however, Sally, like the other girls, was expected to keep her own room clean and neat, take good care of her own clothes and other belongings, and do her share to make her home pleasant and comfortable. These were new experiences which she did not find to her liking.

Sally had been at the school for only a short time when Easter was approaching. Also in the offing was an important occasion for her half-brother. He was to attend his Bar Mitzvah (the consecration of a Jewish boy to his religious duties), a memorable event in any Hebrew household. Major Eastwood told Sally that she would be permitted to leave the school and to go home for the Easter holidays or for the Bar Mitzvah celebration.

Sally chose to go home for Easter, saying that she had no interest whatever in her half-brother's Bar Mitzvah ceremony. When she telephoned her home, however, her mother said, "I'm very sorry, Sally, but it just isn't convenient for me to have you at home for Easter. Besides, I think you ought to be here for the Bar Mitzvah."

Rejected again, Sally decided to run away from the school. She left the grounds and wandered the streets for a time, but finally returned of her own accord. Before the Easter holidays her mother telephoned that she was going to visit Sally at the school. Sally, showing no enthusiasm, deliberately mussed her hair and clothes.

The mother arrived wearing a new Easter outfit, complete with mink stole, and a hair-do fresh from the beauty parlor. When she saw Sally she was horrified.

"Sally!" she exclaimed. "Just look at your hair. And that dress —and those dirty shoes! You know you're sloppy, don't you? You're just a mess. Now you go and get fixed up. I'm taking you into Valley Stream to get a new dress for Easter."

In Valley Stream her mother took Sally to a bargain basement to shop for a cheap frock. Wanting something better, yet too proud to ask for it, Sally held back her tears as she declared that she didn't want any new clothes and insisted that they return to the school, which they did.

A few days later Sally and another rebellious girl packed a few clothes in a suitcase and sneaked out of their rooms after midnight. They walked along the edge of the highway, trying to thumb a ride to the city. A car slowed down, stopped, and a man got out and approached the girls.

"Where are you going?" he asked.

"To Northport," Sally said.

"At this hour of the night? What for?"

The girls glanced at each other. "We live there," Sally said.

"What's your name?"

"None of your business," Sally said, taking her companion by the arm. "Come on, Vicki." They started to walk away, but the man put a heavy hand on Sally's shoulder. In his other hand he showed her a silver police badge.

"This is my business," he said. "Now what are your names?"

They both gave fictitious names.

"Are you sure you aren't from the Wayside Home?"

"The—the Wayside Home?" Sally said. "What's that?"

"I'll show you," the officer said, taking her suitcase. "Get in the car."

He drove the girls to the school, where everyone had retired for the night. He knocked on the door of Major Eastwood's cottage and the Major appeared at the window of her bedroom. "What is it?" she asked.

"Sorry to disturb you, Major," the man said, "but I have a couple of kids here who say they live in Northport." He mentioned the names they had given him. "Would you come out and look at them?"

Major Eastwood identified the girls and took them back to their cottage rooms. Vicki, Sally's runaway accomplice, had joined her because Vicki's mother seldom called her and had never come to the school to visit her.

The next morning Major Eastwood reported the incident to Sally's mother, who came to the school with Sally's half-brother. The three were brought together in the Major's office, where the mother promptly began to scold the girl.

Fed up, angry and resentful, Sally interrupted. "Stop it! Stop it!" she screamed. "You're just a hypocrite, that's all you are, a big hypocrite! You know you've never really loved me, never—so why do you keep telling Major Eastwood that you do? You're lying, lying, lying! And why did you have to bring *him* along?" She pointed at her half-brother. "You're always telling me to act my age. Grow up, you say, grow up, Sally! But down deep you don't really care what happens to me at all. You just don't care!"

She burst into tears and ran out of the cottage. The mother turned to Major Eastwood. "I can't understand her," she said. "I've given her everything under the sun. Everything."

In telling me this story Major Eastwood said, "She gave Sally everything but real mother love."

During the months that followed, Sally made new friends with the girls at Wayside and developed a renewed interest in her high school studies. At the time of my visit she was quite well-adjusted and probably happier than at any time she could remember. Wayside has become a real home to her, just as it has and as it will for scores of other young girls.

As a home, Wayside is far more attractive than the homes many of its girls have known. There are six buildings on the 11-acre wooded grounds, four of which are living quarters, each with a supervisor. These cottages, surrounded by broad, well-kept lawns and trees, are tastefully furnished. The entrance hall is brightened by a floor-to-ceiling multi-paned window. The walls of the hall and large living room are papered in a mural of tree branches in blossom, giving a perpetually-airy and Springlike appearance. A big porch with glass louvers has comfortable chairs and a piano where the girls often play and sing.

The bright modern kitchen has sunshine yellow walls, a stainless steel stove top, and formica work counters.

Each bedroom has a bed, bureau, desk, wardrobe, chair and two lamps. Most are single rooms, but some girls do not like to be alone and therefore have roommates. One room had aquamarine walls with yellow curtains and bedspreads. Another had pink walls with light blue curtains and spreads, and still another had blue walls with pink accessories.

"It seems to me that this lovely home is probably much nicer than those some of your girls come from," I suggested.

"No doubt about it," the Major said.

"Then isn't it a terrible let-down when a girl finally leaves here and goes back to some dingy tenement or apartment in the city?"

"I'm sure it is," Major Eastwood agreed. "But that's something we can't remedy. Our job is to give the girls as much love and understanding, and as comfortable and happy a home as we can."

To do this job Major Eastwood is assisted by four other Salvation Army officers, a fully-trained social case worker, a part-time psychologist, psychiatrist, medical doctor, registered nurse, and one full-time and two part-time school teachers. There are also laundry and kitchen supervisors, clerical help and a maintenance crew. Volunteers teach classes in crafts, ceramics, oil painting, sewing, typing, shorthand and dramatics.

On the grounds the girls may roller skate to music, play tennis, have cookouts, campfires, and in the summer they swim in a portable pool four feet deep, or sometimes are taken to beautiful Jones Beach for an outing.

After a girl has lived at the school for a short time she may enroll in the local public high school if she genuinely wishes to do so. Since many were truants, care is exercised to see that those who go to the high school attend regularly, and that they can do the classwork without another sense of failure.

Length of residence at Wayside is indefinite. Sentences are indeterminate and in most cases the girls remain for more than six months, depending upon their progress. The average stay is for 12 to 18 months.

"Sometimes a kid has been so deprived that she can't be deprived of anything else," Major Eastwood says, "You take her to a movie or for a soda or something, hoping to strike a chord that hasn't been sounded before. What means something to one girl—forbidding her to watch television, for instance—means nothing whatever to another."

Maybe a girl has been expelled from school or never does anything right. She may simply be trying to get attention, but in a negative way. Told that she must earn her privileges, she becomes suspicious because she trusts nobody. "We have to convince her that we love her and that she can have confidence in what we tell her," the Major explains.

Some girls have to be disciplined before they can find any relief. They feel that everything they have done is simply terrible, and yet everybody has been kind to them. In other words, they would feel better if they were punished. One 15-year-old, a chronic truant, told Major Eastwood, "I wanted my mother to swat me and say that I had to go to school. That would mean she loved me, or at least cared what happened to me. Instead, she was more interested in playing Bingo, and she said she didn't care what I told the truant officer—that was my problem."

One girl, Lura, has a stepfather who is a Navy officer and who runs his home on a strict military basis, except for having his wife and daughter salute. Lura's mother is a fashion model whose greatest concern appeared to be her own figure and that of her daughter. "Your figure is your most valuable asset," her mother told her.

When her mother visits Wayside—dressed in the latest modes

154

and wearing heavy make-up complete with purple eye-shadow —Lura is embarrassed. Once she said to the Major, "I wish I had a mother who was a mother."

Lura skipped school frequently, mostly to get attention. When she arrived at Wayside as a truant she became the Number One Showoff. Meals at the school are served cafeteria style. Lura would come in for lunch—soup, sandwiches and ice cream. She insisted upon eating the ice cream first, making enough commotion to let people see that she was being contrary.

A psychologist and a psychiatrist have been trying to help Lura. She delights in this kind of attention.

Assigned to the Wayside classrooms, Lura neglected her studies and ignored her homework. She was then expelled. As punishment she was assigned to scrub and wax floors, clean bathrooms and work in the laundry. Under constant supervision she was kept at work from 9:30 until noon and from 1:00 to 4:30 P. M. daily. At the end of each day she was admittedly "bushed." After two weeks of hard work she asked if she could return to her classes.

"If you behave yourself and develop a cooperative attitude, you may go back to school," she was told. "But the first time you step out of line again you'll be taken out for good."

Lura hasn't stepped out of line since.

One Negro girl, Tanny, 13, left a dirty shack in the South to come to New York to live with her brother and his wife. She seemed unable to learn anything in school, and her only desire seemed to be for food. She was allergic to baths and clean clothes, and when her brother's wife threatened to leave him because she couldn't stand the girl, the courts sent her to Wayside.

"She still steals food from the icebox occasionally," Major Eastwood says, "and she's so fat she looks like Aunt Jemima. We haven't discussed a diet yet, because that might seem like punishment. We did learn that she was a 'mirror reader' and we arranged for her to get special remedial instruction in the Valley Stream schools."

155

The Negro girls at Wayside visit the laundry room once a week to straighten their hair, while the white girls want theirs curled. Using a gas hot plate and a brass comb, Tanny practically burned her hair off her head trying to get out the kinks. Now she is being taught how to do it properly. She has no social graces whatever, never says "Thank you," or "Excuse me," and at meals she never asks for anything, just grabs whatever she wants. Although she is supposed to be in the ninth grade she is studying a second-grade reader.

"It will be a long pull before she learns to live like other people," the Major says, "but she isn't our first difficult case and we've learned that patience and understanding pay off in the end."

When a girl reaches the age of 18 and graduates from high school, Wayside finds employment for her and permits her to live at the home until she can return to her own home or find a suitable place to live. Some, for one reason or another, can never go back home. Linda, for example, is a 14-year-old mother whose own father sired her baby. The baby was born an idiot, with a head too heavy for his body. Linda accused her father of seduction and he was arrested and sentenced to a year in prison, but he swore that if he ever saw his daughter again he would kill her for "squealing" on him.

Some of the girls go to live in foster homes, with foster parents paid by New York's Department of Welfare, which makes investigations of the foster parents. "Most of them do wonderful jobs with the kids," the Major says, "but we have had several girls whose foster fathers have attempted intimacies with them."

During the ten years from 1950 to 1960, about 95 percent of the girls who left Wayside have turned out well and never got back into the courts. One girl who was at Wayside for two years went to live in Rockaway, where she became a member of the Congregational Church and met a boy with whom she fell in love. She told him and his family about herself and her stay at Wayside, and they accepted her. She had an opportunity to be married in the church, but chose to have the ceremony at Wayside, so they were wed in one of the cottages and held a reception in the dining room.

Many girls who leave the home return later with husband and children to visit with Major Eastwood and to show off the place to their loved ones.

One of the first things they see as they enter the main buildings is a wall plaque with these words: "Bless the Lord, O, my soul, and all that is within me. Bless His holy name. Bless the Lord, O, my soul, and forget not all his benefits."

Ironically, Emily Eastwood comes from a staunch Episcopalian family who vigorously opposed her membership in The Salvation Army, and she herself laughs about the way she got in. She worked part time in the YWCA in Germantown, Pennsylvania, as a swimming instructor and life-saver. One day a girl in the YWCA Employment Office told Emily that The Salvation Army wanted to hire a waterfront counselor for one of its camps.

"Not for me," Emily said. "I don't want any part of The Salvation Army. If you think I'm going to stand on street corners and beat a bass drum, you're batty!"

She had been doing secretarial work and studying child psychology at Temple University at night, and wanted very much to work with young people. She was approached several times to take The Salvation Army job and finally decided to see what the Army people were like, so she visited their headquarters in Philadelphia.

"I was in for a shock," she recalls. "They were wonderful, warm-hearted people."

They drove her out to their camp and she was so favorably impressed that she agreed to take the job—as an employee. She and a Salvation Army girl named Alice Grace were assigned to a cottage with 35 children. Their job: Keep 'em happy!

"The more I stayed, the more I saw that these people had something I didn't have," the Major says. "Alice Grace had a real, a deep spiritual approach. I saw how they lived and I wanted what they had, but I wasn't sure what the answer was.

I talked with Alice about it several times, but never once did she suggest that I join the Army. At the end of the summer, Al had a group of Girl Guards, and one Sunday we went to a worship service in the camp. I remember that the person with the message seemed to be talking only to me. The theme was, 'What are you going to do with your life?' At that moment I felt that the Lord was speaking to me and wanted me to do something useful to help others. That conviction has stayed with me to this day."

She began to go to band practice and to study The Salvation Army doctrines. When she finally decided to attend the training college to become an officer, her Episcopalian father actually cried, insisting that she change her mind, but Emily was resolute. "I'm glad to say my father lived long enough to see and appreciate the real work of the Army and was later happy that I had become a part of it," she says.

Chapter 12

THE STRAIGHTENED TWIG

Vincent Bulla lived in a tenement on New York's lower East Side, across the street from the Cherry Street Settlement House of The Salvation Army, a house no longer in operation. When he was thirteen years old he ran with a gang of other unsupervised boys, getting into all sorts of mischief. One of their delights came every Saturday night when The Salvation Army band would leave the Settlement House, march to Chatham Square, and play for an open-air meeting.

It wasn't that Vincent and his pals enjoyed the music. Their "fun" was running in and out among the bandsmen, heckling them and trying to kick the big bass drum. The bandsmen kept playing and the boys were disappointed because the Salvationists didn't try to chase or catch them.

Just before Christmas, Vincent's illiterate mother found a card someone had left under her door, and she asked the boy to read it to her. It said that a Christmas basket was waiting for her at the Settlement House, where she could pick it up.

"I didn't want to go," Vincent recalls, "because I was sure someone would recognize me as one of the kids who kicked the drum, and we wouldn't stand a chance of getting that basket. But my mother made me go with her. I'll never forget how I tried to make myself invisible, hiding behind my mother —and the first person we met at the House was the officer who always carried the big drum!"

The boy wanted to flee, but he seemed rooted to the spot. "I just stood there waiting," he remembers, "wondering if the man would smack me or just order us out of the place. He walked right over to me and I guess I flinched some, but he gave me a friendly smile and put his hand on my shoulder and said he had something to show me. I was sure it was some kind of a trick to catch me off guard."

The officer took Vincent to the downstairs recreation room and showed him several power tools for woodworking. "If you'd like to come in after school, I'll be glad to show you how to make some book-ends or lamp bases," the man said.

Vincent and his mother took their Christmas basket, and Vincent did go back after school to learn something about woodworking. If the officers recognized him as one of the boy hecklers on the street they never mentioned it. Frequently the little band practiced at the Settlement House and Vincent would sneak out of the woodworking shop whenever he heard the music, and would stand outside the practice room, listening. One day an officer saw him there.

"Would you like to play a musical instrument?" the man asked.

"I sure would," Vincent said.

The Salvation Army gave him tuba lessons and gradually he began to attend worship services. One night he answered an altar call, was converted, and became a soldier in The Salvation Army. An officer congratulated him and said, "Now you may wear our uniform."

"I was horrified," Vincent recalls. "I didn't want to wear the uniform. I was still running around with the gang, and I had visions of myself strolling around in a Salvation Army uniform, being hooted at and probably getting beaten up for deserting the guys."

Strangely enough, no one mentioned the uniform again, but Vincent kept thinking about it. Says he, "Finally I decided I had to make up my mind—either wear the uniform or get out of the Army."

He donned the uniform. "And believe me, it took all the

160

nerve I had to go out in it that first day," he says. "Remember, that was a tough neighborhood and I was ready to take on all comers who made nasty cracks. I was surprised when nobody said a word about it. I think that was the day I stopped being so defensive, and I can say in all honesty that since that first day the uniform has been a source of pride for me—a combination of pride and humility."

Vincent Bulla later went through the School for Officers' Training and is today a lieutenant in The Salvation Army. He has also become an accomplished tuba player.

The drum has helped to recruit other youngsters. One day when I visited the Harlem Corps and Red Shield Community Center at 216 West 124th Street in New York City, I struck up a casual conversation with a friendly white-haired Negro officer, Sr. Major Lambert Bailey, who told me that he was 76 years old and retired, but that he enjoyed coming to the Corps to teach music to the children there. He still wears his uniform.

"How long have you been in the Army?" I asked.

"Sixty-three years," he said.

"That's practically a lifetime. How did you happen to join?"

"I guess you could say I joined because of a Sunday-playing drum," he said, and he told me his unusual story.

Major Bailey was born in 1885 in British Guiana, where his father was overseer on a sugar plantation. The family, including Lambert, an older sister and a younger brother, attended the Episcopal Church.

"When I was ten," he said, "I heard the sound of a bass drum in our neighborhood on a Sunday morning. This was pretty unusual, and some other kids and I ran down the street to see what was going on. We found a small Salvation Army group that had hiked sixteen miles to get to our community. When they finished playing their music one of 'em made a talk, and it was that talk that got me interested."

"Do you remember what it was about?" I asked.

He laughed softly. "Oh, sure. You see, my folks were church-going people, and in our church we were always told that a

161

sinner couldn't go to Heaven and that every one of us was a sinner. To me, that always meant that *nobody* was going to get in! But The Salvation Army man, now, he said that we were sinners, all right, but that sins could be forgiven, and to me this made a lot of sense. I joined up right away as a junior soldier."

His sister Lillian also attended Salvation Army services, but their mother disapproved. One day the father came home and found his wife spanking Lillian for taking part in the Salvation Army worship. The spanking was not deserved, he said. Lillian was old enough to make up her own mind. Accordingly, when she was 18 Lillian became a field cadet.

Their mother, investigating the Army's programs for herself, became so interested that she also joined, and before Lambert left British Guiana in 1906 he saw his mother made a junior sergeant-major of the local corps.

Lambert Bailey, a skilled carpenter, sought work in Trinidad, where in 1906 he met a pretty Salvation Army girl cadet named Estava. In 1907 he went to Panama for three years to work on the Canal, keeping his affiliation with the Army. The officer in the corps he attended "backslid" and resigned, and young Bailey decided to apply for officer training. In 1910 he went to Kingston, served six months as a field cadet, then entered the training college and became an officer. He held three corps assignments in Jamaica before he went to the United States.

Estava, the girl he met in Trinidad in 1906, was then working in New York City. She applied for admission to the training college, was commissioned, and assigned to a corps in Charleston, South Carolina. There she learned from Lambert's sister that he had become an officer—and Lambert, in Jamaica, learned from a *War Cry* article that Estava was an officer in Charleston. They corresponded, and in one of many letters Lambert proposed, was accepted, and was given permission to go to the United States to work and to marry Estava.

He was sent first to Washington, where he worked as an assistant to the only Negro officer in that city. Not until April,

162

1915, did he meet Estava in Philadelphia, and five days after the meeting they were married there. The newlyweds were assigned to work among the Negroes in Richmond, Virginia.

This assignment, he says, was very difficult and discouraging. Segregation was wholly new to him. Having to ride in the back of busses made him angry, and he avoided public transportation as much as possible. "But soon I took the restrictions philosophically," he says, "because my work always came before my personal feelings."

The Baileys were paid $25 a month for their support while they tried to set up a corps in Richmond. They had virtually no success in attracting any adults. Major Bailey visited homes, and parents let their children go to Sunday School, but although they themselves promised to attend Sunday worship services they never showed up. One reason, Major Bailey believes, was that the southern Negro was accustomed to the fire-and-brimstone shouting of evangelistic preachers and felt somewhat cheated by the more subdued approach of the West Indian Salvationists. Although the Major played a cornet and Estava played the guitar, this was no substitute for a rousing brass band which might have attracted more people.

"One of the most difficult tasks during my first two years there was having to solicit money door-to-door to raise funds for our work," he recalled. "Since there was virtually no corps congregation, there was no collection-plate income. I felt that asking people for pennies they could ill afford to give was very degrading. I never had to do that in Jamaica."

Another difficulty was that he had to spend part of his skimpy $25 allotment for fuel, but with young children in the Sunday School he felt that a comfortable temperature was essential.

The Baileys stayed in Richmond for one year, during which time the first of their six children, their only son, was born. They moved to Elizabeth City, North Carolina, in 1916, where living conditions were poor and there was no city water system. Lambert was stricken with fever and dysentery from drinking contaminated water and almost died. His illness

163

required him to take a two-year furlough, during which he worked in a factory in Massachusetts and later in the Army's trade department in New York City.

Returning to active officership he served in Norfolk, Virginia, in Brooklyn and Manhattan, and was transferred in July, 1941, to Washington, D. C., where he remained until he retired.

When the Baileys retired they went to New York, where they and their children still live. None of the children are Salvationists today, although they all went through the Corps Cadet program. The Major explained that some of his daughters were once interested in becoming officers, but that when they were in their late 'teens the Army was not encouraging Negroes to seek commissions because there were no appointments to give them. The only possible appointment for any of his daughters would have been an "outpost" in the deep South, working virtually alone.

According to Major Bailey, The Salvation Army in the United States has been principally a white man's Army—not by design, but because of racial attitudes here. He said he knew of British West Indian Negro Salvationists living in New York in the 1920s who had "tactfully" been told by "soldiers" that "colored folk don't come in here" when they tried to attend a service at the Centennial Memorial Temple.

He added, "I'm sure that if Evangeline Booth or any of the commanding officers had known what was said and done, the situation would have been quickly remedied."

He is very pleased that during the past ten years or so, opportunities for service have opened up for Negroes in The Salvation Army and that today the Army is looking for Negro candidates for officership.

Despite Major Bailey's own experience, the historic fact is that The Salvation Army in the United States expressed its opposition to segregation as long ago as 1885, when the then Commissioner, Major Frank Smith, declared that the Army was "determined, by the help of God, to be among the first white Christian communities of America who would . . . break

164

down this wall of partition separating the white from the colored."

Today The Salvation Army is on record as endorsing the anti-segregation decision of the United States Supreme Court, pledging itself to do everything possible to implement the decision. This stand creates serious problems for the Army in some areas of the South where segregation is still a potent issue. In such communities if the Army defies local prejudice it will get no financial or other support from the segregationists and would soon be compelled to cease its ministry. Where prejudice is so strong, the Army, like many other organizations, has chosen to await the gradual lessening of tensions and oppositions, and although its social institutions in many communities are operated on a segregated basis, its officers continue their humanitarian service among Negroes with the same dedication and spirit that pervades Army work everywhere.

The "Junior Soldier" program through which Major Bailey entered the Army is the main line through which a child grows to be a Salvationist. A boy or girl who is not a member of another church may become a junior soldier at the age of seven, signing this pledge of loyalty: "Trusting in the Lord Jesus Christ as my personal Savior from sin, I hereby declare that I will live as His loving and obedient child and that I will be His faithful soldier."

When he is 13 the junior soldier may be enrolled in classes in Salvation Army history and doctrine, and a year later, if he understands and is ready for his commitment, he becomes a full-fledged Salvationist.

According to Brigadier John Waldron, who directs the young people's activities for the Eastern Territory, the Army hopes that the young soldiers will go on into the Corps Cadet program, the pre-training ground for local corps leadership and for commissioned officership, and many do. At the time of my visit there were more than 3000 Corps Cadets in the Army's Eastern Territory alone, and almost 13,000 Junior Soldiers.

Other youth activities are important in the Sunday Schools

and in the Junior Legion, a program of crafts and recreation for children 7 through 13 years of age. The Junior Legion serves boys and girls who are not associated with any church and who may not attend Sunday School. It is aimed at character building through craftwork, supervised recreation, fellowship, and community service work.

Few people are aware that The Salvation Army has several hundred troops of Boy Scouts and Cub Scouts of America, whose aims for upright living and good citizenship combine ideally with the Army's own Christian objectives.

The Army also has an organization similar to that of the Girl Scouts and Brownies, called the "Girl Guards" and the "Sunbeams." The Sunbeams are for girls 6 to 10, the Girl Guards for those 11 to 13, and Senior Girl Guards for girls 14 to 18 years old.

I talked with Captain Frances Clark, a young and pretty brunette in charge of the Girl Guard and Sunbeam programs in the Eastern Territory.

"We welcome all girls in the community regardless of their race or church affiliation," she told me. "We try to help them develop with a four-fold purpose: Spiritually, mentally, physically and socially."

No effort is made to have any girl change her church affiliation if she has one, though the Army is pleased if it can help any girl to make some worthwhile contribution to her own church and community.

Captain Clark told me about a Pennsylvania couple with four children. The parents were having domestic troubles, mostly because of the father's bouts with alcohol, and were on the verge of separating. The mother, a Baptist, was compelled by circumstances to give up her church affiliation. One daughter was old enough to baby-sit and took care of the child of a Salvation Army officer who told her about the Girl Guards. For a time the girl attended Girl Guard meetings and induced her two sisters to go with her.

The three girls enjoyed the meetings so much that they decided to attend The Salvation Army Sunday School. The mother, somewhat shamed by the girls' example, renewed her own church activities, but when her daughters preferred to continue membership in The Salvation Army Sunday School instead of the Baptist Church, the mother decided to see what The Salvation Army was like, and she began to accompany her daughters to the meetings. She and the girls were so enthusiastic about the Army that the father's curiosity was aroused, and he attended a worship service—a service that began to change his whole life. After he and his wife went to several other Army meetings he renounced the bottle, stopped drinking alcohol, and for more than eight years has been an active lay leader in The Salvation Army.

Captain Clark, now in her late twenties, had a Methodist father, a Salvationist mother. The captain's maternal grandmother was a Salvationist when the Army first began work in the United States, although the grandmother's parents were so opposed to her joining that they actually burned her bonnet and uniform.

"I've known The Salvation Army all my life," the captain says. "As a youngster I was a bandsman—I played the cornet."

Because music is such a vital factor in The Salvation Army program, I talked with Major Richard Holz, the tall, black-haired, personable Bandmaster of the 35-member New York Staff Band, which has made yearly network television appearances with such stars as Dave Garroway and Garry Moore. Like all other Salvation Army bands in the United States, it uses brass instruments only.

For the band's appearance with Garry Moore on the TV show called "I've Got A Secret," the well-known composer, Meredith Willson (*The Music Man*) revealed his "secret"—leading the band in a number he composed for The Salvation Army years ago. Willson began his own musical career in Mason City, Iowa, by banging a Salvation Army drum while the drummer in a winter street service went into a nearby building to get warm. The song he conducted for the Moore show is entitled *Banners and Bonnets* and is used by the Army in its fund-raising appeals. Willson even changed his own Christmas plans so that he could take part in the show.

All members of The Salvation Army are encouraged to write music for Army use, and some of the best has come from those who seem the least likely as composers. "Of course there's some music that could never be used, but most of our people get pleasure out of trying to create a song," Major Holz says.

Major Holz stressed the importance of music in Army worship services. "We're a non-sacramental group, much like the Quakers," he points out. "We have no Communion, no baptism. The main feature of The Salvation Army and the Quakers is their service to others—but there is one big difference. We have lots of music and make lots of noise, whereas the Quakers are very quiet!"

In the Eastern Territory's 341 Salvation Army Corps there are 194 senior bands and 115 brass bands for young people. There are 148 fully-organized choirs called "Songster Brigades," and 173 youth choirs called "Young People's Singing Companies."

"Bandsman" is the title of a band member, man or woman, and although there are many female bandsmen, a local Corps may decide to restrict its band to men. An approved band must have at least four members. To be a bandsman a person must be a Salvation Army soldier for three months or more and must pay at least 10 cents a week for the purchase of music, the repair of instruments, and other incidentals. A bandsman must also "fire his cartridge" regularly—that is, make regular contributions to The Salvation Army, as all Salvationists do.

Many of the bands are excellent. In Hamilton, Ontario, a band gives nightly concerts in a park for two weeks each year and receives $4000 for its band fund. Many Salvation Army bands play for Easter Sunrise services, including those held annually in the Hollywood Bowl.

Holz chuckles as he says, "Harriet Van Horne, the TV critic for the New York *World Telegram and Sun,* once said of a certain popular singer, 'She should be accompanied by a steam calliope or a Salvation Army band.' True, we do have a lot of the humblest bands you can imagine. Some are real old Americana. We run the gamut of the scale. We give them good arrangements, but sometimes a poor band will butcher 'em!"

Arrangements for the brass instruments are important, and Army bands will play only music arranged or composed by the Army. One of the finest composer-arrangers is Erik Leidzen, a Swedish Salvationist who came to the United States in 1915, now lives in New York, and is in great demand as a guest conductor. Another famous composer-arranger of Army music is Emil Soderstrom, Chicago music publisher, whose arrangement of the "Amos and Andy" radio theme song is familiar to millions of Americans.

Major Holz himself composes and arranges music. He once wrote an arrangement of *America* which, in England, is the same tune as that for *God Save The Queen*. In his special arrangement he interpolated a few bars from *Yankee Doodle*, and when the number was received and played by the British they often omitted the *Yankee Doodle* portions!

In June, 1960, Holz and the New York Staff Band made a tour of England, opening in London at the Royal Albert Hall, whose 8500 seats were sold out in May.

The New York Staff Band has made several hi-fi recordings. One of the most popular is an MGM label with songstress Jane Pickens and the male chorus of the Staff Band, singing old and familiar hymns. All are on sale, along with various Army publications, in the Army's own bookstore on the ground floor of its National Headquarters at 130 West 14th Street in New York City.

As Territorial Music Secretary, Dick Holz is in charge of The Salvation Army music publishing for all four Territories of the United States. The International Headquarters in London publishes basic music for The Salvation Army throughout the world and issues a monthly choir journal, *The Musical Salvationist,* to which many churches subscribe.

Any local Corps that has a band will teach interested young

people to play instruments, using training material and instruction books supplied by Holz' department. In practically all cases the instruments are the property of The Salvation Army, since an individually-owned instrument might not blend satisfactorily with others in the band.

When a youngster becomes a full-fledged bandsman he will be expected to wear a Salvation Army uniform. Sometimes this is supplied free by the Army, but if the bandsman is able to pay for it he will be expected to do so. Frequently the bandsman buys the trousers and the Army furnishes the tunic. A ready-made uniform, ordered through the Trade Department of the Territory, costs about $50. An officer's uniform, with two pairs of trousers, costs about $100.

Major Holz is one of many fourth generation Salvationists now in service. His maternal great-grandparents were officers in 1882, two years after the Army began in the United States. On both sides of the family his grandparents were officers who met and were married in the ranks. His Grandfather Holz, a German immigrant who joined in 1884, later became Commissioner and head of the Eastern Territory, retiring in 1930.

Dick Holz is married and has three sons and a daughter, all of whom play brass instruments in a Young People's Salvation Army Band. "However," Dick says, "one of the boys—he's twelve—isn't sure whether he wants to be a trombonist or a professional baseball player!"

Music is helping another officer, Major May Adam, to work with groups of Spanish, Mexican, Cuban, Puerto Rican and Negro children in a New York neighborhood in which The Salvation Army is the only Protestant church giving religious instruction.

Major Adam and Lieutenant Geraldine Staples make their headquarters in an old house at 431 East 159th Street in the Bronx. Together they brightened the interior by painting all walls a bright yellow, with white trim for the woodwork. In back of the house is a building which was once a beer-bottling works, then a soft-drink distributing center, and is now used as a chapel and recreation hall by The Salvation Army. It has a vinyl tile floor, light yellow brick interior walls, and folding chairs which can be moved aside to make room for games.

Major Adam's work is primarily with 50 children from two to fourteen years old, most of whom have Spanish-speaking parents.

"The problems of these people are greater than many because they cannot express themselves to others without interpreters," she says. "Much of my work involves interpreting for mothers of the children. For instance, if a mother receives a note asking her to confer with a teacher at the school, she brings the note to me to read and asks me to go with her to talk with the teacher."

Major Adam's training in Spanish came from seven years of missionary work in South America, part of which was spent at an orphanage where no one had ever taught the children to play games of any kind. She started Girl Guard and Sunbeam programs, showed the youngsters how to play dodge-ball, tag, baseball and various kinds of table games.

In her New York post she has 11 band instruments and has already begun to teach four children to play the cornet, hoping that others will become interested.

She also conducts regular school classes for younger children and tries to provide games, craftwork and other recreation that will help to keep the youngsters off the streets and out of mischief.

Some of the parents speak Spanish and no English, and others speak English and no Spanish, so it is difficult to get them together for discussions or friendly meetings. Major Adam is teaching English to mothers at night, in addition to her regular work, and also gives them lessons in knitting and crocheting. On Sunday nights she holds worship services in Spanish, and she makes a special effort to see that some of the children get an opportunity to participate in The Salvation Army camping program.

Every division in the Territory sponsors a two-week music camp every summer, where youngsters get specialized training in music. Boys or girls interested in these camps may get more

171

information about the schedules from the Salvation Army Corps nearest to their homes.

In the Army's summer program more than 20,000 under-privileged children enjoy vacations in 58 fresh-air camps in the United States. One of the best of the Eastern Territory camps is at Star Lake, Butler, New Jersey, where children from the crowded cities go boating, fishing, swimming, hiking, play games, enjoy folk-singing and folk-dancing, and do various kinds of craftwork.

Each year 150 teen-age Salvation Army vocalists and instru-mentalists go to Star Lake for music instruction. All are out-standing performers in their local Corps bands or Songster Brigades. They get advanced teaching in major brass instru-ments, voice, ensemble playing, chorus, band, conducting, transposing, composing, arranging, and harmony, all under the direction of Staff Bandmaster Dick Holz.

Star Lake plays an important part in the program of the Ridgewood Day Nursery and Settlement, located at 227 Knickerbocker Avenue in Brooklyn, New York, where I visited with Brigadier Grace E. Dierolf, the officer in charge of this Salvation Army installation.

The Day Nursery cares for the children of working parents. For fees ranging from $5 to $15 weekly, depending upon the parents' ability to pay, the children get supervised care, hot lunches, fruit juices, afternoon snacks and milk. The young-sters range in age from three to six years, and the nursery is equipped to accommodate thirty of them. In another building nearby, the Settlement House, there are provisions made to care for "after-school" children over six years old.

"We have many children with problems, but no problem children," Brigadier Dierolf says. "Often the problems are caused by language difficulties. The parents speak their native tongue at home and the child speaks English at school. One mother came to me and said, 'Now I must learn English. My Nicky tells me I am stupid because I speak only the Italian.'"

The fact that both parents work means that they spend comparatively little time with their children. One boy has never

172

had the experience of speaking with adults in English at home, since his family holds to the rule that a child should be seen and not heard, and he is barred from the family's conversations. Some children do not speak or understand English at all when they first come to the school, but they pick it up quickly from the others, only to find that it is difficult for them to use English at home.

In an attempt to overcome some of the difficulties, Brigadier Dierolf holds language classes for parents, many of whom are anxious to learn to please their children. One four-year-old girl who came to the school unable to speak a word of English has become so Americanized that she refuses to wear any of the clothing her parents brought from Italy and also refuses to speak Italian to her mother or father.

Another girl, five, when addressed by her parents in their native Polish tongue, keeps saying, "I don't understand you. I don't understand you."

"By the time these kids are about six years old they think they know it all," says the Brigadier. "Language is no longer a barrier. Our trouble is that we don't want them to forget their native tongues, because a knowledge of more than one language will be of great value to them as they grow up. We had one girl, the daughter of a Polish family, who had a terrifying war experience. When she came to us she spoke Jewish, German and Polish, and not a word of English—but when she finished school she could speak English fluently and had forgotten all but a few words of the other languages."

Every summer for two weeks the children from 3 to 12 are taken by bus to the Star Lake Camp. For the first time in their lives some throw stones into the lake, some see frogs and woodpeckers and ferns and campfires.

When the schools are closed during the Summer, the Settlement opens its craft shop and woodwork shop daily from 8:00 A. M. to 5:30 P. M. for boys and girls six years old and up. In the same building they hold Sunday School classes, meetings of Girl Guards and Sunbeams, and boys' clubs for teen-agers, operated in cooperation with the Boys' Clubs of America.

173

In Tulsa, Oklahoma, The Salvation Army Boys' Club was always "white." One day a man telephoned The Salvation Army Corps, identified himself as a minister, and said he would like to bring in 35 boys to join the Boys' Club. The officer in charge said the boys would be welcome at any time. When they arrived he discovered that they were all Negroes, including the minister who had called him.

The officer made no comment. He simply brought them into the Club's quarters and let them mingle with the white boys already there. This was the first act of integration in Tulsa, and when it was reported to the national headquarters everyone "sat back to see what would happen." Nothing did—and the club is operating smoothly and harmoniously.

For both boys and girls over 16 there is the "Future Officers' Fellowship," a group of young Salvationists who intend to be officers. In the Eastern Territory the Fellowship is headed by Major George Nelting and Captain Robert McNally, who hold meetings with teen-agers throughout the Territory to explain the opportunities offered by The Salvation Army for full-time Christian service, in the hope that many of the youths will be inspired to join the Fellowship and eventually become officers.

Captain McNally also keeps in touch with Salvationists in the armed forces, letting them know what is happening in their respective Corps and among their friends, so that they will not feel that they have been forgotten while performing their required military service.

In one year The Salvation Army has direct contact with nearly 800,000 children and young people in the United States. About 425,000 of these are members of Army youth programs, including 72 percent under the age of 15 years and 28 percent ranging from 15 to 21. The Army estimates that it has indirect contact with some four million children through its work at Christmas, in disasters, in social welfare operations and similar activities. It keeps in touch with its own young people not only through local Corps, clubs, scouting and camp programs, but also by means of a great many printed guides, manuals, story papers and little magazines, one of the most popular being *The*

174

Young Soldier, "Official Organ for Young People of The Salvation Army," a 16-page weekly with short stories, inspirational articles, cartoons, photographs, and newsy items about various goings-on in the Territory.

The Salvation Army's work with youth is of prime importance in all 86 countries in which it serves. In England, Brigadier Bernard Watson made this observation: "There is world-wide agreement and action on the need to help teen-agers. As American dead-end kids, British Teddy-boys, South African ducktails, or teen-agers by any other name, they spell challenge. They call for understanding and compassion."

In Liverpool the Army has a full-time center for young people, Aintree's Youth Club, supervised by Lieutenant Arnold Bennett, a former boxing champion. When Bennett first met The Salvation Army he was drunk and in Calcutta. Thanks to the Army he gave up drinking and became sufficiently interested to enroll in the training school in London, graduating with a commission.

Assigned to the Aintree Youth Club he soon found that many of the teen-agers who frequented the club canteen were stealing both food and money. He called a meeting of the members, mentioned the thefts, and pointed out that they were only robbing themselves by making it difficult for the club to operate properly.

One "tough guy" sneered at Bennett, who tried to reason with him. When the boy cursed him, Bennett decided to respond in language they all understood. He grabbed the boy, herded him toward the door and said, "Outside!"

The youth took a swing at the one-time boxing champion, but it never landed. Instead, Bennett tapped him with a right to the jaw and the boy went down. He left the club, but returned a month later asking to be reinstated as a member, and today he is one of the most trusted and active members in the organization.

The youngsters in the club still have two major dislikes—religion and policemen. They are intensely loyal, as a gang is loyal, and when one is in trouble all are out to help. One day a Liverpool detective visited the place to ask Lieutenant Bennett about a certain boy who might be implicated in a robbery. When the policeman walked in, every teen-ager in the place rushed out and stayed away for weeks. Today, at Bennett's request, if the police want to talk with him they ask him to come to police headquarters.

Bennett's career as a British seaman and a champion boxer makes him a hero in the eyes of his young charges, and gradually he is shaping them into better, more responsible citizens. "What they wanted was a street corner with a roof on it," he says. "That's what I'm giving them."

And it works. One boy who came in because he was permitted to strum a Salvation Army guitar now attends prayer meetings regularly. Some fifty others who like to sing have grown to enjoy hymns and the lieutenant's Sunday Bible talks.

In Havana, Cuba, 17-year-old Manuel Izquierdo, who supported his widowed mother, was the ringleader of a teen-age gang that found enjoyment in heckling Salvation Army meetings and teasing the señoritas. In the course of their efforts to break up the meetings, Manuel could not help hearing some of the things that were said by the officers making talks, and after three months of creating disturbances in the hall he suddenly decided that he would sit through one meeting just to listen.

On Manuel's orders his companions remained quiet. When the officer in charge finally invited listeners to come forward and accept Jesus as their Savior, Manuel rose and marched straight to the Mercy Seat, where he asked forgiveness for his sins.

The other boys walked out in astonishment. In the days ahead Manuel met and spoke to some of them on the streets, but took no part in their gang activities. His successor as ringleader was Oscar Lopez, an intelligent boy who was surprised to see that Manuel appeared to be happier than ever before. Oscar asked him what the reason was.

"I can't explain it so good," Manuel said. "It's what happened inside of me, that's all I know."

176

At Manuel's suggestion Oscar began to attend Salvation Army meetings, and three months after Manuel's conversion Oscar, too, sought salvation at the Mercy Seat. In turn, Oscar invited another gang member, Odilio Fernandez, to join him and Manuel, and in April, 1954, the three boys were sworn in as soldiers of The Salvation Army. In their white tropical uniforms they campaigned through Havana, recruiting other young people for Christ. The gang which Manuel and Oscar once led has long since disbanded and most of its members are active in Salvation Army youth work. (In Cuba, as this was written, the Castro government still permitted Salvation Army open-air meetings and other activities.)

In another part of the world, in October, 1957, a pioneering venture of The Salvation Army was inaugurated as a service to young people. The Bantu Youth Hostel, situated on three acres of land in Mofolo Village, 15 miles southwest of Johannesburg, South Africa, marked a new idea in social welfare work.

The hostel consists of three dormitories, a dining hall and kitchen, a library and chapel with reading and recreation rooms, a gymnasium and swimming pool, an administration building, and staff quarters. Its purpose: "To provide for young native men from the Johannesburg area who are socially or morally maladjusted, for whose care The Salvation Army is specially qualified to cater."

Africa has long been fertile ground for The Salvation Army (see Chapter 16). One of the great boons to the African people is The Salvation Army's Institute for the Blind at Thika, near Nairobi in Kenya.

Blindness is prevalent in Africa. In many areas people and animals live together in dirty huts filled with flies that crawl over the faces of men, women and children. Smoke from cook-fires stings the eyes, and irritations and infections rob thousands of their sight. Once blinded, both adults and children do little but beg for food and money.

One day a traveler brought word to a jungle village about a Salvation Army school that could teach blind children to do many useful things, even to read and write. A teen-age boy,

177

Kutu, asked his parents and his tribal chiefs for permission to go to the school, but they refused, saying the story was probably a fantasy, and anyway that Kutu was blind and could not find his way. In the dead of night, however, Kutu crept away and started on his sightless walk south, armed only with a long wooden staff.

Picking his way through the bush he knew from the feel of the earth under his bare feet when he was on the main road. Now which way to turn? A passerby heading for a town guided Kutu to the railroad station and told him a train could take him to the school for the blind.

But Kutu had no money. When the train rumbled into the station he felt his way along a car until he came to steps and bumped into a man who stood near them. He was the inspector (conductor). Hearing Kutu's story, the man agreed to let him ride free to Thika.

In Thika, a strange town to a strange blind boy, Kutu was stopped by a policeman who offered to help him. He wanted to go to the school for the blind, Kutu said. The friendly officer escorted him to the school, where Kutu told his story to the superintendent and pleaded for a chance to stay. Admiring his courage, the superintendent accepted Kutu as a student.

Kutu took a bath, was given new clothes and a bed in the dormitory, where he talked with other blind boys who amazed him with their stories of the school, but most of all Kutu was pleased to learn that The Salvation Army people who ran the school were actually concerned about their blind charges. In all, the school had 150 boys and girls, all under 14 years old.

Each day began with a bath, followed by an assembly at which the children said The Lord's Prayer aloud in Swahili. Then came physical training, setting-up exercises, each new blind student standing with the front of his body against the back of another so that he might follow movements and learn the exercise positions.

Many often stumbled and fell, suffering bruised faces or cut feet or hands, but all injuries were treated in a modern clinic each morning.

Kutu, like the others, was taught to knit, to fasten nuts on

178

bolts, to use screwdrivers and other simple tools. He was given all kinds of objects to handle, to increase his range of experience and knowledge.

In one class he learned to read and write in Braille (in English, because English is becoming the universal language of East Africa).

Geography lessons were given with the aid of a giant relief map on which the students could feel features of the terrain.

Kutu marveled at the machine called a typewriter that printed letters of the alphabet, and in the weeks of his studies he became quite skilled as a typist.

He also learned how to operate a telephone switchboard, how to make mats and baskets from bamboo cane, rope from sisal fiber, and how to plant corn between parallel ropes, with stakes placed one foot apart for proper spacing of the kernels.

Not all time was devoted to work and study. The boys and girls had their share of play, too. They jumped rope, told and listened to stories, played "kick-a-ball," a game played with an inflated ball in a walled area. The ball is kicked by opposing teams, and if it strikes a wall a goal is scored. The youngsters played dominoes by feeling the spots, and many of them learned to play instruments in The Salvation Army band.

Every Sunday a long rope was held by the children in single file as they marched to the meeting hall for worship services. Some who were not Protestants were escorted to the churches of their choice in town.

When their training was finished, Kutu and his classmates were sent out to work or to return to their homes. Now they could earn money as traders, rope makers, furniture makers, craft instructors in hospitals, switchboard operators, typists, or perhaps operating hand presses to make metal tops for gasoline cans. At least each was equipped to perform some useful task for which he would be paid.

Wherever The Salvation Army flag flies there are constructive programs for the betterment of young people, and many young men and women wearing the Army uniform today are living proof of the effectiveness of the Army's youth work.

Chapter 13

LOSERS, LIFERS, AND LOVE

The welfare and rehabilitation of men and women in prisons has been of concern to The Salvation Army since its founding. Frequently the Salvationists themselves were imprisoned for disturbing the peace with their open-air meetings, and while they were confined they sang and prayed and preached to those jailed for other offenses.

Today the Army operates special branches for prison work in each of the four United States Territories and throughout the world. One is the Men's Correctional Services Division, the other is the Women's Correctional Services Division.

In the United States Eastern Territory the Women's Correctional Services Division is in charge of a dedicated Salvation Army officer, Brigadier Dorothy Berry, whose constant association with female thieves, prostitutes and narcotic addicts has made her an authority on the ways and wiles of women of the underworld. Her prime objectives are to comfort those in jail and to rehabilitate them when they get out.

Once when she prepared to hold services in the Women's House of Detention in New York City she was approached by a group of female prisoners whose spokeswoman was a peroxide blonde with a once-pretty face now showing the ravages of time and dissipation.

"Look, sister," the blonde said, "we want to tell you that us girls don't mind you comin' here to visit and preach, but we don't go for none of that Prodigal Son stuff. We've already had three Protestant ministers and three Prodigal Sons. We know we're sinners and we don't want to be reminded of it all the time, so don't lay it on and don't bring no sanctimonious phonies with you!"

Brigadier Berry, with her gray hair and gentle birdlike face, is a familiar and welcome figure to wardens, keepers and female prisoners in eleven Eastern States, for she travels from Maine through Ohio into northeastern Kentucky, conducting chapel services in prisons, listening to the troubles and hard-luck stories of the women, and giving religious counseling if any want it.

Much of her time is devoted to those in the Women's House of Detention in New York City, where she has a special monthly non-sectarian Salvation Army service. One girl, a Roman Catholic, talked with Brigadier Berry and was invited to attend the service. "That is, if your priest has no objections," Dorothy Berry said.

"Aw, hell," the girl answered. "Father doesn't mind us going to *your* service. You ain't got no religion!"

The women inmates think of The Salvation Army as a "helping" organization, not as "religious." As Dorothy Berry says, "We don't think it's good just to preach and pray and go home. These women need real help. They cling to those from the outside who are friendly to them."

When Brigadier Berry held her first chapel service in the Women's Detention House, one of the women in attendance, an Italian, stayed after the service to ask a favor of the officer.

"You good woman," she said. "You stand with the Book. You help me, yes?"

"If I can," Dorothy Berry said.

The woman explained in broken English that she had disgraced her family. She had some money and asked the officer to use it to buy clothes for the prisoner's children, who were with their grandmother in Italy. Dorothy complied. The night before the woman was brought to trial, she asked the brigadier to accompany her to court.

"This turned out to be one of the biggest headline cases," Dorothy Berry recalls. "She had murdered another woman who was mixed up with her husband. She was convicted and sent to State's prison, but was declared insane and transferred to a State mental hospital for life. I visited her there and did what I could to comfort her. Her youngest son, twelve years old, came here from Italy and talked with his mother at the hospital. At her request he came to see me, and when he got ready to leave my office he lifted my hand and kissed it in gratitude for my help to his mother."

In one case another welfare agency was trying to assist a young mother who was unmarried and under parole by the State of New York. She wanted to go to New York City to work and to live with the man who fathered her baby, but the State Parole Office refused to grant the necessary permission unless she were married. The problem was discussed with Brigadier Berry, who solved it by uniting the girl and man in matrimony. (Any couple with the required blood-test certificates and a proper marriage license may be married in New York City by any Salvation Army officer who is registered with the city authorities to perform such ceremonies.) Within a short time after the wedding, thanks to the grapevine, several other girls and young men came to ask the brigadier to marry them. "They discovered that it was both harmless and painless," she recalls with a smile.

The true stories uncovered by Dorothy Berry in her prison work have all the drama and pathos of any best-selling novel or Hollywood tear-jerker. Among the saddest is one she calls "the case of our howling failure," the tragic tale of an "old pro" we'll call Nellie, who was both a drug addict and a prostitute.

Nellie left a good home and went to New York when she was young, fired with ambition to be a great stage star on Broadway. She met with no success, but did meet many other despairing hopefuls who frequented places where working entertainers were often seen, and who lived in drab furnished rooms on the fringes of the Bright Lights. Some of the would-be actors and actresses, seeking cheer and encouragement in any form, congregated in cellar dives or went to "parties" given by new acquaintances who showed them how a few marijuana cigarettes or a slight jab with a hypodermic needle could drive away their worries and give the world a rosy glow.

Nellie went for the rosy glow routine, with the necessary ingredients freely supplied by her "friends." In a short time, however, she discovered that if she didn't continue to use the "stuff," her whole body ached and she writhed in torture. She also found that the drug that could bring relief was now expensive, and that her "friends" were hard and greedy, no longer sympathetic. No money, no dope.

Nellie had a job as a waitress, but her pay was far less than she needed to satisfy her habit, so she sold the only thing she could think of to raise more money—her body. That's how and why Nellie became a whore.

It was inevitable that she should wind up in jail, which she did more than once. It was in Women's Court in New York that Dorothy Berry first met Nellie, charged with prostitution, and offered to help her. The officer said she could get Nellie a job, and the girl was released with the understanding that she would take it. She was reluctant to discuss her personal history with Dorothy, who did not press her for it.

The job involved scrubbing the floors and doing general cleanup work in a sanitarium on Long Island, where Nellie became popular not only with the nurses and doctors, but also with many of the patients. Because of her cheerful and friendly bedside manner she was assigned as a nurse's attendant.

After she had worked at the hospital for three or four years she asked one day to be placed on the night shift. Brigadier Berry, hearing about the request, asked Nellie why she made it.

Nellie explained, somewhat shyly, "Well, the head night nurse used to be a missionary. She's been in so many other countries, so many wonderful places. I've always wanted to see some of them, but I know I never will, so she tells me stories about her missionary work and all the sights she's seen, and that's the next best thing. That's why I want to work at night, so I can be with her and hear about all those places."

Nellie worked in the sanitarium for nearly eight years, and in all that time she never engaged in prostitution. She tried hard to shake the drug habit, but the best she could do was to cut down on the amount and frequency of her shots, which she took so secretly that none of her hospital friends was aware that she was an addict.

One day Nellie met a young man who had been hired by the hospital as a general handyman. They saw a great deal of each other in the months that followed, and finally declared their love. The man then confessed that he was AWOL from the United States Army and was being sought as a deserter. Not disheartened, Nellie urged him to tell the director of the hospital, which he did, and the next day he was taken into custody by the military to be court-martialed.

Nellie tried to be cheerful. "It won't be for long," she said. "Anyway, no matter how long it is, I'll be waiting for you."

They corresponded for a year, writing about plans for their wedding, to take place as soon as he was released. Then one night Nellie got a telephone call from her beloved. He was free and in New York City, and would she come in right away so that they could have dinner together at one of the big hotels?

Nellie was never happier, never gayer, as she primped and dressed and went to Manhattan. In the hotel lobby her sweetheart hugged and kissed her and she kissed him back, heedless of the smiles and stares of the people watching them. As they walked arm in arm into the hotel dining room, with its glittering crystal chandeliers and gleaming silver, Nellie felt that she was walking into a bright new world.

When they finished their dessert and were drinking their second cups of coffee and smoking cigarettes, the man grasped Nellie's free hand across the table.

"I have a great idea," he said.

"Good! Let's hear it," Nellie answered.

"Okay. This is our first night together. I figure it's silly for you to go all the way back to the hospital. Here we are in a nice hotel. We're going to married, aren't we?"

"You know we are."

"Well, then—why don't we just shack up for the night right here? We'll get a nice room high up, and—"

Nellie's face turned ghost-white. Surprise was crowded out of her eyes by disbelief, and disbelief by anger. She withdrew her hand, slammed her cigarette into the ashtray. Without a single word she pushed back her chair, stood up and strode out of the dining room, not looking back even once.

She cried most of the way back to the sanitarium. The next day she spoke curtly to her friends and finally exploded into a temper tantrum in which she swept dishes off tables in the dining room and hurled plates and saucers against the walls. Then she went to her room, packed her belongings and walked back to a life of prostitution on the streets of New York. She was sent to the Women's Detention House several times, and although Brigadier Berry tried to help her, Nellie refused her overtures.

The story ended in 1959. Says Dorothy Berry, "Nellie had just come out of the Detention House. She was 'on the nod'— taking so much dope she was groggy. Apparently she smoked a cigarette while lying in bed, not knowing what she was doing. At any rate, the bed caught fire and before the firemen could save her, Nellie was burned to death."

At the time of my research for this book there were 46 teenage girls in the Women's House of Detention in New York, which is the place of imprisonment for all females arrested in the five boroughs of New York City. Many of these young people find their way out of trouble with Dorothy Berry's help.

"My entree to the prison is through the chapel service," she says. "The emphasis of my Bureau is on the spiritual, but our service is non-denominational and our approach to people in trouble is not by a tract or a prayer—more likely it will be a meal or just a friendly chat. It's different with each woman,

185

and whatever her need is, we try to meet it as effectively as we can."

Often the need is a job for the woman who is released. The State Employment Bureau offered to help those women who were not drug addicts or who had no drug history. "That eliminated about eighty-five percent," Brigadier Berry says. "These are the ones who look to The Salvation Army for assistance."

Dorothy Berry's intense interest in prison work was evident even in her high school days, when she wrote a term paper about Warden Lewis Lawes' honor system at Sing Sing Prison. To get first-hand information for her project, Dorothy and another student decided to get themselves arrested by sitting on a park bench late at night, thinking that they would immediately be sent to Sing Sing where they could make notes for their essays. In the park a police officer sauntered by and gave the girls a casual glance and greeting. When it appeared that he was not going to stop, the girls asked him to arrest them. When they told him their reasons he laughed and escorted both of them to their homes, suggesting that they confine their research to books.

As a child, Dorothy lived on West Fourteenth Street in New York, went to the Methodist Church, and sang in the choir. She often saw Salvation Army officers giving food or clothing to poor children, and she wanted very much to take part in this kind of work. When she was twenty she told her mother that she intended to join The Salvation Army.

"You don't want to belong to that outfit," her mother said. "Everybody knows The Salvation Army is only an organization for bums and drunks."

A few months later her mother died, and a year afterwards Dorothy went to The Salvation Army's School for Officers' Training and became an officer. She has been in charge of the women's prison work in the Eastern Territory since 1945 and has become a lovable and familiar figure in the scores of jails and reformatories she visits regularly.

A counterpart of Dorothy's bureau is the Men's Correctional Services Division, headed in the Eastern Territory by Brigadier

H. Victor Dimond, a native of London, England, who was commissioned from the Officers' Training School in New York City in 1924. Dimond's prison work is the more extensive, because male prisoners in the major correctional institutions outnumber females by about 18 to 1.

Brigadier Dimond worked for years among old people and in Salvation Army residences for young women before taking charge of the prison work in 1955. His branch was then called the "Prison Bureau," and because he felt the word "prison" carried a stigma, he proposed a change in the name to "Correctional Services Division." The change was made in the United States, Canada and Great Britain.

Victor Dimond's prison work among men is similar to that of Dorothy Berry among women. In addition, however, Dimond is a parole officer and at the time of my interview with him he was supervising 38 parolees who do not report to any other parole officer.

One man we'll call Ned had been reporting to Dimond for several years, on parole under an original 40-year sentence for assault with a dangerous weapon. The Salvation Army found Ned a job, had his driver's license restored, and was pleased to see that he was continually on good behavior and reported regularly. After 15 years of Ned's parole, based upon a recommendation of The Salvation Army, the Parole Board saw fit to terminate the parole and sent a certificate to Brigadier Dimond accordingly.

In telling me about this case Dimond said, "I could have telephoned Ned and told him he was through reporting to me, or I could have sent him a letter. But I wanted to see the impact of this news upon the man himself, so I asked him to come in."

When Ned arrived Dimond said, "Ned, why do you suppose I sent for you?"

"Gee, I don't know, Mr. Dimond. I hope there's nothing wrong. It would be terrible if I had to go back after all these years."

"Ned, you may consider this your last parole report." He

187

handed him the certificate. "This means you're a free man. You can live and work anywhere you wish—but be sure you don't get into any more serious trouble."

Ned read the certificate, then sat down and looked up at the officer. It couldn't be said that he cried, but his eyes glistened, and suddenly he jumped out of the chair and laughed and threw both arms around Brigadier Dimond.

"Moments like that make our work pretty gratifying," the brigadier told me.

Dimond visits prisons in the 11 States of the Eastern Territory, conducts chapel services, and invites each man to discuss any problems with him personally, in private. At his New York office he gets voluminous mail from prisoners, some of whom write 400 to 500 letters during their incarceration. Dimond reads each letter, and whereas years ago such mail was answered with mimeographed replies, he has the help of volunteer workers to make a personal typewritten response to each prisoner.

Victor Dimond's prison and parole work has engendered some important questions in his mind and some resultant suggestions of significance.

"For one thing," he says, "I hope they will get modern machinery in prisons that will fit a man for a trade when he gets out. In this area, for example, men are taught to work on textiles, but if a man is to be paroled in New York City, where will he find a job on textile machinery? He probably could get such a job in New England or the South, but his parole officer may forbid him to leave New York."

His point is that the prison rehabilitation programs should be aimed at fitting a prisoner for the kind of work he will be able to do in the area to which he is to be paroled.

"Parolees who once made their living in the entertainment field are forbidden to work in any place where liquor is served," he points out. "This definitely bars them from jobs in night clubs and restaurants, where entertainers ordinarily expect to find work. The same prohibition applies to dishwashers and food service workers. Where else will they go? And do you know that if you want to get a fishing license in New York State you must answer a question on the application that says, 'Have you ever been arrested?' That looks as though the fish want to know who's on the other end of the line!"

As part of his prison program Dimond conducts a correspondence course which he calls "An Introduction to the Bible," consisting of five groups of lessons which are made available to prisoners through institutional chaplains—Protestant, Catholic and Jewish. In 1960 there were 1572 men Bible students in 50 prisons in the Eastern Territory, and 112 graduates of the course.

Through the cooperation of Mr. James V. Bennett, Director of the Federal Bureau of Prisons, U. S. Department of Justice, I was able to get an expression about The Salvation Army and its prison work from Mr. J. C. Taylor, Warden of the United States Penitentiary at Leavenworth, Kansas.

Warden Taylor recalled the case of an inmate named Marty. Before his transfer to Leavenworth from another prison, Marty had been badly upset because his wife and children had been rejected for public assistance and were in dire need. He wrote to the Correctional Services Division of The Salvation Army in Chicago, which assigned a case-worker to investigate. The family's needs were clarified and The Salvation Army saw to it that Marty's wife and youngsters were properly cared for.

Soon after Marty was transferred to Leavenworth his aged and diabetic mother was found sitting on the doorstep of Warden Taylor's home at eleven o'clock one night. She explained that she had been under treatment for diabetes in Wichita Falls, Texas, and that friends there had bought a bus ticket for her to go home to St. Louis by way of Leavenworth and Chicago so that she could see a son in each place.

"I'm going to die soon," she said, "and I want to see my boys before I go."

The Warden gently suggested that she go to a hotel until morning, since she could not visit Marty that night. She couldn't go to a hotel, she said—she had only fifty cents in cash—but she would just lie down on the lawn and sleep until morning.

The Warden helped her into the house, where he telephoned the Leavenworth Corps of The Salvation Army and explained the circumstances. The Salvation Army paid for a room for the woman in a local hotel and for her breakfast, and in the morning the Warden sent a car to bring her to the penitentiary.

During the visit with Marty his mother suffered an emotional seizure and was attended by the Chief Medical Officer. Marty withdrew $10 from his commissary account at the prison in order that his mother might have money to continue her trip to Chicago, where she was to see his brother.

The Warden telephoned Marty's wife in Chicago, asking that she meet the bus, but the wife refused because she said she did not get along with her mother-in-law. Once again The Salvation Army was called upon to locate Marty's brother in Chicago. The old lady was placed aboard the bus, which was met in Chicago by Salvation Army representatives who brought her to the home of her other son.

"While this is only one specific case," Warden Taylor says, "I'm sure you know about the general kind of assistance that is always available to discharged prisoners in the various communities to which they are released. The Salvation Army is one resource that our men can be sure will offer a place to sleep and a free meal when they need it, and I am sure many of them utilize this resource. Some people are not overly anxious to help the discharged prisoner, but The Salvation Army doors are always open to him."

Much of the assistance to parolees comes under the direction of Secretary of the Social Welfare Services Department, Lt. Col. Roy C. Barber, who also directs the Emergency Disaster Service. The employment service originally started as a part of the Correctional Services Division, but today it does whatever is possible to find jobs for needy people. In New York it deals mostly with itinerants seeking day-to-day employment, because many of the men who apply are not stable enough to hold steady jobs.

One man pleaded, almost begged, for some kind of work—any kind. He said he was 51 years old and had to support a

190

widowed mother. He talked with Mr. John Dockendorff, Employment Counselor, a Salvationist who plays in the Staff Band.

"There's a job open for a general handyman," Dockendorff said.

"That's fine! I'll take it."

"It's in Westchester County. About an hour's bus ride."

"Oh. Westchester County? Well—can I let you know later?"

"All right, but it has to be today."

Two hours later the man telephoned. "I'm sorry, but I can't take that job. My mother won't let me go all the way to Westchester!"

Chapter 14

ATTACK ON DEVIL'S ISLAND

The one prison in the world where condemned men lost all hope was (with the possible exception of Siberia) a group of three small islands off the coast of French Guiana—the *Iles du Salut*, or Safety Islands. One was called St. Joseph, one the Ile Royale, and one the Ile du Diable, or Devil's Island.

Devil's Island, a name infamous in penal history, won notoriety as the place of imprisonment of French Captain Alfred Dreyfus, falsely accused in 1894 of supplying French military information to the Germans. Thanks to Novelist Émile Zola and others, Dreyfus was later shown to be the victim of a frame-up and was freed and reinstated. The name of Devil's Island, however, came to be synonymous with hopelessness, terror and death.

Although Devil's Island signified the entire penal colony, relatively few prisoners were confined to this one island, and most of those were political offenders. Others of a more desperate character were kept on Royale and St. Joseph, but most of the prisoners were confined to a part of the Guiana mainland.

A convicted man sentenced to less than eight years in the colony was subject to *doublage*, a system in which he was compelled to remain at liberty in Guiana for a period of time equal to his sentence, working in the colony to earn his passage home. If he was sentenced to more than eight years he was confined to Guiana for life, although when his specific sentence was completed he could work and live in the colony. The men so engaged, and those in *doublage,* were called libérés, and their real status was virtually one of slavery.

When the French government abolished slavery in 1848, plantation owners and others in French Guiana were suddenly deprived of free labor and complained bitterly about the man-power shortage. In an effort to pacify the landowners and solve the problem, France in 1852 began to ship convicts to Guiana, not only as forced labor but also to populate the colony. When a man became a libéré he could learn a useful occupation and would be given a house and land in the hope that he would remain in the colony and raise a family there. Few, however, had the ambition or desire to do so after spending years in shackles and at hard labor, but a libéré needed 2000 francs to buy passage to France, and it would take years to accumulate such a sum.

The hot, damp climate was not conducive to settlement. Tropical diseases killed off prisoners in droves. Millions of mosquitoes carried fever and death in their tiny stings. Convicts were herded together like animals in small, filthy shacks, where fights broke out nightly and were won or lost with fatal stabbings or beatings. Morning generally found a corpse or two or three in the stinking huts. The place was better known as "the dry guillotine."

In 1928 a young Salvation Army officer in France, Major Charles Péan, was ordered to go to French Guiana to work in behalf of the despairing prisoners and to see what might be done to abolish the penal colony, the *Bagne.* It was a staggering mission for a 27-year-old Salvationist.

On a 17-day voyage from St. Nazaire in France to St. Laurent-du-Maroni in French Guiana, young Péan read a great deal about the penal colony which was to be his ministry, yet he had the feeling that the printed word failed to communicate the stark realities soon to challenge him and his mission.

As the mail-boat *Biskra* sailed slowly up the Moroni River, Péan rejoiced in the rich beauty of the jungle, a study in greens, with cocoanut palms curving upward like umbrellas to shield the lacy ferns and masses of brilliant flowers from the scorching rays of the tropical sun.

When he stepped ashore in St. Laurent the beauties of Nature were forgotten, for he found himself in a cruel and tragic world peopled by despondent men for whom Nature had lost all attraction. They were the convicts, and all about them were the foul-smelling huts where men were penned up in groups, and the punishment cell-blocks where many waited in shackles to be transferred to the Isles of Safety (or Isles of Salvation). Men naked to the waist, wearing ragged straw hats and shabby linen trousers, shuffled along the roads. Libérés sat on the ground or worked at unloading cargo or at other arduous tasks, their skinny bodies shiny with sweat.

Péan walked among the murderers, thieves and other criminals, seeing them scowl at his Salvation Army uniform because all uniforms were, to them, symbols of tyranny and oppression. He learned that some 500 men tried to escape each year, but that most were beaten by the jungle and came back half-starved, the last shreds of hope gone forever. A few never did come back, but that was no proof that they escaped, for corpses and skeletons were sometimes found in the jungle, and occasionally bodies were washed up by the sea.

I talked with Charles Péan, now the Commissioner in charge of all Salvation Army activities in France.

"The only way to escape in the penal colony," he told me, "was to get a canoe and go to Trinidad, where the sympathetic police put the fugitives in prison, fed them, and sometimes supplied them with boats to try to get to Venezuela, which had no extradition treaty with France. I think very few ever made it."

Péan saw men whose minds had been warped and destroyed by years of solitary confinement in dank underground cells. In some of the cells and blockhouses he was nauseated by the stench from prisoners who suffered from cancer, leprosy, tuberculosis, malaria, dysentery, and a variety of other diseases, and he was shocked to discover that other men in reasonably

194

good health were shackled with leg irons and housed with the sick and dying.

Péan lived in a small house with seven windows, all without locks, and one of the convicts was assigned to him as a house-boy. His bed was sheathed in mosquito netting, but the wither-ing heat, even at night, made sleeping difficult, and he read law books until he became so drowsy that he could no longer stay awake.

Later, as he roamed the settlement, he discovered that there were three categories of convicts: transportés, rélegués, and deportés. The transportés had been sentenced after conviction for murder, sexual crimes or similar violent physical offenses. Rélegués, ranging in age from 21 to 60 years, had committed lesser crimes of violence. Deportés had actively opposed the government or were guilty of other political offenses, and they made up the "hard labor" crews in the colony.

There were three sub-classes among the transportés—as-signes, who worked for private employers and were paid ten francs per month by the government. The ten francs came from payments of fifty francs per man made to the government by the employers, who contracted to feed, clothe and house the convicts. A second group, concessionaires, lived and worked on small land tracts which were given to them while they were still under sentence in the hope that they would help the community to develop. The third class, also known as con-cessionaires, worked at farming, lumbering, or at some other useful occupation as employees of the government or of some private landowner.

As Péan visited with the men and became better acquainted, he was approached by murderers, robbers and other convicts who had known about the work of The Salvation Army in France or elsewhere and who pleaded with him to try to win their freedom. Many begged him to visit their families and relatives when he returned to France, to say that the con-demned men dreamed of the day when they might be reunited.

One day Péan visited a section of the colony known as the New Camp. At first sight it seemed a pleasant community of huts with white thatched roofs and tiny herb gardens, but behind this façade he was shocked to find some 260 men in various stages of paralysis, tuberculosis, syphilis and cancer, all without hope, all resigned to their inevitable fate. He prayed with and for them, gave them Bibles and copies of Salvation Army literature, and did what he could to strike sparks of hope in the hearts of those who would listen.

Continuing his exploration, Péan toured the New Relegation Camp at St. Jean. Here he discovered conditions even worse than in the New Camp. In St. Jean more than 260 men were sardined into ten small shacks, and although this overcrowding was bad enough in itself, the men were mostly epileptics and imbeciles, with a scattering of consumptives and other sufferers. Here was a community of living dead, for St. Jean was the destination of men expected to die soon.

The convicts who crowded the colony's huts could at least move about without fetters, but Péan found a series of so-called "punishment cell-blocks" in which many offenders were chained and shackled, tormented by pain, thirst and hunger as they paid the price for violence, crime, or rule infractions within the colony.

Churches were "off limits," though Péan doubted that many would go even if they could. On a Sunday afternoon following his inspections, he arranged to have the convicts assembled in St. Laurent while he talked to them for half an hour or more, telling them that The Salvation Army wanted to help them and to improve living conditions on the islands. After the meeting a number of the men wanted to speak to Péan privately, so he remained far into the night listening to their troubles and promising to take messages to their families when he returned to France.

To complete his inspection, Péan made a boat trip to Royale, St. Joseph's, and Devil's Islands, some twenty miles from Cayenne, their only vegetation a few cocoanut palms. Here a thousand convicts worked, ate, slept and suffered.

On Devil's Island, smallest of the three, Péan found only 27 convicts, all serving life terms as traitors or political offenders.

Their food was sent to them by sliding it along a wire strung from Royale Island, and they cooked it themselves.

On St. Joseph's Island, its terrifying dungeons reserved for convicts condemned to solitary confinement and for those who had gone mad, the unearthly screams of the lunatics sickened Péan, but also bolstered his determination to bring them aid and comfort.

Royale Island housed the administration offices, workshops, gardens, and a hospital, in addition to huts for its 450 convicts.

Leaving the Salvation Isles, Péan went to Cayenne, most important town in the colony, and the capital of French Guiana. Among its 13,000 people were numerous libérés, many of whom sought him to pour out their troubles, to ask for help, to tell him how much they appreciated what he was doing in their behalf.

Not all were friendly, however. One day in the center of town Péan saw a row of libérés sitting at the roadside, dressed in rags, their gaunt faces staring at him and his uniform. One of them rose and approached Péan.

"You stand and watch us rot away!" he said. "It would be better if you gave us a crust of bread."

Péan tried to talk to the man, but he turned and strode away.

At his quarters Péan was visited by many of the libérés who wanted counsel and comfort. Talking with these men, wandering through the streets in the stifling heat, and getting all too little sleep, Péan was stricken with fever. Two convicts were assigned to care for him, and as he lay in bed there was an almost steady parade to the house by other libérés, anxious to learn whether or not the fever was subsiding.

After three days in bed Péan insisted upon getting up to attend a scheduled meeting at the Town Hall. Pale and shaky, he told the local authorities about the objectives of The Salvation Army and what he wanted to do for the libérés and others. His message delivered, he staggered to the street and almost collapsed, and was helped to his quarters and put back to bed.

The next day, when the *Biskra* arrived on its monthly mail

trip, Péan went aboard, the first step toward his return to France. A crowd of half-naked libérés, many with tattooed backs, came to see him off and to plead with him not to forget them. It was a plea they need not have made.

On his way home Péan made notes about actions he felt should be taken concerning the penal colony. First and foremost, the entire penal settlement should be abolished, but this would be a long-range target and in the interim there were other more practicable considerations. *Doublage* must go. First offenders and youngsters must be kept apart from old and more hardened criminals.

Cells should be provided for one or two men, to replace the crowded barracks area.

For the libérés some religious, social and recreational activity should be provided, along with a hostel, restaurant and snack bar, and a reading room which could double as a chapel and auditorium. In the hostel clean beds should be available, and there ought also to be a workshop where the libérés could produce articles according to their respective skills and sell them to earn some money.

Péan saw a good use for the natural fruits of the country, such as lemons and pineapples. These, he noted, could be used to produce jams and jellies to be sold by the libérés.

A sizeable garden could be cultivated to raise vegetables for the proposed restaurant and for the market.

Péan's notes contained many other suggestions, the fruit of his terrific urge to wipe out the suffering and cruelty he had witnessed in the colony. There could be factories for soap and rope, a tannery, and a kind of employment agency where libérés could learn what jobs were available in the community.

All these were of vital importance to Charles Péan and aimed not only at rehabilitating the men, but also to provide a way for them to earn the 2000 francs each needed to buy his passage home.

For those who would be repatriated, Péan noted that they would be going from the tropics to the temperate European climate where they would need warm clothing. This could be

198

furnished by The Salvation Army upon their arrival and the Army could also help them find work—this was all simple to write down, but represented a formidable undertaking. Certainly few employers would be inclined to hire known convicts from the colony that was notorious as a scourge upon the earth.

Péan finished his notations on September 12, 1928, the day before he landed at LeHavre.

With his superiors in The Salvation Army he set to work to make his dream a reality. In less than one year after his return to France, The Salvation Army officially approved his plan and asked the French government to support it.

Not all of Péan's time was devoted to the project. To carry out promises he had made to the convicts and libérés, he visited their families and relatives to deliver personal messages. Soon he began to receive letters of thanks from the men in the colony whose families had written them about Péan's visits. Some said they had heard about his plans to improve conditions in Guiana and that they wanted to help. A few said his ideas were very commendable but represented an impossible dream.

For four years Péan and his Salvation Army associates hammered away to stir up public interest in the penal colony so that the government would feel impelled to act. Newspapers and magazines added their editorial voices to promote the campaign, and in 1933 the French government authorized The Salvation Army to begin its work in Guiana.

A special project headquarters was established in Paris, and Péan traveled through villages, towns and cities throughout France, lecturing on what he had seen and heard, and what The Salvation Army proposed to do in the colony. He and his fellow officers solicited contributions of money, clothing, and other supplies that would be useful.

With such funds the Army bought tools, medicines, clothing and other goods to be transported to Guiana in the company of seven volunteer officers led by Péan. They sailed on July 6, 1933, and on July 30 Charles Péan looked again upon the cadaverous faces and bare, bug-bitten feet of the men of the *Bagne,* so forlorn in their pajama-like clothes.

199

Chapter 15

THE HARD WAY HOME

Charles Péan and his companions went immediately to Cayenne, where their arrival caused great excitement among the libérés. Near the dock the officers rented a small shack in which they stored the materials they had brought with them. Saws, planes and other tools were furnished to two libérés who were experienced carpenters and who set to work making beds, chairs and tables.

Next, Péan rented land on the Montjoly Peninsula, a few miles from Cayenne, to be cultivated and planted with vegetables by other libérés. Within two weeks The Salvation Army flag flew over the shack which served as temporary headquarters, and some 20 libérés were at work in the Montjoly camp.

Péan's dream of a hostel, restaurant and garden materialized in Cayenne, where he acquired a two-story building with 13 rooms in the Rue Malonet. One of the officers and a group of libérés swept and scrubbed the rooms until they were spotless. Others cleared away brush and debris from garden space adjacent to the building, and still others set to work making charcoal for Army use and for sale.

September marked an important milestone in Péan's plan, for the restaurant was opened.

"Our first meal was free," he told me. "Hundreds of men came to eat—and when they finished and left, there wasn't one

knife, fork or spoon in the place! They had stolen everything!"
He laughed at the recollection. "I sent a cable to my Paris
headquarters: 'Please send more knives, forks, spoons. All
stolen.' I soon got the answer: 'The Board urges you to watch
more closely what you give those men.'"

Beds manufactured in the carpenter shop were moved into
the upper rooms of the hostel and arranged in dormitory
fashion. For those libérés who had money, a clean bed could
be rented for one franc or less. For those who were broke there
was no charge, provided a bed was available.

At Montjoly the libérés constructed a road from their farm
to the main highway, erected huts, built a kitchen and even
improvised an irrigation system for their garden. The number
of workers doubled and within a few weeks they were selling
fruits, vegetables and charcoal in the town. Pigs and other
livestock were brought in and used both for food and breeding.

In keeping with the primary mission of the Army, the officer
in charge at Montjoly began each day by reading one passage
of Scripture to the men and singing one verse of a hymn with
them. Worship services were held every Sunday morning.

Péan and another captain established headquarters at St.
Laurent, leaving other officers at Montjoly and Cayenne. The
first six or eight libérés Péan brought in to help were emaciated
but happy—so happy, in fact, that two became ill and two
others got into a fight.

From the first day, lanes of libérés formed at Péan's
headquarters to pour their life stories (sometimes vivid with
imagined details) into his sympathetic ears and to seek productive work. A vacant one-story building in the woods outside
of town was converted into a workshop by the libérés, who
also fenced it in and prepared a kitchen garden inside the
fence. Part of the building was used as a dormitory, part as a
meeting hall. One ingenious libéré even built a bowling alley
beside the house.

With the work in progress, the libérés asked Péan for advances on their small wages. As soon as he paid them they
marched into town and to the nearest saloon, where they drank

201

until their money was gone, returning to the Army in two or three days with hangovers and remorse.

When the home was officially opened, the public and government officials were invited to attend. For the special occasion libérés were offered supper for one franc and were told that beds, for which a charge of one franc was normally made, would be free for the night. The cook and houseboy got uproariously drunk, and the libérés who would not have to spend the franc for a bed used the money instead to buy rum and went on an all-night binge.

In the morning Péan, though again stricken with fever, made an inspection which revealed that most of the tools in the workshop had been stolen, along with several bags of charcoal and a quantity of food, all of which apparently went in trade for more rum.

As weeks passed the three settlements at Cayenne, Montjoly and St. Laurent made considerable progress and so did the libérés. There were good crops of pineapples, corn and bananas. Jungle growth had given way to vegetable gardens and even to cultivated flowers. Water was piped in for drinking, cleaning and bathing. Henhouses were built and flocks of chickens were increasing.

Women officers brought by The Salvation Army from France were looked upon with reverence by the libérés. At no time did any of the men attempt to molest any of the women officers. One or two of the women brought their children with them, and the libérés took pleasure in making toys for the youngsters and playing games with them.

Pleased with such progress, Péan again returned to France and again visited families of men in the colony. Some of the libérés who had long since given up hope of going home had also stopped corresponding with their loved ones, but were now beginning to believe that The Salvation Army might really be able to perform miracles. In some cases Péan talked with wives who had not heard from their husbands for several years and had given them up for dead, only to learn that they were alive and might even be brought back home.

202

One day in 1935 a woman called to see Péan in Paris. "My sister is dying," she told him. "She has a son who is a libéré in Guiana and she prays constantly to see him before the end comes, but it will cost two thousand francs to pay his passage and we can never raise such a sum. Is there anything you can possibly do to help us bring the boy home to see his mother?"

With the help of his associates and contributions from other people who were sympathetic to his cause, Péan raised money to have the boy returned to France—the first man to be repatriated under The Salvation Army program that Péan had proposed some seven years earlier.

With the ice broken, Péan arranged for the return of 67 more libérés in 1936—North Africans, Arabs, Indo-Chinese and Frenchmen—all to their respective homelands. Many had found peace and hope at The Salvation Army Mercy Seat and were dedicated to new lives of Christian service. Others were simply glad to get away from what they considered a living hell. Few had any definite plans. Most were skinny and no longer young. The adjustments they would have to make in climate, human relationships and city life were formidable. Many were met by relatives and started on the journey home, while others were taken in by The Salvation Army which fed and sheltered them and tried to find them productive work.

Péan's efforts received wide public attention and the people of France set up a growing clamor for improvements to be made in the penal colony. The convicts were given better food and clean quarters, and morale among them grew increasingly higher. Recreation programs became popular and many men who once drowned their sorrows in rum actually turned to drinking lemonade! The spotlight of publicity which Péan and The Salvation Army had centered on the penal colony brought what the government itself called "severe criticisms" from many sources, and so strong was the public pressure that French officialdom was compelled to take decisive action.

On June 17, 1938, a government report to the President of the Republic pointed out that the *Bagne* had little deterrent effect, if any, and failed to provide opportunities for rehabilitation. Moreover, the prison colony was not the kind of place which added to the prestige of France as a nation. For these and other reasons, said the report, "the *Bagne* should disappear by extinction and Guiana will then be able to adapt itself progressively to a new economy."

When this news reached the colony the convicts and libérés ran from one to another, laughing, shouting, even singing. For weeks there was no other topic discussed throughout the colony, and there were frequent gatherings in The Salvation Army meeting halls to talk about the future and about the incredible achievement of Charles Péan and his Salvation Army associates.

The French government, however, could not simply abolish the colony overnight. It was decided that many convicts serving terms, especially convicted murderers, must remain, and that thieves might still be sentenced to Guiana. The libérés, however, would gradually be repatriated.

Péan made several trips between the colony and France to keep the program moving forward as much as possible, but in the midst of the movement came the Second World War. The Nazis were on the march against France, and the problems of the penal colony were pushed aside and forgotten by all except The Salvation Army.

The colony itself was virtually cut off from the rest of the world. Products raised by the libérés rotted in the fields for lack of export markets. Salvation Army funds were diverted to services among the fighting men, and the camp at Montjoly was closed for lack of operating money.

Under the Nazi war machine France was divided into the Vichy Government on the one hand and the Free French forces on the other. Each side had its sympathizers in Cayenne. In a search for volunteers a Free French officer recruited some 300 libérés from the colony and sent them into French Equatorial Africa with the fighting forces. The Vichy government, learning of this action and seeking to appease the Nazis, laid the blame on The Salvation Army captain supervising the St. Jean camp, where the libérés had been housed, and with his wife and three children he was expelled from the colony and confined temporarily in a concentration camp.

Once rid of The Salvation Army in St. Jean, the warders cut down on food, beat the convicts with whips, and worked them so unmercifully that within a few months the death rate climbed to nearly 50 per cent. Survivors were walking skeletons.

At the other installations, Cayenne and St. Laurent, The Salvation Army remained active, and with the end of the war Péan returned to Guiana to resume his program. The government itself now supplied money for the work and officially requested The Salvation Army to complete its plans.

In Guiana, Péan found his fellow officers weak and weary from years of the hardest imaginable work—cleaning, cooking, ministering to the sick and old, holding Gospel meetings, counseling and consoling friendless men, with never a day off, never any relief.

Péan and the other officers arranged for the repatriation of a number of libérés. Some of the convicts would be transferred to prisons in France where they would still be much better off than in the penal colony. Many libérés, having served their prison sentences, would be housed and fed by the Army when they reached France.

In August, 1946, 144 repatriates docked at Marseilles, each carrying all his wordly goods in his arms. They were taken to a Salvation Army hall and fed. Some had been imprisoned before the First World War, and each man marveled at the changes in his country. Some were met by their families and cried openly in their happy reunion. Throughout the night The Salvation Army put others aboard trains bound for their homes in distant French towns. Each was given shoes, heavy clothing, an overcoat and a woolen scarf.

Month after month men were taken out of Guiana to return to a decent life. Some remained in the colony under sentence, some were hospitalized, but the accent now was on rehabilitation for the prisoner, not punishment alone.

In October, 1952, some 24 libérés arrived in France—the last of more than 2000 taken from the *Bagne* to be repatriated. The

Salvation Army has kept in touch with many of these men, some of whom now hold highly responsible positions in big business firms. Others are happy in menial jobs, many are employed in Salvation Army institutions. Some still come in for help in finding new jobs or for counsel about personal problems. Many, of course, have failed to keep in touch with the Army, perhaps because it is a link with a past which they are anxious to forget.

It is with a great sense of accomplishment and pride that Charles Péan says, "Today Devil's Island is overgrown with cocoanut trees and bushes." With equal pride he wears the symbol of the French Legion of Honor, bestowed in recognition of his tremendous service to the nation and to mankind.

In July, 1960, the French government prepared to auction off the crumbling buildings, the rusting cells and the land where once had walked men without hope. The authorities on French Guiana have asked for the opportunity to buy some of the land, on which they may build beach cottages, a modern hotel and other attractions in the hope that they may induce tourists to visit their "islands in the sun." By the time this book is in print it may be that the underground dungeons once used to keep men in solitary confinement are already being dug out and transformed into swimming pools or sunken gardens.

Charles Péan, a tall, brisk 59 (in 1960), was an agricultural college student of 19 when he first met a group of Salvation Army officers in France and became so interested in their philosophies and programs that he decided to join their organization. As he said to me, "I sold all my books and microscope and tools, and I thought, 'Now I will be a poor man in uniform for the rest of my life.' But if nothing else, the abolition of the Guiana penal colony has made me rich beyond any possible dream."

Chapter 16

CHEER LEADERS

Benny, a Russian-born Jew, was arrested in New York to be tried in Detroit, Michigan, for stealing goods from a factory and re-selling them. Benny was convicted and sentenced to serve seven years in prison and to pay a fine of $10,000. The authorities discovered that while he was out on bail and traveling to Detroit for his trial he had gone via the Michigan Central Railroad through a part of Canada. Under the law and in light of his criminal record he was not eligible to re-enter the United States, and the authorities decided that upon his release from prison he must be deported to Russia.

Benny was frightened, for he knew that if he were sent back he would be persecuted and perhaps killed. Benny was not poor. He had made considerable money in the business world and had married a girl who was an American citizen, living with their children in a comfortable home. He could well afford to hire a competent attorney to fight his deportation, but instead he chose to ask the Immigration and Travel Bureau of The Salvation Army for help, and his request was channeled to the head of the Bureau, Brigadier Thomas Johnson.

When Johnson approached the U. S. Immigration and Naturalization Service for the facts in Benny's case, an Immigration inspector said, "I don't get it. This guy is well off financially. How come he goes to you instead of some lawyer who specializes in these cases?"

"Don't ask me," Johnson said. "I've been doing this work for forty years and nothing surprises me any more."

Later, when Johnson talked with Benny face to face, he asked him why he hadn't hired an attorney or asked for help from some of the competent Jewish welfare agencies. "I'll tell you," Benny said. "I heard from other guys that The Salvation Army could help me best if anybody could, and that if they couldn't, they'd tell me so."

After a study of the facts, Brigadier Johnson arranged for Benny to take up temporary residence in Canada and eventually to re-enter the United States legally and join his family.

The Salvation Army's Transportation and Immigration Bureau of the Eastern Territorial Headquarters in New York provides a unique service nationally. Since it has no counterparts in any of the other three Territories, if those Territories get cases involving immigration or naturalization problems they try to refer them to other local welfare agencies. If that does not work out, the Immigration Bureau in New York is asked to help. Travelers' Aid, the International Social Service, and similar agencies also refer cases to Brigadier Johnson, who is an authority in the field. He represents The Salvation Army on immigration matters in the United Nations, is chairman of a New York Committee on Immigration and Naturalization, and a member of the Immigration and Naturalization Conference, a national body.

"Deportation started with Adam and Eve," Tom Johnson told me. "Adam had no passport and Eve could produce no valid birth certificate. They had to hire a lawyer who turned out to be a snake in the grass!"

One of his most interesting cases involved a Frenchman named Henri who had enlisted in the United States Army in World War I and had served with the Philippine guerillas in World War II. (His service, at the time Johnson received the case, was not considered service qualifying for citizenship.)

Henri had a wife in California who, he learned, was unfaithful to him. He obtained a Mexican divorce by correspondence with a Texas attorney, and the ex-wife later remarried.

When World War II ended, Henri prepared to return to the United States and was given necessary official papers. At the Panama Canal an Immigration inspector checked Henri's papers and told him they were temporary only, and that he could not remain in the United States.

Henri went to Washington, checked again with Immigration headquarters there, and approached various Senators and Representatives to introduce a private bill that would make him an American citizen. He was unable, however, to obtain affidavits he needed for such action.

Somewhere he heard that if he were to marry an American citizen he would automatically become a citizen. In the tenement where he lived on New York's West Side he met a woman who had borne two illegitimate children. He married her and sired a third child.

He took his case to Brigadier Johnson, who sifted the facts, corresponded with the authorities in the Pacific, and spent time intermittently for five years to help Henri. It was finally decided that a hearing would be conducted in the U. S. Immigration Office and that it would probably be arranged for Henri to go to Montreal, get a visa, and enter the United States legally.

At the hearing Henri showed his marriage certificate and was asked if he had been married before. When he told about the Mexican divorce, they turned down his plea because the Justice and State Departments did not approve of proxy divorces. Henri's second marriage, in other words, was bigamous, and he was in more trouble than ever.

Brigadier Johnson communicated with The Salvation Army in Reno, Nevada, and arranged with the officer there to get Henri a job in a Reno hotel. An ex-judge who was a member of The Salvation Army's Advisory Board in Reno agreed to get Henri a proper divorce. He lived in Reno for six weeks until his divorce was granted, then his second wife went to Reno from New York and married Henri again.

Now the situation was quite in order and Brigadier Johnson was re-processing Henri's case when a new law was enacted providing that any man who had served in the Armed Forces during World War I was eligible for American citizenship. That included Henri.

Brigadier Johnson took Henri to the Federal Court in the Southern District of New York and stood at his side while he took the oath of American citizenship.

"Henri and his family are still living in New York and getting along very well," Johnson says.

Not all the work of Johnson's bureau deals with immigration and deportation. Travel service is also provided, and although most of it is rendered for Salvation Army personnel, it would be made available to anyone in need of help or advice.

Take a purely hypothetical case of a person preparing to make a round-the-world trip—you, for example. If you needed help which you might not otherwise obtain, The Salvation Army would check as to the time at your disposal, how long you wanted to stay at each place, and would contact transportation companies concerning portions of travel beyond their own lines. The Salvation Army would send you a form showing the documents you would need—passport, health certificate and so on—and information about the countries you would visit. They would tell you about currency regulations and Customs duties. If necessary, the Army would notify its offices in those countries to have someone meet you upon your arrival. For those not capable of doing it themselves, the Army would make necessary transportation reservations, get tickets (with your funds, of course), and see travelers safely off. Those who travel in groups such as Cook's Tours would obviously look to the travel agency and tour master for any assistance, and not to The Salvation Army. No fees are charged for the services rendered by the Army, though voluntary cash donations have been offered and gratefully received.

In 1959 Brigadier Johnson's Transportation and Immigration

Bureau served 1190 travelers. Of this number only about 55 were from the public at large, the others being members of The Salvation Army. The Army wants it known that it does not solicit travel business, though it is always ready to be of service to those travelers who genuinely need assistance.

Assistance of another kind is given to a different variety of travelers through another Salvation Army operation—Scandinavian work. In its early days The Salvation Army built up a strong and successful program in the Scandinavian countries which still exists. In 1884 three Swedish women Salvationists came to the United States from Stockholm, settling in Brooklyn, where they made friends with other Scandinavian people and attended worship services at a Brooklyn Salvation Army Corps, only to find that they had difficulty in understanding the English in which the services were conducted. Accordingly, the girls obtained permission to conduct a service in Swedish, and it was so well received that they rented a vacant store and held similar meetings regularly, paving the way for The Salvation Army to establish its first official Scandinavian Corps in December, 1887, headed by Captain Mary Hartelius and her sister Annie. Other Scandinavian Corps were subsequently opened in several other cities, followed by Corps aimed at bringing salvation and service to Germans, Italians and Chinese in their native languages.

Sr. Major Olof Lundgren, whose speech, mannerisms and delightful humor make him a kind of Salvation Army Victor Borge, has spent many years in Scandinavian work which, along the East coast, centers around Scandinavian seamen who come to the United States as members of crews of various ships and who seek out The Salvation Army as a home away from home.

In the Brooklyn Scandinavian Corps the sailors sing traditional songs in their own languages, get help from the officers in writing letters home, attend Scandinavian Christmas services and receive Christmas gifts from the Corps. For those who happen to be aboard ship and at sea on Christmas, The Salvation Army furnishes gifts to the ships' captains before sailing, to be distributed among the men on Christmas Eve.

Major Lundgren, who speaks Swedish, Norwegian, Danish and English, has been an officer for some 30 years. At one time he headed the local Scandinavian Corps, and he told me about a case which symbolized the kind of help the Army might give to Scandinavian seamen.

He received a telephone call from a Swedish friend, a woman, who had visited the prison hospital on Riker's Island and had seen two Swedish boys who had been brought there from Bellevue Hospital in New York. It seems the boys had gone out on a spree, got drunk, and were arrested. They could not speak English, so they were sent to Bellevue, then to Riker's Island, where they would stay until someone called for them or perhaps for life.

Lundgren promptly went to the Swedish Consul, who said he was unable to help the boys, so the Major and Mrs. Lundgren went to Riker's Island and talked to the sailors. They were horrified at being confined and terribly frustrated because they could not make themselves understood.

Through the Army's Prison Bureau, Major Lundgren met the Warden, who agreed to release the boys if The Salvation Army would be responsible for them. The Lundgrens took them to their own home, where Mrs. Lundgren prepared a typical Scandinavian dinner, then the Major got them a hotel room for the night. Next day he went to one of the seamen's unions and got both boys jobs on ships bound for Sweden. Later he received letters from one boy and from the mother of the other, thanking him for his help.

A few days before I talked with him, Major Lundgren had gone to a pier of the Swedish-American Steamship Line to see a friend off. On the dock he noticed an Italian boy soliciting telegrams, speaking English with a strong Swedish accent. His curiosity aroused, Lundgren stopped the boy.

"Were you born in Sweden?" he asked.

The boy laughed. "Naw! In the Bronx." His Swedish accent had vanished.

"That's a pretty good Swedish accent you've worked up."

"Ain't it, though? It's a business gimmick. But you ought to see when I work the Italian Line." He lapsed into an Italian accent. "'Atsa where I'm-a make-a the mon'!"

Accents and nationalities, colors and creeds are of little significance to The Salvation Army, and women of many kinds find a haven in its Women's Lodge at 11 Dominick Street in New York City. This is an attractive residence for women who are retired or earning low wages or being supported by welfare agencies. Although the age bracket is supposed to be 18 to 80, one resident is 89 years old and Brigadier Gladys Phillips, the officer in charge, says, "We sometimes break the rule to meet the need."

Brigadier Phillips, who has a youthful and sweet face, white hair, blue eyes and long, slender fingers, is frequently asked to take in a mother with children on a temporary basis. Most such referrals are made by Protestant, Catholic and Jewish welfare agencies, by after-care clinics in city and State hospitals, by correctional institutions, and by Travelers' Aid.

One Friday afternoon Brigadier Phillips received a telephone call from Travelers' Aid to the effect that an old lady had alighted from a plane at Idlewild Airport from Puerto Rico, expecting her children to meet her there. They had not appeared, and the woman could neither speak nor understand English. She was at least 80 years old, wore a little shawl over her plain blue dress, and indicated that relatives had put her aboard the plane in Puerto Rico. No one quite knew what to do with the old lady, but Brigadier Phillips agreed to give her a room at the Lodge until her problem was solved.

At the Lodge the women called her "Grandma" and tried to make her feel at home, but she cried often and was very upset because she felt that her daughter had deserted her. Since Grandma was unable to be understood, Brigadier Phillips looked through her luggage and found a letter from the daughter which showed that the old lady was supposed to have flown to Chicago instead of New York!

The Salvation Army got in touch with the daughter and put

Grandma aboard a plane to Chicago, where the two finally met.

One young girl referred to the Lodge by the Army's Family Service Bureau was very disturbed emotionally. After several months at the Lodge she came to Brigadier Phillips one day and said, "I'd like very much to have my mother with me for Christmas."

The girl's mother was an inmate of a State mental hospital to which she had been confined for 17 years. Brigadier Phillips called the hospital and learned that the mother was well enough to be discharged, but had no place to go and could not be released until the hospital authorities were sure she had a protective home and someone to care for her. Brigadier Phillips, working through the Family Service Bureau, arranged for the mother's discharge and to permit her to live at the Lodge on a trial basis.

Leaving the hospital the mother was quite overwhelmed by the sense of hurry, the noise, the crowds of people in the frightening outside world. At the Lodge she and her daughter hugged each other and cried and laughed and talked. Brigadier Phillips hovered close to the mother for weeks, leading her gently into social activities with other guests and letting her know that she had friends who cared about what she did and how she progressed.

The mother became so well-adjusted that the Army's Employment Bureau found her a job in the Men's Social Service Center. Subsequently she and her daughter left the Lodge, rented a small apartment which they enjoyed furnishing together, and today both are employed and happy.

Brigadier Phillips' job at the Lodge is not easy. Besides supervising her staff of 24, she is responsible for 110 women in residence, and although some have lived there for two years or more, others may be admitted on an emergency basis for two or three days at the request of other welfare agencies or the courts. About two thirds of the women are 50 years old or over. The others are young girls. The total includes whites and Negroes, Catholic, Protestant and Jewish.

214

The Salvation Army charges $12 a week per person for two in a room, $14 for a private room at the Lodge, which includes two meals daily. If a woman accepted at the Lodge is destitute, she may live there free until such time as she is able to pay her way.

The Lodge is as nice a hotel-like home as anyone would find in New York. Situated about a block from the entrance to the Holland Tunnel, it comprises a six-story main building and an adjacent five-story "emergency" building.

The main lobby is a large room with a big fireplace and comfortable chairs and sofas. On the window drapes is the design of a waterfall, and sometimes the more elderly guests straighten the folds of the drapes just to look at the picture as though it were a real waterfall. "This is such beautiful scenery," they say.

One woman whose room overlooks a huge automobile parking lot was to be transferred to another room, but pleaded not to be moved. "If I go I won't be able to see all those automobiles with all those lovely colors," she said. Watching the parking lot and cars was her greatest enjoyment.

The ladies at Christmas time in 1959 were all thrilled to be taken on a bus trip from the Battery to Columbus Circle in New York, taking picnic lunches. Many of the women have seldom seen the open country, and at the time of my visit Brigadier Phillips was hoping to find some way to finance a bus trip to take her guests on an outing in New Jersey.

Besides the comfortable lobby there is a sizeable clubroom with upholstered chairs, bookcases, and a grand piano, used for old-time songfests.

A large room that was once a gymnasium has been converted into an auditorium where worship services and meetings are held and where the women are given instruction in ceramics and other crafts.

There is a television room for those who are video fans, and every Thursday night they have movies. Once a month they invite oldsters from the neighborhood to a silver tea, "But we have no silver," Brigadier Phillips says with a grin. When this first started, many of the Lodge guests had never before attended a tea, did not know how they should dress. One 70-year-old lady sought fashion advice from a friend and was told she should wear a hat and gloves. Although she lived in the Lodge and rarely went out, she came downstairs to the tea wearing her best dress, a hat, and white gloves.

Every Monday evening there are vesper services which invited ministers and Salvation Army officers attend as guest speakers. A group of the ladies formed a choir and wear white choir robes made for them by their friends in the sewing classes.

Brigadier Phillips showed me their "roof garden," which consists of a few window boxes with plants on the roof. "If anyone has any plants they would like to give away," she says, "we would be most grateful for them. The ladies like to come up here and look at the few flowers we have, and they know each bloom so well they almost have names for them!"

A few of the Lodge guests call Brigadier Phillips "Mom," but most call her "Brigadier," and she thinks this is probably better in the interests of maintaining discipline. A native of Cleveland, Ohio, Gladys Phillips was brought up in the Reformed Church. One day a Salvation Army captain called at her parents' home, said he understood that Gladys played the piano, and asked if she might play it in the Salvation Army Sunday School. The local Corps had just been opened and had no song book, so Gladys brought her own hymnal. She immediately became interested in The Salvation Army youth program and in 1929 became a soldier in her 'teens. She has been at the Women's Lodge since 1956 and is on 24-hour duty, for the place is never closed and on Sundays and holidays when people in trouble cannot reach other welfare agencies they can always find a helping hand at The Salvation Army.

The Army operates another kind of unusual residence in New York City, officially dubbed "The John and Mary R. Markle Memorial Residence," but popularly known as the

216

"Evangeline Residence," one of 51 similar places in the world, 15 of which are in the United States.

John Markle, son of a Pennsylvania anthracite pioneer, was a coal tycoon whose memorial to his deceased wife and whose respect and admiration for The Salvation Army took the form of a gift of $500,000 to be used to build a residence hotel for young business women in New York, a place with the same objectives as "Evangeline Residences" in other cities. (The "Evangeline Residences" are named for General Evangeline Booth, who inaugurated them to provide respectable homes in big cities for business girls earning modest salaries.)

Now worth an estimated $2,500,000, the Markle Memorial Residence is an 18-story building at 123 West 13th Street, New York City, with 260 single and 65 double rooms, accommodating about 330 business women under the age of 35 years. Average age of those in residence at the time of my visit was 22-25 years. It offers sewing facilities, a huge main lounge, a library, a gymnasium and swimming pool, a laundry, a television room, kitchenette, a number of "practice rooms" with pianos for study or amusement, exercise rooms, a typing room equipped with typewriters, and a secluded roof garden. A dining room, supervised by an experienced dietitian, provides a cafeteria breakfast and dinner at night. For room, meals, and use of all of the facilities, a girl in a single room pays from $18.90 to $22.40 weekly. Girls in larger double rooms pay from $17.90 to $22.40 weekly.

The girls, both white and Negro, are Protestants, Jews and Catholics, mostly from cities and towns other than New York. They are employed as secretaries, typists, physical therapists, dressmakers, singers, actresses, artists, and in a variety of other occupations. Residents have included TV star Anita Bryan from the George Gobel Show, and Eileen Farrell of the Metropolitan Opera Company.

The building is managed and maintained by a staff of 70 people under the direction of Brigadier and Mrs. Harold Anderson, assisted by Brigadier and Mrs. George Baggs. It is not supported by public contributions made to The Salvation

Army, but is self-supporting, operating primarily within the income received from its girl residents, although the swimming and gymnasium facilities are rented at specified times to churches and schools.

There are certain qualifications for guests. A resident must take both room and meals and cannot rent a room only. A prospective boarder fills out an application accompanied by suitable references and is personally interviewed to answer questions that will help them determine whether or not her admission to the residence will actually fill a need for the girl.

"If a business girl is making enough money so that she could afford to rent a small apartment, we would probably turn down her application to live here," the assistant manager told me. "If we were to accept her, we might be depriving some other girl, who is earning much less, of a good place to live."

Although there is no arbitrary salary limit for applicants, it appears that a girl earning more than $70 or $75 a week would not be admitted. There has never been a time when the place was not filled to capacity. If a girl applies for a room and none is available she is referred to various approved rooming houses in the city. Vacancies occur when some leave to get married or to live in apartments when they can afford to do so.

As part of the Markle Memorial Residence, The Salvation Army operates "Evangeline by the Sea," an ocean resort at North Long Branch, New Jersey, where business girls and women may enjoy a seaside vacation on a modest budget. Daily rates are $4.00, covering room, breakfast and dinner. The weekly rate for room and two meals daily is $24.00. For this the girls also get sun and surf, have beach parties, play shuffleboard, croquet, ping-pong, go bicycling, and relax in bright and happy surroundings.

For many people bright and happy surroundings are the exception rather than the rule, especially in crowded New York neighborhoods such as Harlem, where the population is predominantly Negro and Puerto Rican. Here The Salvation Army fills a real need with its Harlem Corps and Red Shield Community Center, located in the heart of Harlem at 216 West

218

124th Street, where I talked with Lt. Abraham Johnson, a pleasant young Negro officer, and with Loften Mitchell, also a Negro, who directs the Community Center for New York's Department of Welfare. The Welfare Department provides the staff to administer affairs of the Center, and The Salvation Army provides the building and facilities.

One of the main programs of the Harlem Center deals with the senior citizen. Elderly men and women, white and colored, enjoy classes in sewing, painting, carpentry, choral singing, public speaking, lip reading (about 80 percent are hard of hearing), and other crafts of therapeutic value. Average age of the group is 75 years.

In 1960 the old folks of the Harlem Center staged a fashion show with the help of Zelda Wynn, an attractive Negro girl who is considered one of the outstanding couturiers in New York. The oldest member of the Center—and the oldest model at the show—was Alice Brown, who is 106 and a former slave from Lexington, Virginia. Youngest model was 60. Fashion models are not supposed to sit down while waiting to appear on stage, to avoid wrinkling their gowns. Because of Mother Brown's age her friends tried to have her seated as she awaited her turn, but she said, "No, sir—I'll stand, like everybody else." She was the twelfth to appear, and she modeled a black moss crepe dress with a lavender dickey, a lavender straw bonnet with a pink tone, black shoes, black gloves, and a cane.

A reporter from the New York *Times* asked Mother Brown if she was feeling all right, or whether anything hurt her. "Well, sir," she said, "my feet hurt some, but I found out that in this life something's got to hurt now and then, else we don't appreciate it when the hurt's gone."

Those who attend the Community Center may get lunch for 25 cents. Non-members pay a dime more. Some who are destitute are fed without charge. Sample luncheon: Tunafish loaf, spinach, mashed potato, bread and butter, dessert, coffee.

The oldsters have a recreation room with card tables and a piano, and are trying to build up a library, including books

219

in Braille for the blind. Once a week a volunteer comes in to read aloud.

In the Sewing Room I met several Negro ladies hard at work on various projects. One of them, Mrs. Bradley, had embroidered several beautiful quilts, one with a picture of The Last Supper, one with figures of the Disciples, another with brightly-colored butterflies.

There is a dark room where those studying photography may develop and print their own pictures. In the studio for Arts, Crafts and Ceramics there are several paintings and ceramic figures which the instructor, a professional artist named Paul Spyropoulos, says reflect portions of the lives of his students. I saw one ceramic log cabin which Spyropoulos explained was a miniature of the cabin in which the ceramicist once lived.

An important part of the 5-story building is The Salvation Army Corps, or chapel, on the first floor. Here, as in all Salvation Army installations, the visitor is impressed with the neatness and cleanliness of the room, with its highly polished light oak pews, light-colored tile floor, green walls and maroon drapes. The chapel seats about 250, but Lieutenant Johnson told me that the Sunday morning attendance averages about 100. In addition there are about 105 children in the Sunday School. "We could have two hundred if we could only get the necessary teachers," he said.

All young people get enthusiastic attention at the Center. They have a game room where they play volley ball and other supervised sports; there is a body-building class for boys 12 to 16, a woodworking shop with power tools, and a machine shop.

The machine shop area was protected by heavy wire screening. "We had to enclose the equipment with the screen to prevent thefts," Lieutenant Johnson said. "If we didn't, some of the dope addicts in the neighborhood would come in and steal everything and sell it to get money to buy drugs."

A day camp is conducted at the Center in July and August for young boys and girls at a cost of $5 each for the entire season. The camp is operated by a staff of four paid workers and six to eight volunteers who give instruction in arts and crafts, home economics, woodworking, and Bible study. The children are taken on outings and given free lunches, and all activity is aimed at helping them to become good citizens and good Christians.

Part of the Center is used for The Salvation Army's Home League, an organization similar to the Ladies' Aid Society, where women create and work on projects in sewing or other home arts that will produce something of service to those in need.

The Home League, founded in 1907, has nearly 300,000 members in all parts of the world, including about 49,000 in the United States. Its expressed objectives as set out in 1907 were "to combat the growing tendency to neglect the fostering of true home life and to encourage thrift and hygiene." It was formally launched in London by Mrs. Bramwell Booth, daughter-in-law of General William Booth.

Throughout the world the Home League exists in virtually every Salvation Army Corps and in such places as missionary hospitals, in leper colonies and in hostels for the homeless in some European cities. Women living with service-men husbands far from their homeland welcome the weekly League meetings.

While most League meetings are held in the afternoon, the cool of the evening is a better time in tropical countries. In Nigeria, where women work all day in the fields, they have their meetings at six in the morning.

In Punta Arenas, on the Straits of Magellan at the tip of South America, The Salvation Army is popular among the 35,000 inhabitants and the Home League is a welcome activity to many of the Scottish, Czechoslovakian and American families in the area.

Punta Arenas is always windswept, and being close to the Antarctic Circle it is usually cold or chilly. Bad weather sometimes discourages open-air street meetings, but they are held whenever possible, and then the wife of the commanding officer ties on her bonnet with a scarf and is perhaps the only Salvation Army lassie to wear *pantalones,* because the whipping wind makes a skirt inadvisable.

Home League members attend meetings in heavy clothing and huddle in a circle around a pot-bellied wood-burning stove, where they plan their work. One project undertook to provide food and clothing for a fast-diminishing tribe of poverty-stricken Alakalufe Indians living on a remote island near Tierra del Fuego

The Home League in France proudly displays a Home League banner whose design was voted the best among many submitted in a contest. The members wanted to make the new banner of expensive material, but their tiny budget would not permit such extravagance. One day the Home League Secretary showed the banner design to another woman officer and said she hoped that sometime they could buy enough satin to make it and find someone to embroider it.

Later that week a uniformed chauffeur in a Rolls-Royce stopped at Salvation Army headquarters and delivered to the Home League Secretary a package wrapped in white paper and tied with a beautiful white ribbon. In the package was enough satin for the new banner and a gift card from Madame Schiaparelli, world-famous *haute couturière.*

The banner design was skillfully embroidered by a mother and daughter who were Rumanian refugees. Once wealthy, they had lost their home and possessions through political tyranny and had fled to France, where they lived in a dilapidated shack with no heat, light or water. Hungry, lonely and despondent, they made a suicide pact and planned to drown themselves in the Seine.

On their way to the river they saw a Salvation Army lassie selling copies of *The War Cry.* "What a sweet face she has," the mother said. "If we had met someone like her when we first came here, perhaps things would have been different."

"We can talk to her now," the daughter said.

"No, not now. It's too late."

"No, mother, it isn't."

"We have never asked others for help. I shall not begin now." The mother's pride was standing in her way.

"Then I will!" the daughter said.

She ran from her protesting mother to the Salvation Army officer and rapidly and tearfully blurted out her story. The officer persuaded both women to come to Salvation Army headquarters, where they were fed and given beds. In the course of their conversation the mother and daughter revealed that they were skilled at embroidery. An officer mentioned the Home League banner, and the women asked that they be permitted to embroider the design as an expression of their appreciation to the Army. Today the satin banner with its embroidered emblem is a prized possession of the Home League in Paris.

The League program is adapted to national and local needs. It may be a lesson in simple hygiene for primitive Maori women, or a washing machine demonstration in some village or suburb. In some missionary lands the Home League meeting marks the occasion when a woman handles needle and thread for the first time and triumphantly produces her first home-made garment. Often, too, she gets her first lessons in family diet and baby care.

In service to the community, a group of Home League members in Tennessee erected a much-needed bus-stop shelter. In Germany, members do the mending for welfare homes. In India's Lushai Hills the Home League provides food and clothing for motherless babies who, in former times, were left to die. Members of a Home League in Rhodesia made 50,000 bricks to raise funds to recondition their meeting hall, and in Natal four Home League women themselves built the hall in which The Salvation Army holds its worship services.

Volunteers in another humanitarian activity are members of the Army's League of Mercy, a group of men and women who do their utmost to bring cheer and hope to those who are ill and lonely. I talked with the Secretary of the Greater New York League of Mercy, Mrs. Brigadier John Phillips. (This title shows that Mrs. Phillips' husband is living. If she were a widow, her title would be "Brigadier Mrs. John Phillips.")

"To become a member of our League of Mercy, a woman must be a Christian, must be able to pray, must be neat in appearance and kindly in manner," Mrs. Phillips said. "Many are Salvationists and many are not. We have 183 members in the Greater New York area, and one Salvation Army officer leads each group."

At New York's Welfare Island, a county hospital for the destitute and for some children with muscular diseases, League of Mercy members keep patients supplied with stationery, clothing, slippers, robes, or various necessities.

At Bellevue Hospital the ladies of the League chat with patients, perform little acts of kindness, and pray with them if they are asked to do so.

At King's County Hospital, just before my visit with Mrs. Phillips, members of the League had visited 825 patients in 15 hours, distributed candy, toys, puzzles, 350 copies of *The War Cry* (to those who asked for copies), 4 copies of the New Testament. They also used their own money to buy special candy for 22 diabetic patients, first obtaining permission from the doctors.

In Veterans' hospitals, among other things, the League holds birthday parties each month for all those having birthdays during the month. They furnish birthday cakes, sing songs, tell stories.

In the St. Albans Hospital the League members bring shaving cream, toothbrushes, toothpaste, soap, writing paper and stamps to the patients.

In Harlem Hospital and in the Welfare Island children's wards the League of Mercy distributed Easter baskets filled with candy. The children were especially thrilled when they discovered that the baskets had been prepared and donated by the Radio City Music Hall "Rockettes," whose incomparable precision dancing has won them world-wide fame.

Every Christmas the League of Mercy buys gifts for scores of men in the armed forces. In 1959, for example, they handed out hundreds of pocket notebooks with a telephone index, fitted with a ball-point pen. The 1960 gift was a leather pocket case containing a comb, nail file and nail clipper.

One Salvation Army officer has chosen to make more than 10,000 artificial corsages for women hospital patients every year.

In weekly and monthly hospital visits the League members give children copies of the Army magazine, *The Young Soldier,* and three lollipops if the youngsters are permitted to have them. No gifts of any kind are made to patients unless hospital authorities approve the giving.

One man, as a League of Mercy volunteer, in one month gave patients at Welfare Island 2 table model radios, 20 wallets with ball-point pens, 10 calendar-covered scratch pads, 30 razor blades, perfume for 3 patients, several pairs of house slippers and socks, writing paper and envelopes, and 10 pounds of candy. In addition he has taken patients back and forth to movies, has written letters for them, and fed five patients lunch and supper in bed. He takes patients to visit friends in other wards, talks with those who like to talk, and reads the Bible aloud to those who ask him to.

Mrs. Phillips gave me a copy of her annual statistical report for the year 1959, showing that the League of Mercy in Greater New York, with 183 members, had spent nearly 3400 hours visiting 113,389 hospital patients and distributed a total of 237,205 gifts, all designed to bring happiness to people who are ill or friendless and lonely.

Chapter 17

THE GLOBAL FIGHT

Elephants and hungry lions were bad enough, but the lizards, gnats, scorpions, cockroaches, mosquitoes, sand-fleas and white ants of Africa were even worse. All, however, were unimportant to some twenty or more natives standing in line outside the door of a small building in the Congo—men, women and children, each wanting help from the person who lived there.

A husband wanted to get back his wife, who left him because he refused to give her soap and matches. A tall, skinny man wanted to borrow money to repair a bicycle. A short, pudgy African policeman wanted a cloth badge sewn on his uniform. A youth waited with a girl his own age, and someone in the line asked what he wanted.

"I will show my girl to the Major," he said, "and if the Major approves I will marry her. If not, I'll find another."

The Major is father, mother, sister, brother, Beatrice Fairfax and guardian angel to these people and scores like them. Moreover, the Major is a woman—Major Ruth Siegfried, of The Salvation Army.

An Alsatian, Ruth Siegfried has lived and worked in the Congo for so many years that she regards Africa as home. "If you wander about the world, your homeland is the place where you can give your heart away," she says.

Her job is "to lead my boys to Christianity." She adds, however, "I don't serve merely to save people from Hell. I aim to make them happier here on earth, to lead them to light— but it's easier to walk on the edge of a knife blade than to live out integral Christianity here. I'm really making it possible for these people to earn money. The more they know, the better jobs they find and the more they enjoy life, and for that they need neither our mission nor Christianity."

Typewriting, says Major Siegfried, is one of the few occupations held "in honor," because it pays enough for the typist to buy a European suit, a hat, a bright necktie, a camera, and a record-player. The natives think that most Europeans are rich and mean, are out to exploit Africa, and with money can get or do anything they wish. For this reason Ruth Siegfried uses parables to teach her flock. Christ is the Sun who gives light. *Mama Alanga Njembo* is Mother Earth, on which they thrive. The students learn that they have no real light of their own and that it is their duty to radiate the light they receive by serving others. This, the Major tells them, is the chief object of education, not learning typing so that they may buy felt hats and bright neckwear.

In July, 1960, the Belgian Congo that Ruth Siegfried called home became The Congo, a new republic given its independence by Belgium. Within a few days Congolese troops revolted, attacked Belgian men, women and children, and the new nation was plunged into chaos. Troops were dispatched from Belgium to protect Belgian nationals, and subsequently a United Nations force from several UN countries was flown into the Congo to restore and maintain order.

In the midst of the pillaging, murder, rapes and beatings, officers of The Salvation Army stepped up their efforts to "save and serve." The Salvation Army in the Congo, with headquarters in Léopoldville, has a rather extensive operation, with 210 officers, 22 cadets, 295 employees, 75 Corps, 252 outposts, 5 dispensaries and clinics, and 72 educational centers, all under the direction of Territorial Commander Colonel Victor Dufays.

Reports of Salvation Army activity in the Congo revolt were

227

just beginning to reach General Wilfred Kitching at International Headquarters in London as this book was in preparation, but I was able to get a general idea of developments at a time when the whole situation was still fluid.

Colonel Dufays was preparing to go to Paris to join his wife on homeland leave, but when the rebellion broke he chose to remain in the Congo to encourage and guide his officers and people. General Kitching was able to keep in touch by cable with Colonel Dufays and with Lt. Col. Marcel Beney, commanding the Salvation Army territory of French Equatorial Africa, adjoining the Congo, and learned that all Salvation Army missionary officers were safe, including 40 working in or near Léopoldville.

According to International Headquarters, "It has been necessary to evacuate wives and children of certain missionary officers on the advice of the Embassy. They are generally officers from Switzerland and The Netherlands. This upheaval has caused a situation which is being met by our officers in various other centers. The evacuation of so many thousands of people has presented a problem, but Salvationists in Brussels are at the airport day and night welcoming and helping the refugees as they arrive from the Congo."

The report adds, "An official camp has been set up in Brazzaville for the refugees, and here we must pay a warm tribute to the work of Lt. Col. and Mrs. Beney."

In East Africa, The Salvation Army was asked to house, feed and otherwise help hundreds of refugees from the strife-torn areas.

In an effort to obtain more detailed information about Salvation Army activities in the Congo, I asked its national headquarters in New York to communicate with international headquarters in London, which subsequently answered that it had only one detailed report. Published in *The War Cry* for the information of all Salvationists, here is the report:

"Major Gabrielle Becquet arrived back home in Léopoldville from her furlough on August 28 [1960]. She was arrested by 20 Congolese soldiers with guns, and taken to court. The Congolese judge before whom she appeared designated her as a spy, probably because she was Belgian, and stated that she would be imprisoned and eventually deported to her own country.

The Major asked to speak in her own defense. She told the story of her great love for the black people and her 25 years of devoted service and sacrifice on their behalf. Major Becquet explained the purpose of the Army and its school work, as well as its evangelistic program.

Her deep sympathy, emotion and love broke down the resistance of the judge, who was even brought to tears and stated, 'Your love for our people is even greater than our own.' He released her from custody and put his own chauffeur and car at her disposal for return home. The judge also stated that the government, in spite of its financial problem, would continue subsidy for Army schools. The subsidy is currently being received and our work in the schools carried on without any disturbance to program or people."

In Southern Rhodesia, where The Salvation Army has 384 officers, 738 employees, 194 Corps, 83 outposts, 12 boarding schools, 176 day schools, 2 night schools, 2 hospitals, 6 dispensaries and one leprosy settlement, uprisings drove a thousand or more refugees out of Salisbury to Bulawayo. The Salvation Army enlisted the help of various residents to provide food and shelter for the evacuees and distributed food and clothing brought to the refugee center by airplane.

I wonder what effect the uprisings will have upon the work being done by Major Ruth Hacking, a British missionary nurse working in The Salvation Army's Tshelanyemba clinic, 120 miles from Bulawayo. Her little bush hospital, with its 35 beds, is three miles from the nearest village and 23 miles from the nearest doctor. With her 13 years of experience she must do much more than is expected of any nurse—dentistry, forceps deliveries, the treatment of wounds. One man was brought to her clinic with half his nose almost split from his face. Using the sensitive skill that comes only with knowledge and practice, Major Hacking stitched the nose, which healed perfectly with only a faint scar. So far as I know she is still continuing her service to the natives.

A short time before the African uprisings began, I talked with Captain and Mrs. A. Lyndon Taylor, who were on leave in the United States from their assigned task of training school teachers at Howard Institute, a Salvation Army institution 50 miles north of Salisbury in Southern Rhodesia. Captain Taylor is British, his wife American. This young couple, parents of two boys, are grandchildren of Salvation Army officers, and at the time of our visit had served for more than five years at Howard Institute.

Howard Institute is not only a school for teacher training, but also encompasses a hospital, a central primary school, and a training college for Salvation Army officers. The Taylors live at the Institute, along with several American, Canadian, Norwegian, Scottish and British officers.

In Southern Rhodesia certain areas are set aside for Africans only, and by special permission Howard Institute is situated in an African sector. It serves about a thousand people, many of whom are children. The Institute operates its own farm, raises vegetables, chickens and cattle. One officer in charge of the Agriculture Department teaches agriculture in the mission schools and also runs the Institute's farm.

The Institute has one of the only three Domestic Science Departments in the entire country, and also has a modern woodworking shop for boys.

At their home the Taylors raise sweet peas, roses, zinnias, gardenias, poinsettias, carnations and hibiscus. Tropical fruits include the mango, pawpaw, avocado, lemons and oranges.

In its teacher training the Institute educates African youth to teach and preach. "The ultimate objective is to train young people and to persuade them to follow Christ," Captain Taylor says. "We try not only to tend to the needs of the body and the mind, but also needs of the spirit, through The Salvation

230

Army as part of the Church in Africa. Mainly this is done through education. If the Christian church does not do the educating it will be done by non-Christian agencies, and if the African's education is entirely secular there will be nothing to replace the ancient superstitions and ideas that he has left behind in the bush. Christian teachings make a satisfactory replacement for these."

Superstition creates obstacles for the African teacher. Under Salvation Army doctrines, if an African accepts Christ he must burn all magic charms and other materials he may have to drive away "devils," and "devils" take many forms in the primitive African mind. One boy was suddenly taken ill in class, and although he knew he should go to the hospital he tried to remain in school to finish his final examinations. He finally felt so sick that he left the classroom, went outdoors and cut deep gashes in his arms "to let out the evil spirits." If he had not been found and treated promptly he might have bled to death.

Superstition may also interfere with classroom discipline. As an example, an African teacher might be reluctant to discipline a boy in his class for fear that the boy's family would retaliate by casting an evil spell upon him. Potential teachers in training at the Institute must be able to accept discipline themselves, else they cannot be expected to discipline others.

"If a boy in teacher training should disobey some rule he is put out digging a ditch for two or three days," Captain Taylor says. "If he were in a government institution he would be thrown out completely. We've found that infractions don't happen often, and that if we show that we will enforce a strict rule we generally don't have to use it."

One boy hit another over the head with a chair and was punished by being made to dig a ditch for a week. After a couple of days of digging he rebelled and was promptly dismissed. About two years later he returned to the Institute, much more mature and determined to make a success.

Says Taylor, "Often they don't develop in character until they reach some crisis which brings them up with a start and changes their lives. Sometimes they resent it, but more often we find that discipline may bring about a healthful turning point in the life of the one being punished."

By tribal custom in the primitive bush, if a boy did something wrong like "spoiling" a girl (as they call it), he would be killed immediately, so that under these customs they were held to a rigid code of morals by fear alone. When they learn about Christianity and hear talk about the forgiveness of sins, their old native beliefs begin to fade and their new philosophy is, "Now if I do anything wrong I won't be beaten or killed. I'll be forgiven." Without firm discipline they get the mistaken impression that they may do anything they please without punishment.

Applications for teacher-training number about 800 a year, of which about 250 are from Salvationists. About 50 to 60 applicants are accepted each year, ranging in age from 16 to 27 years. There are two courses, the "lower" and the "higher." The lower course trains students to teach the first five years of school. The higher course is for those who will teach children throughout the first eight years of school life.

The African children go to village schools for five years, though plans are under way to provide a full eight-year course for each village school. Those five-year students who show the most progress are sent to boarding schools in larger mission stations for three more years.

There is one Salvation Army secondary (high) school in the area, carved out of virgin land in the busy country. The Army caused roads to be bulldozed, put in electric power, installed a pump in a river to get water, and built a 30,000-gallon tank for a reserve water supply. Buildings and facilities were completed within one year with African labor under supervision of the Institute, and the school is today a showplace in Southern Rhodesia.

The over-all educational system is controlled by the government, which pays the salaries of the teaching staff for each mission, including the Salvation Army missions. They may teach their own religious doctrines, but all other subjects are government-controlled. A single girl Salvation Army officer with a Master's degree may receive a salary from the government of a thousand pounds Sterling (about $2800) a year. Of this she would actually receive about 200 pounds ($560) a year, plus 150 pounds ($420) for maintenance of her house and furnishings, as her Salvation Army salary. The other 650 pounds goes to The Salvation Army and is put with other funds to maintain all buildings, clerical expenses, and to promote its educational work.

The Salvation Army, according to the Taylors, is attractive to the African, who likes the colorful uniform and flag, the loud brass horns, the bass drum, the tambourine and the singing. "They have a wonderful sense of rhythm and harmony," Captain Taylor says. "Their children can actually harmonize when they're only five years old. And the African has a very strong leaning towards reverence in prayer."

A Salvation Army band marching through the African settlement in the city of Salisbury, some 50 miles from the Institute, draws a great crowd quickly, mostly because there is no incentive for the people to stay at home, and because they like the music. Accordingly, there is endless opportunity to preach the Gospel.

In discussing the population generally, Captain Taylor estimated that there are about 2½ million Africans in Southern Rhodesia, making about 13 Africans to each European. Most Africans are unskilled laborers, he said, working in factories, driving trucks and busses, although there are many clerical workers in firms such as Lever Brothers, and many policemen, firemen and mail carriers. As in other parts of Africa there is a breach between white and black. Europeans want African workmen to get the same pay as white workmen, but this would mean that the African would have to be equally skillful, which he isn't. Under such a policy, thousands of Africans would lose what jobs they have, for which they are now paid much lower wages than white men doing the same kind of work.

The men in the towns drink native beer, which is not very

strong. One of the first crises in a multiracial state is, "Should European liquors be sold to Africans? Should Africans have access to hard liquor?"

"The church is in an awkward situation," Captain Taylor points out. "If it answers 'No,' it can be accused of supporting the color bar. If it says 'Yes,' the result may be to its great disadvantage. There is a lot of social drinking among Europeans in Africa, and there are heavy publicity campaigns designed to induce Africans to drink beer and smoke cigarettes."

The African still practices polygamy. When a man wants to marry he is expected to pay a "lobola," or "bride price," probably including money and cattle, so that an African father enjoys having many daughters, each representing a dollar sign. Since many cannot or will not pay, they are secretly intimate with girls and create serious moral problems. The African is cautious about marrying a well-educated girl, because he must pay more for her and will have less obedience than he would get from an ignorant wife.

According to native custom a man is married as soon as he makes his first "lobola" payment. Often when his wife becomes pregnant he brings her to The Salvation Army to be married by Christian rites so that everything will be proper in the Army's eyes.

When I talked with the Taylors they were enjoying their first home leave in five years. Every five years The Salvation Army foreign missionary gets five months' home leave, but gets little time off during the five years. In one five-year hitch the Taylors had about 24 days off. "But on a missionary's salary we can't afford a car, so even when we get a little time off we can't go much of anywhere," Mrs. Taylor told me.

What of the future? I asked this question when none of us could know about the bloody African uprisings soon to come.

"Modern civilized ways are a great strain on the African people," Captain Taylor said. "Once the men lived leisurely, doing nothing, making no progress, having no real culture. Now they must work to be educated. They see the world whizzing past them. They hear our talk about interplanetary

234

travel and space exploration, something which is far beyond their simple understanding. But a new generation of African children will soon learn the new ways and acquire modern knowledge, and they will be quite different from their parents. In time, as the African gets more and more education, he will take on more and more responsibility for the welfare of his people and his country."

People in all countries know and appreciate the work done by The Salvation Army in their behalf, but comparatively few realize the extent and variety of this work, or that The Salvation Army, because of its international nature, is classed as a non-governmental agency related to the Economic and Social Council of the United Nations, working with the World Health Organization, UNESCO, and other specialized UN agencies in various countries.

In Germany The Salvation Army has ministered to thousands of displaced people, feeding the hungry, treating the sick, comforting the dying. One Austrian Salvation Army officer, working in an area with 786 refugee camps, wrote in his diary: "In one of the worst camps we found a family of fourteen in two poor rooms with hardly any bedding. Another room was divided by sheets hung up on string and three families live in it. One child is sick and the father is in a sanitarium. The clothing we brought was received like a gift from Heaven. A gypsy refugee camp was a veritable hell. The people live in a dirty stone barracks, caravans, an old boat and an old omnibus. No wonder so many of them are ill. The clothing we distributed and our songs and prayers were much appreciated."

In its command in Hong Kong, China, The Salvation Army has eight Corps, a young men's hostel, three medical clinics, two day nurseries, a home for delinquent girls, a "street sleepers'" shelter, three primary and two sub-primary schools, and a rehabilitation center for men.

The Salvation Army is also active in Ceylon. In one location its meetings were attended frequently by a local drunk who, despite his wobbly condition, was always made to feel welcome. One day he surprised everybody by walking to the

Mercy Seat to accept Christ as his Savior. The officer in charge put his arms around the man, said a prayer, then suggested that the penitent pray for himself.

"I'm sorry, but I don't know how to pray," the man said. "I can whistle, though."

"Then you whistle a prayer," the officer said, and the new convert whistled beautiful bird songs which were heard and answered, because he became a sober and active Salvationist.

In Japan, where The Salvation Army has 249 officers, 14 cadets, 271 employees, 58 Corps, 64 outposts, and 18 institutions of varying kinds, clothing, food, medical supplies and fresh water have often been distributed to victims of floods and typhoons. In the winter season the Army's officers patrol the streets of Tokyo offering food and shelter to men who have neither.

One of the most dramatic episodes in Salvation Army history took place in Japan in 1900 and is worth recording here. At that time prostitutes in Japan were licensed, and thousands of young girls were held in virtual slavery in "legal" bawdy houses. In Tokyo, one licensed part of the city boasted 5000 prostitutes, none of whom were permitted to leave an establishment without written permission of the brothel keeper and the manager of the licensed quarter.

Colonel Henry Bullard, then in charge of The Salvation Army's work in Japan, discovered a clause in the law under which the girls could be released. He decided to mobilize his forces and march on the most notorious quarter in Tokyo to bring this news to the girls and to offer them the shelter of a Salvation Army rescue home.

Bullard and his fifty officers spent most of the night in prayer. At dawn they assembled with The Salvation Army flag and a big bass drum. They carried copies of *The War Cry* which told how the girls could get their freedom. With flag flying and drum beating they marched into the sin-soaked neighborhood. The thumping of the drum brought the girls to the doors and windows and then into the streets, where the

236

officers gave them copies of the magazine and asked them to seek their freedom.

When the brothel keepers realized what was going on they gathered their minions and thugs and waded into the Salvationists with clubs and fists. One brothel keeper seized The Salvation Army flag, ripped it from its staff and savagely tore it to shreds. Another drove his foot through the bass drum, yanked it away from the drummer and jumped on it to smash the wooden frame. The police finally broke up the fight and the girls returned to the houses—but not for long.

The Salvation Army used other drums for more "invasions" and became so persistent in its battle against organized prostitution that within two months the Emperor signed a decree permitting any prostitute who wanted freedom to make her wishes known at the nearest police station. More than 12,000 girls took advantage of the decree within the first year.

Today, in Indonesia, Korea, Malaya, New Zealand, Pakistan, Ceylon, in Africa, South America, Europe, the United States —in all countries of the free world—The Salvation Army carries on activities such as those you have read about in this book. It even has its own navy!

The Salvation Army's fleet consists of five vessels—the *Noah Maru* ("Noah's Ark"), the *Febe,* the *William Booth,* the *Salvo,* and *La Peniche* ("The Barge").

The *Febe,* a converted pleasure yacht, cruises the extensive inland waterways of The Netherlands, bringing the Gospel to thousands of men, women and children.

The *Noah Maru* generally remains at anchor in the Kyobashi River at Hiroshima, Japan, where as many as 70 hungry and destitute men come aboard nightly to attend worship services and to get food and a place to sleep.

La Peniche is also a floating shelter on the Seine in Paris. It has beds for 75 men, but in wintry weather its officers permit as many as 200 homeless men to come aboard for food and warmth. For some ten years *La Peniche* has been skippered by a woman, Major Georgette Gogibus, whose kindness and generosity is known to some 40,000 men who walked her gangplank.

The *Salvo*, a 72-foot motor vessel, cruises England's inland waterways throughout the year, giving special attention to the men and families living on coal barges in British canals.

The *William Booth* is familiar to many Alaskan Eskimos and sourdoughs, for it has carried Salvation Army officers to villages and towns along the coast to conduct worship services and Sunday Schools. With the growth in population of the 49th State, officers of The Salvation Army may soon relinquish the *William Booth* and travel by air to settlements in the interior, but the good ship remains a symbol of the Army's efforts to spread the Gospel to remote parts of the world.

Chapter 18

MEN AND MEANS

It is notable that in its "fleet" The Salvation Army does not have an Admiral. Its officers carry the standard ranks of The Salvation Army, from Lieutenant to General. There is only one General in The Salvation Army, and as this is written he is General Wilfred Kitching, appointed in 1954, and the seventh to serve in the top post. His International Headquarters are on Queen Victoria Street, London, E. C. 4, England.

The Salvation Army procedure in electing the General is to assemble its Commissioners and Territorial Commanders from all parts of the world. Behind closed doors in London this group, known as the High Council, casts ballots and by a process of elimination chooses the world leader.

General Kitching was born into a Salvation Army family. His father, the late Commissioner Theodore H. Kitching, had joined the movement as a youth and had served for many years as private secretary to General William Booth.

As a boy, Wilfred Kitching became known to an unusually wide circle of Salvationists through his musical talents. At nine he enrolled as a player in the local Salvation Army band. At fifteen he had become known as a promising song composer. A year later he formed and led a young people's band, also accepting the deputy bandmastership of the senior band and a post as Corps Secretary.

239

His officer career began at the age of twenty-one, when he received his commission from the International Training College in London (in 1914) and was placed in charge of a Wiltshire (England) Corps with the rank of Captain. In the next several years he served as Divisional Young People's Secretary, Divisional Commander, and Field Secretary.

In 1946, as a Colonel, Kitching was sent to Melbourne, Australia, as Chief Secretary and second in command of the Australian Southern Territory. Two years later, as a Lieutenant Commissioner, he became Territorial Commander of Sweden, one of the Army's largest and most important territories. In 1951 he was recalled to London to take charge of the evangelistic work of The Salvation Army throughout Great Britain and Ireland as a full Commissioner. It was from this position that he was elected to the top rank.

As an international leader General Kitching has traveled extensively. In his first year in office he became the first General to visit the African Gold Coast (now Ghana), Nigeria, The Belgian Congo, and French Equatorial Africa. A second African trip, made in 1958, took him to Kenya, Rhodesia and South Africa. With Mrs. Kitching he has also visited India, Pakistan and most European countries, and has made five trips to the United States, the latest in 1960.

Mrs. General Wilfred Kitching, who was Adjutant Kathleen Bristow when they married in 1929, has been closely associated with the General throughout his career and has taken an active share of the Army's responsibilities and duties. She has a special interest in work among women and is world president of The Salvation Army's organization for women, the Home Leagues.

In the United States there is a National Headquarters at 130 West 14th Street, New York City, and four Territories, with Territorial Headquarters in New York, Chicago, Atlanta and San Francisco.

National Commander of The Salvation Army in the United States is Commissioner Norman S. Marshall, a forceful energetic leader who grew up among the drums, trumpets and prayers. The son of Salvation Army officer parents, one of seven children, Norman Marshall was born in Worcester, Massachusetts, and traveled with his family to Maine, Illinois, Oregon, Washington State, Missouri, and Minnesota. In Minneapolis, where the family lived for eight years, Norman entered training for officership.

Actually his Army activities began much earlier. He and his brother Ernest, thirteen months older, were often mistaken for twins. Their mother taught them to sing, dressed them in red sailor suits which they called "our captains' uniforms," and let them take part in open-air meetings, standing together on the drum and singing. Later they had blue suits trimmed with silver braid, which they called "our adjutants' uniforms."

When they were about ten years old the brothers, for a few weeks during the summer, were the singers for a traveling revival group, pitching a tent wherever they stayed, and relying upon the generosity of the townsfolk for their food.

One night the food supply ran out. The officer in charge announced this at the meeting and held a prayer service. The officer told the boys, "Don't worry, now. We have great faith in God to provide for our needs. In the morning you'll open the door and see more food than you can eat." In the morning they rushed to the door and there on the steps were five baskets of food—a sight which made an indelible impression upon their young minds.

The first instrument that Commissioner Marshall received as a Junior Bandsman was a very old and badly dented baritone horn which he was told he could use if he could straighten it out. "Going home on the street car," he remembers, "I was ashamed lest people think I had so little regard for the instrument that I had dented it myself, so I tried to hide it under my coat! At home I worked on it for two days, straightening it out and polishing it."

He was a member of several bands and solo cornetist with the Chicago Staff Band, with which he went to England in 1914. He credits his band experience with having carried him "over fool's hill," for that fellowship held him to the Army many times when he might have become disinterested.

Commissioner Marshall recalls returning from a band concert one night on the elevated railroad on the South Side of Chicago. Seated next to him was a captain with a large Sousaphone bass horn with a very large bell, and across from them were two youthful smart alecks and their dates. The boys sought to entertain their girls and the other passengers by heckling the Salvation Army officers.

"Hey, Captain," one said, "which end of that thing do you blow into?"

The captain smiled. "Well, sonny, I use this little end here," he said, pointing at the mouthpiece, "but if I had a mouth as big as yours I'd certainly use the other end."

Commissioner Marshall laughs as he remembers his first post of duty after his commissioning. He and his lieutenant, whom he called "Huffy," were assigned to Sioux Falls, South Dakota. They planned enthusiastically for their welcome meeting, despite a heavy snowfall which they feared might cut down the attendance. They were right. Not one person showed up! The following Sunday three people came to the morning meeting, but after that the hall was again empty.

Undaunted, the youthful officers held meetings by themselves. They marched up Main Street with Norman carrying the flag and playing the trumpet, and Huffy following with the drum. They held open-air meetings, too, trying in vain to form a circle of two.

One night they were meeting in the hall alone when they heard the door squeak open. In came a man who was obviously drunk, seeking relief from the cold.

Norman whispered to Huffy, "You can't carry a tune, so I'll sing while you talk to this man."

Somehow they impressed their "audience" so favorably that he was actually converted. With pride and spirit the boys sent a written report to *The War Cry*: "Wonderful results of our work here—100 percent of our congregation converted." After all, it was the complete truth!

Commissioner Marshall is an active member of the U. S. Conference of the World Council of Churches, the National Institute of Social Sciences, the American Protestant Hospital Association, the National Conference on Social Welfare, and is

242

a vice president of United Service Organizations, Inc. He is also a member and past director of the New York Rotary Club, a member of the New York Chapter of the Military Order of World Wars, and of the Newcomen Society of North America.

Commissioner Marshall is ably assisted by the National Chief Secretary, Lieutenant Commissioner Llewelyn W. Cowan, who is also a "son of the Regiment." His father came from Lockerbie, Scotland, and his mother from South Shields, England. In 1893 they were among a group of young officers chosen by General William Booth to be part of a pioneer party bound for America. They met on the boat, fell in love, and were married in 1894 in a huge "hallelujah wedding" at a camp meeting on Labor Day. When Llewelyn Cowan was born, his parents were stationed in the Harlem Corps in New York City.

"In my childhood the family was continually on the move," he says. "The Salvation Army was growing very fast in those days, and officers were transferred much more frequently than is the case today."

Before he reached high school Commissioner Cowan had attended ten different grade schools. His education started in a Texas prairie school where his parents had to pay a dollar a week for his tuition, but he soon transferred to a new public school 1½ miles from his home and walked there every day to save the dollar, which was hard to come by in the early days of The Salvation Army.

As Divisional officers his parents traveled extensively through Oklahoma during the days when oil towns were booming, and travel by train meant riding in the caboose, as there were no passenger cars. Commissioner Cowan recalls sleeping in barns in the hay with oil derricks all around, and being frightened during thunderstorms lest the lightning set fire to the wells.

When they were still small boys the Commissioner and his brother, Bob, were taught to sing by their parents. Both were lifted to the top of the drum in open-air meetings and would sing duets. Once they were taken to a revival meeting conducted by the well-known Doctor Wilbur Chapman in Portland, Maine, and were seated in the front row of the balcony. When the hymn-singing began the brothers sang out so loud and clear that they were invited to the platform to sing a duet before the revival gathering.

The Commissioner says that his wife had similar experiences. She was one of six girls in her family, and they all attended open-air meetings. The youngest girl played the mandolin, Mrs. Cowan played the guitar, and an older sister played the violin. In those days it was considered sinful to sing any music not arranged by Salvationists, and this made a variety of songs difficult, so Mrs. Cowan's father found an old German Salvationist musician who worked out arrangements for them.

Lt. Commissioner Cowan has immediate supervision over all Territorial departments and bureaus mentioned in earlier chapters. According to statistics available in 1960, the United States has 5121 Salvation Army officers, 181 Cadets, 12,675 paid employees, 1107 Corps (churches), and 484 institutions. While there is no accurate figure available for the number of people who are "soldiers" and those "adherents" who attend Salvation Army worship services, it seems reasonable to say that they would total about 250,000 in the United States.

Only six direct descendants of Founder William Booth were active in The Salvation Army as of 1960. William Wycliffe Booth (1895-   ), grandson of William Booth and son of William Bramwell Booth, is Territorial Commander in the Dominion of Canada, holding the rank of Commissioner. He has four children who are Salvation Army officers.

Muriel Booth-Tucker, daughter of Frederick deLatour and Emma Booth-Tucker and granddaughter of William Booth, was born in 1903 in New York City when her parents were National Commanders in the United States. Now a Colonel, she heads Salvation Army work in Ireland. Her father, Frederick deLatour Tucker, like other men who married into the Booth family, adopted the famous Booth name to use in hyphenated form with his own; hence the name Booth-Tucker.

In these pages you have met some of the Salvation Army officers and learned something about what they do. A natural question is, "What are these people paid for this unselfish and humanitarian work?"

The Salvation Army is a quasi-military organization, and this

244

resemblance obtains throughout its structure, including salaries and allowances for its officers.

Each officer, as in military life, is provided with furnished quarters which are maintained completely by The Salvation Army.

Added to this arrangement is a base salary which ranges in the present scale from a minimum of $28 per week for an unmarried officer who has just completed his training, and $45 per week for a married couple who have just completed training, to $35.50 for unmarried officers and $60 for married couples after they have given forty-five years of service.

Any allowances or benefits in addition to the salary are based on such qualifications as Long Service Award (25 years of unbroken service), the number of children in the family according to their ages, health needs and other allowances to meet expenses arising out of the demands of an officer's appointment. It is to be remembered that the wife of a Salvation Army officer is expected to be equally available at all times for regular duties and service.

The entire system is based on need rather than reward, for every Salvation Army officer has dedicated his or her life to service in the organization because of religious conviction and not for personal gain. The system is admittedly paternalistic, but is so arranged as to be adequate for an officer's needs.

To pay these salaries, to continue to bring "soup, soap and salvation" to needy multitudes, and to maintain buildings and equipment, The Salvation Army depends upon contributions from people like you and me, either as individuals or as part of community fund campaigns, but it also derives funds from other sources, including its Evangeline residences for business girls, thrift stores, hospitals, fees for Family Service and other welfare units, and contributions from its own officers and soldiers.

At its International Headquarters in London The Salvation Army administers The Salvation Army Assurance Society, Ltd., which has nearly two million policy-holders in England and Scotland. To collect premiums Salvation Army officers call at more than 400,000 homes weekly, providing opportunities to talk with families about their problems and thus carry forward the work of the Army. Each policy-holder is considered not only a client but also a person about whom the Army cares, and the officers representing the Society have been called "padres of the people." In 1895 the Society had 38,500 policy-holders and total funds of £14,039. In 1959 members numbered 1,901,715 and funds amounted to £21,290,325 (nearly $65,000,000). The Society has 360 active officers, 1112 employees.

Another British activity is the Salvation Army Fire Insurance Corporation, Ltd., which writes fire insurance policies not only for the general public but also on all buildings and contents belonging to The Salvation Army in the United Kingdom. The company also issues policies on household comprehensive, burglary and plate glass coverage, and insures motor vehicles. It has eight active officers and 13 employees.

In the early days of the Army, General William Booth organized a "Bible and Tract Department" and also published a Christian Mission magazine. From these grew the present Salvationist Publishing and Supplies, Ltd., a department which later included production of uniforms, bonnets and other supplies used by Army personnel. A large portion of the work involves the repair and manufacture of brass musical instruments. The Salvation Army produces "Triumphonic" instruments of high quality, meeting the meticulous requirements of soloists the world over and also able to sustain the rough wear and tear demanded by continuous service of Salvationist bandsmen.

In London, The Salvation Army Trust Company operates The Reliance Bank, Ltd., which has special facilities with other banks in the British Isles for the convenience of customers. Various types of banking service, including collections of bills of exchange, annuities, dividend and pension payments, are available. Demand deposits receive 2½ percent interest, fixed deposits 3 to 3½ percent, depending upon the length of notice necessary to make withdrawals. This bank has a capital of £60,000 and deposits totaling £2,519,019 (as of March, 1960). It has 15 active officers, 10 employees.

At Hadleigh, Essex, The Salvation Army Farm Colony, located on the Thames Estuary, includes a Roman site and the remains of Plantaganet Hadleigh Castle, which is a tourist attraction. Chief purpose of this colony is the uplifting of men who need the Army's help and training in modern agricultural work, while adequate provision is also made for their spiritual and physical welfare and recreation.

Among the colony's activities are farming, stock raising, truck gardening, fruit growing, dairying, and operation of a nursery and greenhouse. Its "Castle" herd of British Friesian dairy cattle is on the attested register for the production of tuberculin-tested milk. Latest farming machinery is in use and up-to-date methods are followed. The colony has 4 active officers, 30 employees, and 21 colonists who have come from other lands to work and learn.

In all of these British activities no fees are paid to directors, and all profits are paid into the central funds of The Salvation Army for the advancement of its humanitarian work.

In the United States, The Salvation Army's income flows from many sources. As an example, I obtained a financial statement showing the Army's finances in the New York area in a recent year:

Institutional Earnings

From the Army's social welfare institutions and residences for business women; city and county grants made to women's and children's institutions; and earnings on endowments bequeathed by wills to specific institutions $4,583,936.44

Appeals and Special Gifts

Annual maintenance appeal; contributions from special appeals such as Christmas Funds; members' contributions and sundry donations.

Special grants—administered by New York Community Trust Company—Laura Spellman Rockefeller Memorial Community Trust Fund; Wilhelm Loewenstein Memorial Fund; Mildred Anna Williams Estate; James Foundation of New York, Inc.; Staten Island Community Chest; and New York City Youth Board 1,296,955.09

Endowment Earnings, Legacies, etc.

Appropriations from endowment earnings and principal and earnings from trust funds; Nassau and Suffolk Counties Service Unit income; and discretionary funds raised throughout the Eastern Territory not applicable exclusively to New York City........................... $ 760,136.58

Total income $6,641,028.11

Expenditures, totaling this same amount, were made for these purposes:

Maintenance of (5) women's and children's institutions.
Maintenance of Booth Memorial Hospital.
Maintenance of (5) Men's Social Service institutions.
Welfare work.
Civil Defense and Red Shield Services.
Maintenance of summer camps.
Group work centers.
Maintenance of Residences for Business Women.
Maintenance of School for Officers' Training.
Community Relations and Administration.

One rather unusual source of income is The Salvation Army's Gift Annuity Plan, in which donors give a sum of money to the Army and receive in return a guaranteed income for life. The New York State Insurance Department has granted a special permit to The Salvation Army as a New York corporation to receive such gifts and to pay such annuities, and all funds in the plan are supervised by the New York State Insurance Department.

The minimum amount acceptable under the plan is $100.

248

There is no maximum. The income rates to be received by the annuitant are on a graduated scale ranging from three per cent (for those 35 years old or younger) to 7.4 per cent for those 80 and over. The agreements may be made for an annuitant and a survivor. For this reason many people consider the plan as a good investment, simpler than a will and better than a trust fund because there are no trustees' fees to be paid and no legal entanglements.

Some people, in making a Last Will and Testament, have specifically provided that the Executor of the estate will purchase a Salvation Army Gift Annuity for a beneficiary. Numerous others, in their wills, have made outright bequests to the Army.

Whatever its sources of funds, The Salvation Army uses them for one magnificent purpose—to help people who need help.

Asked what he considered the most important activity of The Salvation Army, Commissioner Norman Marshall said, "I'm not in a position to answer that arbitrarily. If you asked this question of an unwed mother, she would probably consider her own case the most important. If you asked a man who was fighting alcoholism in the Bowery Corps, he might well tell you that his problem was paramount. What do you think a homeless mother whose children have been killed in an earthquake would tell you? The point is that each person in real need and seeking a solution to his own troubles is really the most important activity of The Salvation Army."

Perhaps the fitting close to this story is appropriately found in the Holy Bible (Matthew 25:35-36): "For I was an hungred, and ye gave me meat: I was thirsty, and ye gave me drink: I was a stranger, and ye took me in: Naked, and ye clothed me; I was sick, and ye visited me; I was in prison, and ye came unto me."

This is the way of the warrior in The Salvation Army.

GLOSSARY OF SALVATION ARMY TERMS

Articles of War: The undertakings which every prospective soldier is required to sign before he enrolls.

"Blood and Fire": The Army's battlecry. It refers to the Blood of Jesus Christ and the Fire of the Holy Spirit.

Cadet: A Salvationist in training to become an officer.

Cartridge: An envelope for the weekly contribution of officer, soldier or recruit toward corps expenses. (Similar to offering-envelopes used in most Protestant churches.)

Corps: A Salvation Army post established for the propagation of the Gospel; generally with its central meeting-place and under the leadership of one or more officers.

Division: A number of corps grouped together, under the direction of a Divisional Commander.

Fishing: Speaking with individuals during a prayer or after meeting, in order to help them decide to follow Christ (See Matthew 4:19).

General, The: An officer elected to supreme command of The Salvation Army throughout the world. All appointments are made and all regulations issued under his authority.

Home League: An association to influence women in the promotion of a happy home life and toward a personal experience of salvation through Jesus Christ.

Junior Soldier: A boy or girl who, having professed conversion and proved satisfactory for at least one month, has signed the junior soldier's pledge and become a Salvationist.

Knee-drill: A prayer meeting, held generally on Sunday morning.

League of Mercy: Salvationists who, in their spare time, visit prisons, hospitals, and needy homes.

Officer: A Salvationist who has left ordinary employment and, having been trained and commissioned is (until retirement) engaged in full-time Salvation Army service.

Outpost: A locality in which Army work is carried on from time to time, and which it is hoped will eventually develop into a society or corps.

Penitent-form, or Mercy Seat: A bench (usually in front of the platform in an Army hall) at which persons anxious about their spiritual condition are invited to seek salvation or sanctification, or make a special consecration to God's will and service.

Promotion to Glory: The Army's description of the death of Salvationists.

Soldier: A person at least 14 years of age who, giving evidence of salvation, has, with the approval of the census board, been duly enrolled as a member of The Salvation Army, after signing the Articles of War.

Sunbeam Brigade: An organization for girls aged 7-11.

Territory: A country, part of a country, or several countries combined, in which Salvation Army work is organized under a Territorial Commander.

Young People's Legion: A branch of the young people's war which aims at training and winning the young for God and the Army.

INDEX

260